SURVIVING EVIDENCE

MEMOIR OF AN EXTREME
HAUNTING SURVIVOR

Gina —
Thank you for
speaking with me!
My best
Ch

By CHRISTOPHER Di CESARE

Surviving Evidence, Memoir of an Extreme Haunting Survivor

Front cover art and design by Mara Katria

Copyright © 2014 Dark Moon Press

Published by

Dark Moon Press

Copyright Dark Moon Press

ISBN-13: 978-1496079169

For a full catalogue of Dark Moon's publications refer to

http://www.darkmoonpress.com

Or send an SASE with $8.00 USD to:

P.O. Box 11496, Ft. Wayne, Indiana, 46858-1496

To contact the author, please refer to the publisher's website:

Or send an SASE to:

Dark Moon Press

P.O. Box 11496, Fort Wayne, Indiana 46858-1496

All messages will be forwarded on to the author, however publisher cannot guarantee a response

Man ... cannot learn to forget, but hangs on the past: however far or fast he runs, that chain runs with him. – Friedrich Nietzsche

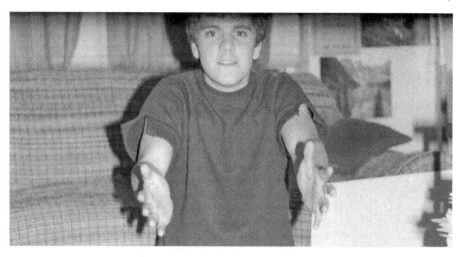

TABLE OF CONTENTS

8

Acknowledgments

The passage of thirty years from the events detailed in this book has afforded me ample time for reflection. In those intervening years I have learned more than a few valuable 'life lessons'. Perhaps the most vital realization has been to better appreciate the many extraordinary people who, either through chance or choice, found their way into my life. Along with that has come the understanding to appreciate them before they, or I, shuffle off this mortal coil. As a youth, I believed that I could achieve virtually anything I desired to on my own. I recognize now, through wisdom gleaned by the passing years, that it would never have been the case. For even if I had been able to accomplish all that I set out to when I made my way to college as a hopeful, buoyant, and determined teenager, without the people that I care about (and those who care for me) to share those experiences, any achievement would have been less complete, less meaningful. It is important that I acknowledge individuals such as John Jeff Ungar, who meticulously recorded the terrifying 1985 events via the "C2D1 Journal Notes", and who risked it all to ensure that proof would exist, and that I would survive.

There were others who braved those frightening months in Erie Hall as well. Thank you, Beth Kinsman, for taking actions that helped me bridge the gap between fear and progress, and Craig Norris, for challenging me to face my greatest of fears that fateful morning in April of 1985. To Paul A., my first Erie Hall C2D1 roommate, you have my eternal gratitude for enduring the nightmare for as long as you were able to.

I am also grateful to Father "Charlie" (Charles) Manning, for the trust that he placed in two very frightened young college students, and to Dr. Lawrence Casler, PhD, for offering all of us an initial roadmap to understanding the events swirling around us.

The importance of the strong moral and familial foundation provided me by my parents cannot be understated. To my father, Vito Di Cesare, thank you for taking that long drive, on a moment's notice, and for being there for me at the most important times. To my mother, Patricia Di Cesare, I am eternally appreciative for your insistence that I should 'do the right thing' at all times, even in the face of insurmountable adversity. A special debt of gratitude also needs to be expressed to my sisters, Nicole and Melissa. You both helped to make my childhood a fun one, and taking that positivity and laughter with me to college helped me to endure the darkness I would face.

The eventual decision to share this experience was not made lightly, nor was it made overnight. The path towards public dissemination, at no point a certainty in my mind, was made possible largely through the support, encouragement, and efforts of both trusted friends and experienced professionals. I remain deeply appreciative of both Alan Lewis and Lori Bowles Nazos, who provided me with the very first unrestricted votes of confidence the years following the haunting, and Timothy T. Shaw, who stayed on the trail of this Western New York 'urban legend' for several decades and who would author the first book on the topic: *"Please, talk with me"*.

Many things can change over the course of three decades. And whereas happenings like those that occurred in Geneseo were once considered the 'occult' and largely unspeakable, today they are more often analyzed, researched, and discussed. I would like to strongly commend SUNY Geneseo, for allowing us to share these events publically, and for their support and sponsoring of my speaking engagements there, and to Joshua Gregory (host of the *Edge of the Unknown*) who served as Master of Ceremonies on the very first occasion. To Eilfie Music and Chris Edwards, thank you for opening the door to the future. Likewise, it is essential that I recognize the tremendous boon the telling of these happenings have received due to the work of actor Ian Way, producer Andrea De Brito, and writer Mora Stephens, in addition to the executive producers Mark Burnett, Julie Insogna, and Seth Jarrett – not to mention the Jarrett Creative Group, for their noteworthy *SyFy School Spirits: "Dorm Room Nightmare"* production (2012). That finely crafted, commonly lauded, one-hour episode shot this extreme haunting into the national conscience.

I was not prepared to find myself signing autographs the very next morning, nor quickly becoming a welcomed commodity on the convention and lecture circuits. Fortunately, producer Bill Edwards and director Mara Katria provided me with a loving, insightful, and moving venue by which to better express the powerful meaning of the haunting: the multiple award-winning independent film, *"Please, talk with me"*. In watching the performance of Kyle Shea, reliving my darkest moments, I finally saw the true value of sharing my experience: human spirit.

Thanks must be afforded to author Corvis Nocturnum, and *Dark Moon Press*, for encouraging me to add my own personal experience and insights to the paranormal lexicon, and for bringing this labor of love and survival into your hands. To the band Attention for providing me with an unofficial theme song, "Ocean of Stars" from the SyFy episode, and to John Tobin and Brian J. Cano who have given freely of both their time and talents to support the educational value of the experiences you will soon read about; also to Chip Reichenthal, Mark Keyes who referenced these events in publications of their own, and to Dave Delise who thirty years later got me on that *Wheaties* box!

I suppose we all must be doing something correctly, as the outpouring of love and support since we survivors have 'gone public' has been nothing short of astounding. To longtime friends Michael Lewis and Kerry Lyon, thank you for your assistance in helping me navigate this incredible, and unexpected, journey. And to all those who have been inspired by our ordeal, know that your care and kindness to us are equally inspiring.

My final acknowledgments are to the reasons that I will continue to fight for every single breath, and every waking moment, for as long as I am able: my family. To my wife Rita, my daughter Susan, and my son Matthew, please know that whatever challenges life creates for you, and however you choose to face them, you have my undying love.

"Somewhere, something incredible is waiting to be known." — Carl Sagan.

Foreword

The fire I had built was small, and it was smoky. I was kneeling before it as I ripped the pages from my journal to keep it going. Thirteen years had passed since the haunting – almost fourteen years since I had recorded the events in 1985. There was a feeling of conviction about the moment. I watched the pages as I tore them out and tossed them in. The leaves curled, charred and turned to ash. When I finally threw the spiral binding of the notebook into the flames, the spine did not melt. There was a great sadness in sacrificing the past this way, burning all that I'd labored to protect, breaking the soul-tie to my interest in the whole paranormal realm – particularly my role in the haunting. Yet, a facet of this was a misplaced hope that this would bring relief from the self-imposed responsibility of being the archivist and chronicler of the C2D1 Haunting.

"Chronicler." It always felt as though I had fallen short of deserving such a title as that. It was partially out of a sense of duty that I began the writing of the "C2D1 Journal Notes" – as they have come to be known. I never meant them to be any more than a quick sketch to aid in recollection and analysis. Even before the supernatural "came calling" at my college dorm-mate's door (room C2D1, Erie Hall, SUNY Geneseo), I felt it was important to keep a record of significant events. And, when

Chris Di Cesare, my friend and suitemate, arrived in a panic at my room next door that fateful night in February of 1985 – I was ready.

The decision to help Chris was a given. I did not need the type of conviction that comes with planning. The moment I glimpsed the terror in his face, there was no question; I was determined to help if I could. It was there: a commitment to see him through this. Nor was the urgency to record the events lost on me – they had exploded like a supernova, swift and violent, leaving only a brief window of time in which to conduct a spectral analysis of the afterglow. It was incumbent upon me to react immediately to record, and help cope with, each aftershock caused by the ghost, as reported by Chris, the person who would become my best friend.

So then, why did I burn my journals? As I said, the responsibility to glean some meaning from what happened to us weighed heavily, anchoring me to the darkness and confusion of the phenomena that my scribblings described. Between 1985 and 1998 (the year of the burning), the legacy of the haunting seemed entirely negative, and I wanted to be free of it.

Despite my attempt to destroy the past, however, I received a call in late 2009. A film production company was interested in making a movie about what had happened and wanted permission to use my notes as the backbone for the screenplay. The writings I made in the early days of the C2D1 Haunting had apparently survived as photocopies – that they survived in any form was a stunning revelation to me. So successful had I been in distancing myself from the trauma of those dark days and nights at Geneseo that I struggled to recall even having written them. But, this was a story that wanted to be told.

Through my involvement with that film, entitled *"Please, talk with me"*, my friendship with Chris was rekindled. For that I am forever grateful. The process was one of healing that allowed light to shine back on those times. A veil had lifted to reveal the intervening years had actually been necessary, that the time and distance were required in order to gain much desired perspective. Things had come full-circle. What once was so detrimental now had a silver lining.

It was Chris who was the focus of the ghost's horrific attentions back then. Now, it is he who will share with you, dear reader, what those experiences were like. It was a privilege that he placed his trust in me more than a quarter century ago when I did my best to help him survive. It is an honor now to add my humble foreword to this, his memoir, so aptly titled: *Surviving Evidence*.

J. Jeff Ungar
5th February 2014
State College, PA

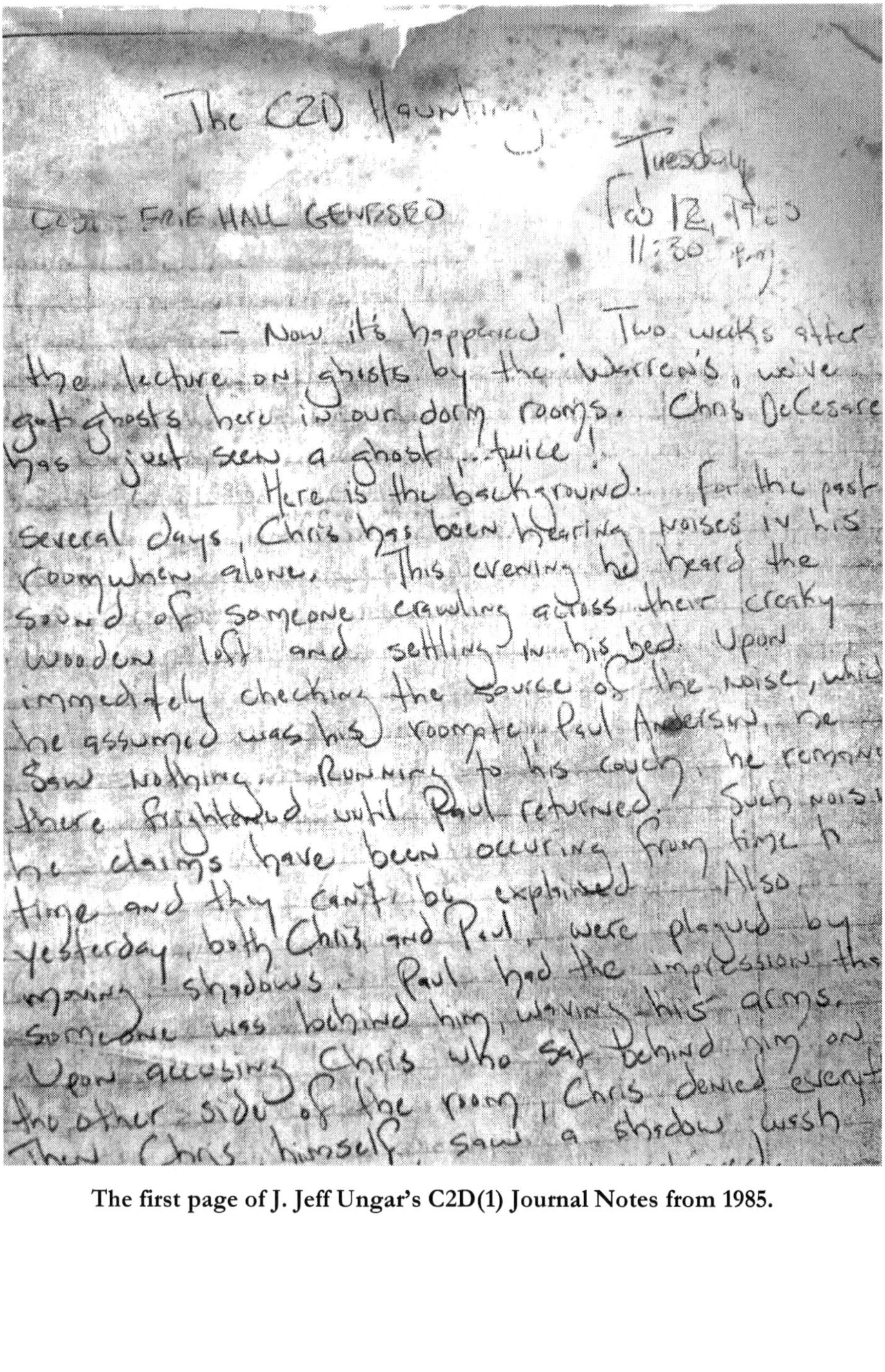

The C2D Haunting

CO2 - FRIE HALL GENESEO

Tuesday
Feb 12, 1985
11:30 pm

— Now it's happened! Two weeks after the lecture on ghosts by the Warren's, we've got ghosts here in our dorm rooms. Chris DeCesare has just seen a ghost... twice!

Here is the background. For the past several days, Chris has been hearing noises in his room when alone. This evening he heard the sound of someone crawling across their creaky wooden loft and settling in his bed. Upon immediately checking the source of the noise, which he assumed was his roommate Paul Anderson, he saw nothing. Running to his couch, he remained there frightened until Paul returned. Such noises he claims have been occuring from time to time and they can't be explained. Also, yesterday, both Chris and Paul were plagued by moving shadows. Paul had the impression that someone was behind him, waving his arms. Upon accusing Chris who sat behind him on the other side of the room, Chris denied everything. Then Chris himself saw a shadow whish

The first page of J. Jeff Ungar's C2D(1) Journal Notes from 1985.

"There are some things you learn best in calm, and some in storm." – Willa Cather, *The Song of the Lark*

Introduction

Tuesday, October 30th, 2012 – 3AM. Hurricane Sandy is devastating the northeastern United States of America, and I sit on the timeworn brown rug of a first floor apartment one hour's drive north of New York City. There is no power. None has been available for seven and one-half hours. It flickered off – with a few uneven, intermittent stutters – for the duration, at 7:26PM the evening prior. Some like darkness. It can provide a temporary protection from the burning rays of the Sun, or perhaps the disapproving stare of a neighbor. This particular darkness may afford to some an unexpected reprieve from a long work day or the chance to rekindle a love that has long suffered under all those things that the light reveals.

I don't like the darkness ... *not since the haunting.*

My wife, still auburn-haired and beautiful in spite of the quarter century that has passed since I met her, had gone round in her bathrobe and lit an un-matching assortment of candles. She scattered them throughout the modest living space. Some were scented, some were not. I found the largest candle – from which a sweet cinnamon smell emanated – and placed it on the sturdy, old wooden coffee table in front of me. Its once lustrous surface was scarred from countless human motions and its edges worn just the same. I had considered placing it out on the sidewalk for the bulk trash collection on more than one occasion, due largely to the questionable stares it would elicit from our guests. But on this unscheduled occasion it was sturdy and reassuring, the marks of aging were washed away as it held – with purpose – the one bright point of physical light in my world.

I choose to wait up through the night, in the event that one of my two children decides to make the dangerous trip home. They might need my help. I am their father. That's what good fathers do. I wonder to myself if they think I *am* a good father.

Outside.

The moon is there, I know, because it always is. It has silently observed the rise of the Great Pyramids; the expansion and collapse of mighty empires; and the excited beginning and teary-eyed end of every single human relationship. And from a perch canopied by countless stars above, eventually it beheld the illumination of a forever-darkened Earth night by humanity's artificial fire: the light bulb.

Oh, but even its eternal gaze was now blotted out by tumultuous fast-moving clouds of medium and dark gray on this night. Amongst the bowing trees, there are no street lights to guide anyone home now. There is no method by which to look up into the stars and chart one's course, one's destiny.

Inside.

My window offers no comfort, other than to reflect distorted sections of my own pensive image back to me. The shadows cast by the candle dart and flit and dance across the plain walls.

The memories – long locked away – are knocking again. I hear them, but they are faint as though light rain drops on bending grass. My mind begins to race, to connect the strands of memory, to calculate the numbers. There is one thing that I *do* know: I don't want this, I don't want to start counting with the number 'one' again!

A silhouetted figure in a 2002 Oldsmobile Cutlass drives down the road, and the beams of the car's headlights – as they cut through the falling rain – serve to refocus my straining synapses. A few long seconds pass and then I let loose an exhale born of cerebral achievement: It has been twenty-eight years, six months, and ten days.

This is what I do. I count.

A more advanced math had long since replaced the 'count to ten' method that was featured prominently on the SyFy Channel's *School Spirits* episode just four months prior. It was the method my maternal grandmother, Anne Marie Hubley, had taught me as a child. It had worked back then.

One of my sisters had been screaming and crying to the point that her face turned red as she gasped for air between tear-laden whines. My grandmother took both of my sister's hands into her own, and then placed them on her wise face. She looked into her eyes and told her: "Count to ten."

My sister, perhaps intrigued by the request, did so. Her crying stopped; she sniffed back some tears, and then asked for permission to feed the dog who had been hiding under the table in an attempt to escape the noise. I was dumbstruck.

I walked repeatedly around the perimeter of the Long Island backyard. For several hours the world moved on happily without me. Then, and only when I had planned out what I felt was a satisfactory line of questioning, I pushed my hair back off of my forehead, climbed up the three cement steps of the porch, and entered the house.

The Great Sage was occupied: frying potatoes in a pan, chopping up cucumbers, and checking on the meat in the oven.

"Grandma?"

Her hair was pure white, and it seemed to me that no grays or browns would ever dare to besmirch it. And though aspects of her physical form showed the wear of having raised six children, having lived for five-plus decades and worked through most of them, her light blue eyes remained sharp and focused. She half-turned and afforded me a welcoming glance.

"There he is! I was watching you walk around all afternoon. What's on your mind?"

I smiled. Wisdom.

I stood by her side, with my hands clasped behind me, as she fine-tuned the evening meal. I was mesmerized for a short time by the speed and accuracy with which she chopped up stalks of celery. I watched her fingers peel the head of lettuce. I noticed that her apron, which no doubt years ago was worn to protect her clothing, was now nothing more than an ornament. Nothing. Not one drop of water, one bead of grease, or one cucumber seed tarnished it.

And as the sun began its glorious gold, orange, and pink descent behind the treetops of the flat Long Island horizon obscured only by the wooden fence that secured the back yard, she explained to me that by counting to ten, you can put some time, some space, between you and the event. She explained that after my sister had counted to ten she realized that she was fine, that there was no emergency or crisis, and that things often are not as bad as we first perceive them to be.

I cannot remember much, if anything, about the meal itself, but I do recall helping my grandmother wash the dishes afterwards. I recall because she turned to me, while my young mind focused on the now heroic – and seemingly overwhelming - chore of getting every speck off of the silverware, and said to me: "I am glad that you are a good person, Christopher."

Then.

In deference to my grandmother, and more specifically the counting technique, I had a large purple-faced, monocle-wearing 'Count' hand puppet, the one from *Sesame Street* who would engage in some counting exercise with each appearance. I placed the puppet at the foot of my bed each night, until I was sixteen and the family dog decided she would eat it.

But the routine that had served me so well in achieving both athletic and academic success, and for so long, would eventually fail. It would fail – utterly and outright – when some terrifying *thing* willed itself through the walls of my college dorm room and into what had been a promising young life by any standard of measurement.

Then again, maybe it was I who had failed. Maybe I should have counted *longer* at 9:16PM on February 12th, 1985, as the room's temperature dropped and that *thing* was materializing behind me. Maybe I should have pushed past the number 'seven' before I turned to see what it was that sent a strong, pronounced chill of pure dread up my spine. Before I gazed into a face that …

Now.

I count further. I count back the days, thousands of days. I count and it makes the memories recede. It takes away some of the responsibility, and the shame of a long ago failure that simply will not heal.

Then, at the precise moment when I know they will evaporate away, like they have for the last 10,419 days, they rise up in the darkness like a tsunami wave, and wash an aspect of my mind up onto the hard, wet, unforgiving beach … left vacant, unattended, decades ago. I land hard, feel paralyzed; my breathing becomes more forced. It feels like my brain hurts, under the skull, in the back, on the right. Just like before.

Oh, God. Not like that!

As there is no electricity, there is no heat in this old Victorian-style home and the room's temperature has dropped noticeably. My skin is now cold to the touch, I check to be certain. Just like before. My fingers begin to lose sensitivity. Yes. Just like before. Just like 1985 … in my college dorm room … when the ghost came.

This is my story.

"Peace begins with a smile." – Mother Teresa

Dedication

It was early May 1985. I had just returned from college at the State University of New York at Geneseo. The ten-week period between February 8th and April 20th (which is the focus of this book) had been the strangest, most horrifying time of my life, and I was quite relieved to have survived it.

Once unpacked, one of my first thoughts was to visit with my great-grandmother – who was by then in her eighties. She was a humble and plain woman by almost any contemporary standard: with only a primary school education, no career other than tending to her family, and standing at less than five feet in height. But there should be no indignity in that.

Roses, my great-grandmother loved roses.

In the heart of the ghetto on the eastern side of the city of Newburgh, New York (the site of numerous recent FBI anti-gang raids) you could find her rose garden. Nestled between untended, debris-strewn dirt lots in any direction the eye dared to look, she would methodically make her way with a spouted watering can in one hand, trimming sheers in the other, to her beloved floral sanctuary. My great-grandfather, Pasquale, had passed away almost a decade earlier shortly after their fiftieth wedding anniversary. She should have been moved out of the area long before and more than a few relatives had become exasperated trying to convince her, but she steadfastly refused.

I parked in front of her aging, but well-maintained, two-story home. She made me some homemade meatball and rice soup after which I set out to mow the grass of her tiny back lawn. I enjoyed speaking with her and she always seemed thankful for the company. As I wheeled the old lawnmower out of the basement, she stopped me, pulled my hand into hers, and with a quiet steady determination led me to the thickest patch of red petals.

"Do you remember what I told you when you were little, honey?" she asked me, her gray aging eyes staring intently into mine through her wire-rim glasses.

"About flowers being like children," I asked.

"That's right honey," she smiled. Her eyes grew bright and she nodded her head in approval: "Tell me."

The conversation that she was making reference to had occurred in a similar spot, when I was a mere four years old. It remains one of my first cogent memories:

I had mistaken a plastic decorative grape for the real thing and almost immediately began to choke on it. My great-grandmother retrieved the object from my mouth and later informed me that "Not everything that looks real ... is." That alarming thought would replay itself time-and-again in my mind as I journeyed through adolescence, through the haunting and well into adulthood.

We made our way out to her garden. It was a stinging hot, bright, summer day and I was startled by a blue-tinted dragonfly that flew noisily past my face just before she placed my child's fingers onto several rose petals.

"Flowers are like children," she had whispered gently to me. "If you talk to them, and touch them and feed them, they will grow." She was looking directly into my eyes. I clearly remember nodding in order to communicate that I understood her, even if I didn't. But — even at the tender age of four — I knew that this was something special.

I relayed the story back to her, now, some sixteen years later. She puckered her lips and kissed me firmly on the cheek, "good boy". Then as she disappearing back into the silence of the old home, I cut the grass.

My great-grandmother is gone now. Her roses are gone, too. I can no longer physically show you either. But she — and her rose garden — still lives on inside of me. I hope to share them with you.

This book is dedicated to Mary Rose Di Cesare ... and all of her flowers (children).

Battle not with monsters, lest ye become a monster, and if you gaze into the abyss, the abyss gazes also into you. – Friedrich Nietzsche.

1. Fear

Some say that there are two instinctive reactions to a crisis: flight or fight. My experience teaches me otherwise. There is only one true, instinctual reaction to a crisis: fear. And when we fear, we freeze. It is the most natural, and logical, of responses in that it provides our mind with potentially vital time to understand what is occurring around us. Over time we can train ourselves – or be trained – to fight or to flee in a crisis. Firefighters are trained to run into burning buildings, while those who have suffered through a prior fire will typically run from it. But most of us will just stare. We stare with horrified expressions, and watch the building burn ... to ashes.

It is March 10th, 1985. The digital clock in room C2D1 reads 3:31 but I am not there to see it. I am lying face down, stark-naked, shivering wet, and bleeding on the floor of a bathroom some thirty feet away. My eyes are open, wide, but they are not focusing. A numbing cold is creeping through my 19-year-old body, a body that has been honed by preparing for – and racing in – nine 26.2 mile marathons. But the source of the icy cold is not the square-tile covered floor that presses uncomfortably up against my face, my chest, and my thighs. Rather, the sensation is spreading from an area near the center of my back ... an area where the wounds are: the scratches and the blood. My toes are cramped from the pressure of being pressed unnaturally upwards by the floor since I fell. But I am too exhausted to shift my feet in order to relieve the pain. My breathing remains steady in spite of my growing fear, possibly because my body is shutting down. My mouth is open, slightly, just as it was at that precise moment when I looked into the mirror, above the sink, and first saw the three 'impossible' scratches.

I am beginning to panic.

My thoughts race frantically from synapse to synapse, trying to make a connection that makes sense, which will help me through this; whatever this actually *is*. But a manic negativity has now seized control. Why did I choose to come here to Geneseo anyway?

Death is here.

Less than an hour ago I was running at a brisk 6:00/mile clip along the dirt roads that separate the local farming fields. The azure sky was lined with wispy clouds of white who were being hurried along by an unseen wind current. It was so peaceful. Almost a month had passed since I was last able to stretch out my runner's legs like this. But things were different now. The priest, Father Charlie Manning, had done his blessing, and the thing ... that horrid thing ... was gone. In the three and one-half days since he had raised up his cross, whispered his sacred prayers, and cleansed my college dorm room, my life had returned to a healthy normalcy. Approximately 3.5 miles out, I turned left onto Rt. 20A and headed back east, over a metal-railed bridge, and up the rolling hills to the college.

The air inside the dorm was noticeably stale as I climbed my way up the stairs to the second floor. But better that than the sense of dread that had emanated here only 72 short hours ago. Order had been restored.

I untied my left shoe when I reached my door and slid the room key off of the lace. Normally my roommate, Paul, would be inside sitting at his desk, his head bobbing back and forth as he listened to the local rock station wearing his thick, padded, head phones. But things had turned ugly in room C2D1, and Paul was now determined to spend most of his free time at home with his parents. I could not blame him. It would likely have been my course of action as well if I lived less than an hour away like he did. As it was not the case, I often became the lone human occupant, and I soon got into the habit of tying my room key onto my shoelaces, so that I could lock my door when I went out. It was very important that the door remained locked!

I pulled off my royal blue and white wool cap, and tossed it onto the old couch that sat quietly in front of the room's lone window. My hair, which was so famously thick that my Aunt Roe once joked that she broke her thinning shears while trying to cut it, was matted down and a bit darker than its usual shade of sandy blond due to perspiration. Peeling off my layers of sweat-laced running clothes, I placed them in the plastic bucket at the bottom of my closet and retrieved a white towel, some shampoo, and a bar of soap.

The D-Quad bathroom was directly across from my bedroom and a heavy, two-inch thick, wooden door (on a floor-based roll track) guarded the bathroom entrance. It would rattle as it was slid open and closed, due perhaps to its sheer weight, which made passing in and out of the bathroom without notice impossible. This was a fact that would soon become vitally important.

Two photographs of the C2D bathroom in Erie Hall where the March 10th attack took place. Note the sliding wood door and the mirror above the right sink.

Entering the bathroom, I switched on the overhead lights and proceeded to the lone shower stall. A cheap, thin, largely ineffective plastic shower curtain hung from a shiny metallic crossbar. The speckled shower stall floor was lean, cool, and dry. It had not been used for several hours.

The warming spray of shower water relaxed my muscles as it washed away the salt from my pores. I lathered up my hair, still taking the time to make the pointy Alfalfa/*Little Rascals* shape that my mother used to when I was young.

There was no question that my afternoon training run had gone very well, and if my body continued to respond in such a manner, I would be returning home in just eight short weeks to what should be a very successful road-racing season.

My peripheral vision caught sight of a minor fluctuation in the light that was entering the shower stall. The shower curtain certainly was no help and it probably cost fifty cents to replace. If anyone chose to shoot a glance into this shower stall, they would be able to see at least two-thirds of the occupant at any given time. And it would happen from time-to-time, especially on Parents' Weekend, when someone's mother or sister would wander onto the 'wrong' floor and be confronted with sights unexpected.

Sights unexpected.

This external movement didn't tear me from my thoughts right away, as the 1985 Montgomery Summer Track Series was a prime focus. I wasn't a great hot-weather runner, perhaps due in part to my light complexion. Conventional wisdom stated that the darker one's skin the better able one was to run in hot temperatures (think Kenya or Brazil) and the lighter one's skin, the faster you were in cooler conditions (think Norway or Great Britain), but I had held my own the previous year, winning three of the five scorching, hot, cross-country runs. The races were long enough to allow me the chance to 'out-strength' my opponents, but not *so* long (typically three to five miles) that I would bake in the sun's rays.

Reflecting as I was, it occurred to me that it had not rained once during any of last year's races, and I couldn't recall one run under even cloudy conditions. How welcome some shade would have been, even if for just one race! *Heck, I would have settled for the shade I had right now!*

Right now?

A sense of uneasiness grew over me. I glanced up towards the ceiling, and there – through the steady stream of water – I saw a human-shaped shadow. It was silently gazing down at me. My eyes squinted, watching as it swayed ever so slightly: shoulders, skull, a tilted neck …

Impossible.

The priest had arrived, as he had promised, on Wednesday the 6th at 8PM, dark briefcase in hand. I had been there as he chased away the evil with his blessed water and his commanding presence.

Afterwards he spoke to me about the mysteries of God and I had asked him if the ghost could somehow come back.

"Only if you invite him back," he had answered without hesitation.

"*That's* not going to happen!" I assured him.

For as the cleric put away his belongings, I could state with an honest heart that there was no possible scenario in which I could imagine me doing so.

"Call me if you need anything else," he had said as he walked out the door.

But there was no need to call. The strange closed-room breezes; the flashing clocks; the whispering voice that people heard calling my name; the empty creaking loft; the missing items; the cloudy white mists; the shadows washing across the walls; the cold finger tips touching my neck; the opening – while latched – closet door; the zones of cold that people claimed clung to their legs; the tug-of-war with an unseen opponent for my pillow; the self-activating tape recorder; the full-bodied apparition that would rise from Paul's stereo or hover over me as I slept, breathing in my breath … were all gone now.

Using both hands, I cleared the water from my eyes, only to see the shadow moving away, across the ceiling. With the speed and reflexes that had recently helped me run a 2:09 half mile, I sprinted from the misty shower stall, and came to a sliding, bare-footed, halt in the center of the college dorm bathroom.

"Hello?"

Nothing.

Ignoring my nakedness, and the immediate discomfort caused by the rapid change in air temperature, I checked inside the toilet stall and under the sinks. My slightly pruned fingers clenched and unclenched nervously as pools of water began to form around my feet as it dripped down my legs. The pools of water on the floor were good, I reasoned. For if, in fact, someone *had* actually mastered the art of opening the bathroom door in silence, I would certainly hear them splash through the newly-formed puddles if they decided to foolishly return. It wasn't the ghost.

The priest had sent him away.

Returning to the comforting warmth of the shower, I began washing the lathered shampoo from my hair, rationalizing that perhaps the shadow was nothing more than an 'afterimage' caused from inadvertently rubbing my eyes with my hands.

I watched as the steady stream of white shampoo bubbles gathered around my ankles as they prepared to make their unavoidable journey down the shower drain into darkness, never to be seen again.

The water running down my torso soon became clear again when I noticed the skin on my right arm abruptly darken from a stark absence of light. I shot a quick glance up to the ceiling.

The shadow was back.

Now, suspended directly over me, the shadow seemed to move a bit closer, as though it were trying to get a better look. I darted – a second time – out into the middle of the bathroom, nearly losing my footing in the puddles that I myself had left behind just minutes earlier. As I skidded across the room, certain that this time I would see one of my college mates silently cowering in the toilet stall after having failed to prank me, I said aloud: "There is *no* way you're getting away. I can outrun *all* of you. It's done, it's over."

Empty.

The bathroom was empty.

I checked the heavy, wood, bathroom door. It had not been moved. At this point I recognized something of great relevance: the room's lights were on the ceiling. This meant that any shadow cast by them would be located on the *ground,* just as the sun's light casts shadows to the ground during the daylight. There could be no shadows on the ceiling unless there was an active and continual light source on the floor. The pulse in my neck quickened with the sudden understanding that regardless of my efforts, I would *never* catch one of my friends by chasing shadows on the ceiling. This was because they would be incapable of casting such a shadow.

But if it wasn't a person, then …

No.

I'm not ready to accept this. Everything has been fine for three and one-half days, remember, Chris? The priest blessed the room. I looked up at the now shadow-free ceiling and blurted out:

"The hell with you!"

I trudged back, as defiantly as one can be while wearing no clothes, into the warming shower to rinse off one final time. I turned the water off with my right hand. My left hand had remained free, but it didn't matter.

There was no time to react.

No warning.

My eyes, instinctively, closed as my face hit the hard shower wall. The wall tasted gross, like soap powder, but I was thankful that my top teeth were not hurt from the swift and sudden impact. And whatever had just been used to stab me, in the back, just below my neck, was used with such force that my right foot was momentarily lifted off the ground.

I thought I would scream out, but I didn't. There seemed to be some strong countervailing – perhaps primal – 'knowing' that released an adrenaline surge that now rushed through me. And I knew: the next actions I take might very well be my last.

But I wasn't a fighter by nature.

I once had a conversation with my friends in the cafeteria during my senior year of high school in which we were challenging each other to label ourselves as either a 'lover' or a 'fighter'. It was a typically meaningless discussion primarily meant to help us push our way through the awful, spongy, meatball sandwiches. The conversation had been no doubt brought on by a popular song called "The Girl is Mine" (sung by Michael Jackson and Paul McCartney) that was getting huge amounts of air time.

Most of my friends, who it should be pointed out, were too slow for track, too short for basketball, and too weak for baseball, claimed to be 'fighters'. My guess was the only thing that they would be fighting anytime soon would be a bad case of indigestion from the sandwiches. But I liked them. They were creative and funny, and were willing to put up with the fact that, as a competitive athlete, I didn't have much time to socialize after school or on weekends.

For my part, I claimed to be a 'lover'; not that I could prove it. But I certainly wasn't a fighter I told them, which surprised them given the long-surviving 4th grade rumor that I knew karate.

My claim would bear itself out in dramatic fashion just a few months later:

The 3.1 mile road race in historic Cornwall, N.Y. was one that I had been looking forward to for some time. When I had stepped out of the family car in the nearby Bank of New York parking lot a half hour earlier, I told my father that I felt 'good' and that I was 'primed' to contend for the victory. Greg LaMothe, a pleasant and bespectacled gentleman, welcomed us as we registered. A marathoner himself, it was his first year as the race's chair and director, and his efforts were being supported by the Newburgh YMCA Road Runners.

As the start time drew near, I made my way up to the front of the one-hundred-plus assembled runners, as is the established custom in the running community for those who are considered to have a realistic chance of winning.

Maybe it was my matching, name-brand, navy-blue, racing outfit (which were a gift), or perhaps it was my supposed haughtiness at having dared to proceed up to the front as the starter's pistol was about to be fired.

At the starting line. Jeff Murphy (bending with hand on knee) lines up next to me (far left). Murphy came to my aid in the Cornwall 5K race.

Or maybe the guy was just an ass.

As the race director made his last minute announcements through a tinny-sounding blow horn, I felt a finger jab into my right shoulder. I turned with a smile on my face and extended my right hand, expecting to see someone who wanted to shake my hand and wish me 'good luck'. It was not an uncommon occurrence for me to win my age group category (16-19 on that day), if not the entire race, and we Di Cesares were well-known for racing several times in any given week. I recall one week in the summer of 1984 when we raced five times in seven days. There usually wasn't a race in which 'Vito and his kids' didn't bring home some type of victory hardware.

But the face that greeted me was not smiling. His large, square teeth were clenched under a thin black mustache and he shot me a squint-eyed stare. Very confused, I pulled my hand back, and I refocused my attention to the race as the pistol fired.

It was a glorious mid-April morning. Newly-opened, light green, leaves on the maple and oak trees that lined the streets and the fresh smell of the first cut grass of the season wafted from the suburban environment and made me feel very much alive.

I would try to win today, the whole thing.

The lead pack consisted of three runners, only one of whom I recognized. I followed, approximately five yards back, with a secondary pack that included a local, well-known, runner named Jeff Murphy. If you have even the most basic knowledge of distance running, then you know that the most important aspect of success is properly pacing yourself. The most common mistake new runners make is going out (starting off) too quickly. But I knew better. My father had trained me to run, successfully, from the tender age of eleven. From that first day when he chased me (for three miles) with a stick to get me out of my room … It's all right. I ran 18:11 that day, a high school varsity time; he seemed know what I was physically capable of.

My dad was a genius.

I typically preferred holding back and watching the leaders during the early sections of a race. Then as the miles passed by, I would watch carefully as the perspiration seeped through their shirts, as their legs began to tire and their turnover slowed. I noted with a practiced accuracy when their arms began to drop at the elbow, and when their form broke. I listened to their breathing as it became a more labored and painful effort. And when they began to slow, I would surge past them.

Strategy.

I took no water from the makeshift stand at the two-mile mark which was being successfully maintained by two young girls. They were clearly dedicated to the task asked of them as they had spaced out each cup equally. Rather, I picked up my pace around a corner and began my move towards the lead pack.

Corners are important.

Jeff Murphy chose to go with me, running just a few feet off my right shoulder. It was a decision that buoyed my spirits because he was a veteran racer who knew how to win. Together we moved into third place, picking off a tall, bony-thin, runner in a red singlet who looked to be about my age.

'A track runner with good leg speed, who is not used to the distance,' I silently counseled myself.

His determined facial expression indicated that he wanted to keep pace with us, but his body had no effective response to the surge that had moved us well in front of him.

A short-haired, gray, terrier — that must have gotten off of its leash — briefly caught my attention. I watched as it sniffed around the base of a nearby mailbox when violence inexplicably came from behind me.

I didn't feel the pain from the elbow that jabbed my neck, at first, but it did succeed in staggering me to a grinding halt. My hands on my knees, trying to catch my breath, I watched as the angry, poorly-mustached runner, the one who had jabbed my shoulder at the starting line, made unmistakable eye contact with me.

He had struck me down, and he clearly wanted me to know.

In spite of the throbbing pain that stopped just below my jaw line, I ran after him. Still, I was afraid; 'I'm a lover, not a fighter.'

Jeff Murphy, who had seen the spineless move, was having none of it. He was no taller than me, but now in his mid-twenties, he had filled out the way a man should. He was street strong. His curly beard presented my mind with the image of Greek demi-god Hercules, who he seemed an awful lot like, as he deftly swiped the legs out from under the runner who had just attacked me.

Thud.

Jeff Murphy kept running, never once looking back at his deserving victim.

I started running again, trying my best to work through the lingering pain and to regain a steady stride in spite of a newfound stiffness.

The guy with the poor mustache kept running as well, but he stayed back now, keeping his distance. Looking shamed, and with no bounce in his step, he crossed the finish line a good two minutes after Jeff and me, and hastily departed the race area.

It was perhaps his first smart move of the day.

After the awards had been handed out, I thanked Jeff. He seemed completely unfazed by the whole ordeal as he added: "This kind of crap happens all the time."

He was a fighter.

Now, I *had* to be.

I had just been attacked in the shower, and I had decided that I was going to break someone's nose, even if it meant breaking my own hand (which it probably would) to do so. I tried to remember to protect my face. I wanted to make sure that if I was killed that there could be an open casket, having read somewhere that it was better for emotional closure.

My mom would prefer that, I reasoned.

I drew in a deep breath with my runner's lungs and with every ounce of strength I could summon, unleashed a powerful left-handed haymaker into the area that I estimated my assailant's head might be.

I had the passing thought to pull the weapon out of my back, in order to use it against my attacker, but I was uncertain about the potential blood loss in doing so.

My brain tingled with exhilaration as my fist, mercifully, came into contact with something tangible. I made sure to follow through with my motion; there could be no letting up.

This was a very important moment.

There was a tearing sound, which was followed by an odd, soft, flutter. I had vanquished my foe: the thin shower curtain lay at my trembling feet, utterly defeated.

Damn.

The only audible sensation was the soft tap of water dripping from the shower head directly behind me. No shoes, sneakers, or feet were visible in the toilet stall on the other side of the brightly lit room; the only possible hiding place.

The bathroom was empty.

Or was it?

Kicking the wet, plastic, curtain aside, I stepped into the center of the room once again.

Without question the area seemed even colder now.

"*Who* are you?" I screamed, looking about frantically as I did so, "W*hat* are you? God? The devil? Show yourself, you *coward*!"

Total silence now reigned. Even the repetitive drip of the water from the shower head had stopped.

At that precise moment, the sheer lunacy of the situation gave me pause. I half-smiled and considered that maybe none of this was actually happening. Maybe there was no shadow, no attacker ... and no injury. Perhaps this was all some type of psychological flashback.

Was it possible to simply 'disbelieve' everything?

It hadn't worked that way when the *thing* first appeared in my room back on February 12th.

But maybe, this time, it would work. One shouldn't lose faith in a crisis.

Slowly, I turned my head towards the rectangular-shaped mirrors fastened above the two porcelain sinks. The uneasy hope that I might simply be losing my grip on reality (in spite of the pages and pages of notes in Jeff's journal and the photographs that strongly suggested otherwise) was still very much alive inside me. It was an easy way 'out' of this nightmare. The only acceptable course of action that I could see: *there is no wound ... I am crazy.*

Damn. Damn. Damn!

There they were: three, long, uneven scratches! Their edges, cuts in my soft, human, skin, were beading up with blood; my blood.

This was clear proof that something had just viciously attacked me. Proof that – priest or no priest – something ... perhaps dead ... was winning.

I had now crossed my own personal Rubicon. And like Julius Caesar – who marched into Rome in 49 B.C. to lead gloriously and die epically – there was no turning back for me either.

. . .

This is *real*.

. . .

My mind races under my skull, which now, strangely, feels too tight. The spinning in my head, the turning, is too fast right now.

Vertigo sets in.

I had read about vertigo once. Unfortunately, it turns out that understanding what something is doesn't always help in dealing with it when it actually occurs!

I look one more time at my reflection inside the mirror. I look *so* sad. I feel bad ... for myself ... as I weakly drop to my knees, and then fall down onto my face.

It is March 10th, 1985. The digital clock in room C2D1 reads 3:31 but I am not there to see it. I am lying face down, stark-naked, shivering wet, and bleeding on the floor of a bathroom some thirty feet away.

I'm too busy dying.

"You don't make a photograph just with a camera. You bring to the act of photography all the pictures you have seen, the books you have read, the music you have heard, the people you have loved." - Ansel Adams.

2. J. Jeff Ungar

John Jeff Ungar arrived at SUNY Geneseo in the fall of 1983 from Webster, a suburb of nearby Rochester, N.Y. His father was an accomplished architect who designed – among his many projects – the Margaret Woodbury Strong Museum. Known simply as 'Jeff' to his friends at that time, he was rooming with Edward S. in C2D2 when I first arrived at Erie Hall on September 3rd, 1984.

He was extremely intelligent, keenly observant … and emotionally reserved. There was the air of royalty about him. And if you were to ask me to describe his character all these years later, the answer would be no different had you asked me thirty years ago: "The power of doing anything with quickness is always prized much by the possessor, and often without any attention to the imperfection of the performance" – Mr. Darcy, *Pride and Prejudice*, Chapter 10.

Jeff was an accomplished writer and photographer, and it is largely through his writing (the "C2D1 Journal Notes") and photography that there remains some empirical evidence of the haunting. Lord knows I never wanted to keep any reminders of it!

Often a creature of habit, Jeff would rarely leave his room without his trusty 35mm camera, a notepad, and several writing utensils at his disposal. I would meet Jeff a week or so into that fall semester.

My new roommate, Paul, and I had walked into the D-Quad common (or Suite) room to find a large group of boisterous collegians playing pool. A few of the faces I had seen before, most I definitely had not.

The second floor of Erie Hall was comprised of a centrally-located common area, surrounded by four sections of dorm rooms called 'quads'. Each quad had a smaller common area, three bed rooms, and a bathroom. The D-Quad was where I found myself placed, with Paul, by the college housing administration. We were perhaps the only new students to the quad; the rest were all returnees from the prior 1983-84 school year.

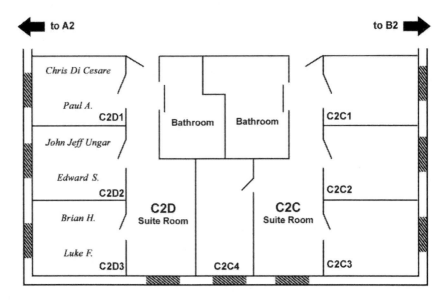

Above: A partial floor map of the second level of the C Building of Erie Hall.

Being that we both 'weighed in' at roughly 5'6" and 130lbs. ... ding!-ding! ... And neither of us had any (or the ability to grow) facial hair, the assumption was made by those who had returned, that Paul and I were freshmen. It looked to them that we needed to be quickly 'schooled' in the ways of college.

When I attempted to share with them the fact that neither of us were freshmen, a disbelieving laughter rose up from the gathering of roughly a half-dozen, the smell of beer radiating off of most, and something else from a few others. One of the returnees took a particular interest in questioning me and stated with full confidence that I didn't look like I was old enough to have finished high school, much less be a college student.

"What are you, like twelve years old?" he exaggerated, pointing a finger in my direction.

This bothered me.

Only two weeks prior I had completed my ninth 26.2 mile marathon at the Empire State Games in Baldwinsville, NY, and I probably knew a great deal more about life and success than this guy did, I just didn't brag about it. So I wasn't about to be dismissed away so casually.

I cut through the smattering of laughter by interjecting that I was a Three-Year Baccalaureate Student, who – because I did so well on the test (in the areas of humanities, natural sciences, and social sciences) – had received automatic credit for my entire freshman year. Thus, having essentially 'skipped over' an academic year (and saved thousands of dollars in the process), I was now considered 'accelerated' and was technically beginning my junior year, well ahead of all of them.

More aggravating guffaws and incredulous rejection followed my pronouncement, and Paul was now getting annoyed as well.

"This is stupid."

He had no strong interest in socializing in the first place (it was my idea) and seeing now that half of the guys were inebriated, he would have been just as happy turning around and heading back to the room and listen to some classic rock music on his state-of-the-art stereo system.

"I can vouch for him!" a sudden voice from the corner of the room to my left interjected.

It turned out that someone else in the room had taken the test as well.

The voice, one that I had not yet heard amongst the din, came from a lightly-bearded and bespectacled student who was perched – not unlike a panther in the wild might be – on the back of a lone chair which was placed in the only quiet, dimly lit corner the room offered.

Corners are important.

Whoever this person was, he apparently had enough social heft, without having to fight for it, to bring the room's activities to a sudden and grinding halt.

I liked that.

"How do you know, Jeff?

"You know these guys?"

Jeff, wearing blue jeans with a button-down shirt under a sleeveless vest that looked to me like it might have survived military maneuvers in Vietnam back in the 1960's, hopped off of the chair backing and walked into the center of the room.

"I saw his name on the list."

I had absolutely no idea what was going on, it felt more like a scene out of the movie *The Deer Hunter*, than any social encounter I had ever experienced.

I remained silent.

If nothing else, he was buying Paul and me some valuable time to figure out what our next move would be.

Jeff walked over to me, permitted himself a close-mouthed smile in order to express an element of brief pleasure, and then shook my hand.

"Nice to meet you," he stated succinctly.

In what can only be defined as serendipitous, after a short discussion, it was discovered that Jeff and I had taken the same exam (Three Year Baccalaureate) on the same day (June 30th), in the same room (Newton Lecture Hall, room 202), and at the same time (12:00 noon). We just did not know each other then. Jeff, in an effort to take his mind off of the multi-hour task ahead, had taken a moment to examine the list of student names beforehand. Apparently my name was unique, or interesting, enough to attract his attention.

Di Cesare: It sounded Latin.

It was this particular characteristic, his ability to remain observant and project a sense of calm, even when fast-paced events unfolded, that would leave a lasting and profound impression on me that evening. It was an impression that I would eventually choose to act on, and an impression that would eventually change everything ... for both of us.

We would develop a friendship over the next few months that was primarily based upon our shared desire to understand the world around us (even if we had differing approaches to getting there). We had a shared appreciation for artistic achievement (I enjoyed drawing and he photography), history, and the guilty pleasure of roleplaying in the form of the classic dice game *Dungeons & Dragons*.

Controversial at the time due to the circumstance of a teen committing suicide following a role-playing session in 1982, some media outlets began the attempt to link the practice to satanic cults and societies. The mother of the deceased teen sued his high school principal claiming that a D&D curse had been placed upon her son, but the law suit was quickly thrown out by the courts.

For Jeff and I, and the few others who would on occasion join us, it was simply an entertaining problem-solving exercise. One that allowed for risk-free application of concept to varied and challenging dilemmas.

```
15.   arcadia is a large town with a pop.of about 3,000.there are two
inns.the happy mans inn,and across the street the arcade,which is
much larger and ornately decorated.a member,rn,spots a person who
he/she thinks is astrologer,going into the arcade.
16.   upon entering the inn,they will be approached by a small frail
old man,who looks very much like the horse salesman.he asks the party
if they would like to put thier horses in the adjacent stable,a gp/
horse.if asked if he knows the man who sold them the horses he will
say no.the clerk a large dark man will then call,is there a lord
valarian party here? message for a lenuvician party!when asked for
the note he will ask him for some proof.if he gets none he will tear
up the scroll.if it is pieced together the clerk will open the
door and allow the wind to scatter the paper about the room.if viol-
ence erupts and someone is severely hurt,astrologer will apear on
the scene and heal the wounded.when he is finished he will give a
strong glare to the leader of the group.then walk out the door,to
disappear into the crowd.
```

A sample of my D&D role-playing notes that Jeff and I used in the fall of 1984.

On occasion we would role-play until the wee hours of the morning, and I could not help but to burst out laughing when at approximately 2 a.m. one weekday morning Jeff mournfully lamented that it seemed "Time's passage functioned proportionately converse to one's desires."

I noticed early on in the friendship that there was no obvious ego guiding Jeff's actions.

It was never about who won, or who was better at some task. Rather, he embraced variation of interest, belief and accomplishment. He admired the achievements of others with the same honest passion that he held for his own. In fact, he would often take inspiration from the success of those around him.

As an athlete whose sole goal was often victory, or at the very least besting as many opponents as I possibly could, this was a refreshing change of pace for me. I admired that his sense of self and happiness were not exclusively driven by accomplishment, and that he could see value in efforts beyond his own.

For his part, Jeff was once asked what his impression of me was when we first met and he replied with a straight face: "He strikes a lot of people as being off-the-wall, but he's actually intelligent."

To inadvertently back up his observation, when asked the same question, I replied that Jeff had what I liked most in a good friend: a body temperature of 98.6°... and holding.

"Raskolnikov", an image of J. Jeff Ungar by Chris Di Cesare

Jeff quickly became a trusted friend after he had helped save me from an awkward social situation that warm September night, as the summer's number one song (ironically) "Ghostbusters" by Ray Parker Jr., echoed out through the college hallways above the reverie.

. . .

Now it is March 10th, 1985 – and I need *real* saving.

It has been a good ten minutes since I headed off to the quad bathroom for a warm shower. Now, I am lying face down on the chilled floor, bleeding, and not doing very well.

I can still feel the sting of the three cuts that run vertically down my tightened back. My feet and toes continue to ache because of the way I landed when I collapsed onto the floor.

Summoning what energy I have, and with great difficulty, I turn my head to the left, taking the ever-increasing pressure off of my chin and neck. With my head now tilting down, I attempt to focus my eyes.

There is a fairly large, unmoving, white mass near my feet that soon comes together for me as the impractical shower curtain that I had torn off of its bar while trying to defend myself. An inch or so from the curtain, I notice that the toes on my left foot are bent upwards and are very pale from an apparent lack of circulation. My carefully trimmed nails – a distance running necessity – are pressed deep into the meat of my toes. I concentrate for a moment, and then signal my left thigh to 'lift'.

My running teammates in high school used to outwardly marvel at the musculature of my legs, now it was time to put this much vaunted attribute to use. A slow, deliberate command travels from my brain, down my spine, and into my leg. I can see my thigh muscle tense up and I am relieved that it seems to be working. The movement creates enough space, enough opportunity, for my foot to spring quickly back into its natural position, and allow my toes to relax.

Finally!

The effort pays off beyond my initial expectations and I find that my entire body has shifted just a bit. I am now lying, partially, on my right side. This allows for the possibility of a continued physical inspection, like a mechanic 'checking under the hood' of a car to see if it is still able to run. And for a split second I wish that I was back on my run. I wish I hadn't stopped and returned here …

My straining gaze makes its way from a now thankful, but aching, foot and travels up my legs. I pause every few seconds to protect my neck from the difficult turn that it is currently making. I do *not* want to lose consciousness; the *thing* is probably still in here watching me as I lie helpless.

Waiting and planning.

A full month had passed since 'it' had arrived, uninvited, and I still had no idea what it wanted … other than to cause me to suffer.

I notice that a barely audible 'sigh' of relief escapes my drying mouth as I confirm that there is no visible damage to my legs … the 'meal tickets' are intact.   Although I have already established that I have very little control over them … that's going to pose a problem.

I am now able to isolate at least one source of pain at the base of my pelvis: my sack is tight like a fist … and it aches.   I'm not sure why.   Even worse, my member is visibly compressed down into what I am sure is a cold, germ-infested, puddle on the bathroom floor.   This observation absolutely *disgusts* me.   The thought (whether possible or not) of bacterium floating their way into my urethra and slowly ascending up into my kidneys, makes me want to vomit.   My stomach muscles convulse in response to this concept, but my body is too exhausted, too traumatized even to vomit.   Since I cannot move, all I can do is hope that being circumcised will reduce my risk of infection.

"Pale Death with impartial tread beats at the poor man's cottage door, and at the palaces of kings." — Horace

There are visible lines of water that cover the side of my stomach up to where my left arm obstructs the rest of my view.   The arm … my arm … is bent at the elbow, and there is a throbbing pain here as well, the result of my flexed bicep pushing uncomfortably into my forearm.   The fingers on my hand – which are trembling uncontrollably – are fully extended much like a bug's legs on the water's surface.

Are you kidding me, God … why is this happening? I have been so good. Where are you?

It is a very selfish plea, and I should know better than making it.

After all, how many Jews had their prayers answered at Auschwitz or Buchenwald? I am no better than they were, no more deserving.

Yet, I make the plea all the same.

Lying there, I recall seeing WWII concentration camp photos in my history class, of stacks of emaciated corpses piled dozens high. A sickening recognition brings my thoughts to a halt: They were killed in the showers.

I want to give up, to go to sleep on a large, round, smooth, rock in some primeval forest. I want the crows to knead my skin with their sharp claws; to heat my ears with the breath from their pointed beaks; to carry my tired eyes away.

Fight.

My eyes are the only parts of my body that are able to function without an extreme effort. They spy upon a single droplet of water. It is hanging down, tentatively, from my left wrist which rests not far from my face. It looks almost pear-shaped. It is holding on for dear life … just like I am. I can see the inverted image of the bathroom floor being reflected in its bulb-shaped base.

It is mesmerizing.

And just as my childhood fascination with the movement of the stars had kept my mind enthralled well into the early morning hours, my mind begins to examine this near-transparent construct of two parts hydrogen and one part oxygen.

Refraction.

That's the word. That's why the image is inverted in the water droplet. I hold onto that concept, my mind concentrates on it.

But the Universe is a constantly changing place, and I watch the droplet fall without a sound … just as I had moments earlier … and flatten against the unyielding floor.

Gravity.

I notice too that the droplet's moisture has darkened the grout between two of the bathroom tiles near my hand: the natural result of liquid hitting the porous grout.

Moisture.

It is a compelling awareness; that I am literally 'observing' my mind putting itself back together.

Metacognition.

Without actually making the conscious choice to do so, I am also experiencing the restoration of who I am and what I know. But the sheer weight of this effort leads once again to despair with the understanding that I will never have the cerebral strength required to do this, again and again. The *thing* is going to wear me down; it's going to kill me. Because no matter how fascinating the process, I cannot put my mind back together each time it moves to destroy me. It is a losing proposition.

I want you out of my life.

I shut my eyes and again I wait for the crows.

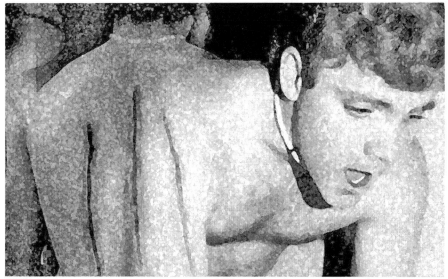

"When you compare the sorrows of real life to the pleasures of the imaginary one, you will never want to live again, only to dream forever." — Alexandre Dumas, *The Count of Monte Cristo*

They do not arrive, but *something* does. The sharp squealing of the door's metal wheels rolling on the metal track is almost deafening in my current state. A wave of much drier air arrives. I feel it glide over the back of my tired heels. I hear sounds, someone is speaking. The voice is nervous and unsure, but not panicked. I want to trust it.

"Chris ... Chris ... are you all right?"

I am able to blurt out a soft "mmm ..." but not any words.

Now there is a flutter of movement, the noise of sneaker bottoms starting and stopping on a wet bathroom floor. There is also the sound of nervous breathing. But it's not *my* breath.

I open my eyes when I sense I am being pulled up by two hands that are clasped together near the middle of my chest. They successfully pull me up onto my knees. But the arms attached to the hands seem to be trembling a bit from the strain.

They cannot do this alone.

There is a quality of friendly determination to them ... I trust them. I command my legs to stand. They refuse, but the effort shifts my balance enough that the arms are now able to prop me up against the wooden door which rattles angrily as I lean into it.

"Chris, can you *hear* me? You're bleeding, what happened?"

A towel is wrapped, very tightly, about my waist. The warmth it creates around my lower half is welcome. I mumble out a weak: "Thankssss."

"No problem. Are you OK to walk? Here, just lean on me."

I follow the words to Jeff's face, and I can see that he has worry etched deeply across it. Seeing him now, assisting me in this manner, makes me regret that I was willing to accept the crows only moments beforehand.

I never want that to happen again.

Jeff navigates me across the hallway into the safety of his room. Ed is standing as we enter. He looks concerned. I am shivering uncontrollably now from the cold, or the fear, or the exhaustion; maybe all of these things.

"And ...?" Ed queried, raising both of his eyebrows in expectation.

"He was attacked, in the bathroom."

I stop looking at Ed when I hear him issue a pained and confused response: a long drawn out almost cynical "Whaaat?"

I have nothing to say.

And as Jeff carefully sits me down at the foot of his bed, my cold and wet feet leaving imprints on his floor, Ed apparently catches his first glimpse of the cuts.

"Oh my God ... Oh my *God!*"

There is a pause.

"All of this is *real*, isn't it?"

"Dwell on the beauty of life. Watch the stars, and see yourself running with them." – Marcus Aurelius, *Meditations.*

3. Geneseo

I should have gone to Marist College, Marist accepted me first.

That's what was running through my head as the reality of the five hour commute from my home to the college in Geneseo finally began to sink in. There would be no 'quick trips' to places I know, and I would have no car.

No, I could never go there. I didn't win that race. I was supposed to win.

That side stich had been ferocious. It hit the underside of my ribs as I crested a hill with just three-quarters of a mile to go in the high school invitational race. With it went any chance of winning. College scouts would be there we had heard beforehand, scouts that awarded fast runners scholarships. A scholarship sounded plenty good to me.

My training had been going well, many of the other top area runners were racing down at Van Cortland Park in New York City, and the course (winding and hilly) seemed made to order for a strength runner such as myself.

Working my way up to the lead pack as we reached the second mile mark was easier than I thought it would be, and my legs still felt strong and fresh. I was so relaxed and so confident at that point that I allowed myself a few moments to take in the Marist College landscape. What surprised me more than the majestic and scenic vistas overlooking the Hudson River were the multiple bed sheets hanging out of dorm windows, the number of crushed plastic party cups on the grass lawn, and the overall lack of students out cheering for the runners. It must have been some party last night! I wondered, as Marist was a Catholic school, if there would be severe repercussions for such unruly behavior. Right then, as I began to pump my arms to begin my surge to the finish line, the cramp hit.

Afterwards, I sat dejectedly, on a bench in the men's locker room. I understood all too well that there would be no scouts and no scholarships for me that day. My coach found me. He helped to console me, got me dressed, and walked me onto the team bus. Perhaps being aware of how much doing well in this race meant to me, my teammates left me alone. It would be easy, now, while sitting inside the bus as it wound its way down the road, to enjoy the majestic and scenic vistas overlooking the Hudson River; but I no longer wanted to.

I did have several road racing victories to my credit, but that still did not mean that losing was acceptable, particularly while representing my school. Thankfully I was trained to believe that being a competitive runner was a process, not a result. So it was never a question of whether or not I could accomplish something that I wanted to, it was only a matter of how I would change my routine in order to achieve it.

The truth of the matter was that the 'side stitch incident' turned out to be important because it reminded me of a valuable understanding: in order to succeed in life you need to be able to work through the pain. So, I set a valuable goal for myself: to learn how to run through even the most agonizing of cramps.

Apples, pears, nectarines … I now brought any type of cramp-inducing foods that I could on my training runs. I would tear bites out of them with my young teeth between breaths as the miles passed underneath my fast-moving feet. I was doing it – purposely inducing cramps – in training so that I would learn how to run through them in races. And I did.

The result of my newfound dedication was improved running times.

Following my disappointing finish in Poughkeepsie that cold, crisp Saturday morning, I clicked off a 33:59 10K (6.2 miles) in Port Jervis, logged a strong 15:45 5K in the twilight at New Paltz, and then set the new cross country course record for my high school on a very difficult and hilly course ... the kind that I liked.

Chris DiCesare leads Vikings to victory

Chris DiCesare recorded the first win on Valley Central's brand new 5,000-meter course to lead the Vikings to victories over Cornwall and James I. O'Neill in the Orange County Interscholastic Boy's Cross Country League Tuesday.

Valley Central turned back Cornwall, 24-32, and O'Neill, 27-28, in the initial race on the new course.

Tom Scott of O'Neill captured second place with his time of 18:34 and Bob Jurgens of Valley Central was third with 18:36. DiCesare's winning time was 17:50.

The icing on the proverbial cake was running stride-for-stride across the finish with a future U.S. Olympian. John Trautmann – who would represent the United States of America in the 5000 meter event (round one, heat three) in the Barcelona Olympic Games in the summer of 1992 – walked up to me before the race, and in front of my friends and teammates, announced that he was going to break the course record; which at time was *my* course record.

Trautmann was a freshman phenom whose running achievements were already being talked about with relative disbelief in the local high school locker rooms. But his impetuousness reminded me a lot of Alberto Salazar, the hot-headed Oregon State runner who told the world he was going to dethrone four-time winner Bill Rodgers, my running hero, in the 1980 New York City Marathon. "I intend to beat Billy Rodgers at his own game."

A strong tail wind had pushed the elite runners along at a brisk pace through the New York City streets, but at the 14-mile mark Rodgers' legs got tangled with another runners and he fell to the ground. By the time he got up the other runners had a good eighty yards on him. He would finish in fifth place; his attempt at five consecutive victories was over. Salazar, now tagged 'The Rookie' in the press, won the race, shaving thirty seconds off Rodgers' course record to add insult to injury.

I fumed.

If Salazar had any class, I informed my bored friends the following day on the bus ride to school, he would not have mouthed off to the press beforehand, and afterwards he would have talked about the large crowds supporting his effort along the way, not a dismissive "I don't want to add to the myth of the marathon. It's just a distance, not a shrine." and "I don't think I proved anything to myself, but I imagine I did to a lot of others."

The marathon was an event steeped in history, drama and tradition from the famous battle of the same name in 490 B.C. when a Greek soldier, Pheidippides, ran all the way from the battlefield to Athens to deliver the message: "Niki" (victory); to the barefooted the victory of Ethiopian Abebe Bikila in the 1960 Olympics in Rome, the city that had conquered his nation.

Just a distance, more like selfish ignorance?

Now, this high school rookie had just called me out (on a much reduced but, to me, no less meaningful stage).

I replied that he was welcome to try, but what was running though my head was: *What a jerk!*

Above left: On my way to a 1:20.41 half marathon finish in Middletown, NY, at the age of seventeen. Above right: A caricature drawn by Brian Peters of New Windsor in 1984 looks spot on (except for the tattoo).

It was a devastatingly hilly cross country course, the type of course, and terrain, that rarely offers a runner the chance to settle into a steady pace. On a flat track his leg speed would have easily left me in the dust. In fact Trautmann would go on, at 46, to set a world age group record for the mile in February of 2015 – as I was putting the finishing touches on this book - with a time of 4:12.33.

But give me some hills, or tack on a few more miles, and watch my leg strength – born of years of marathon training – do the trick! I also had the advantage in two other key areas: I had better knowledge of the course; and, whereas he was running for a very fast time, I was now running for my (and by imagined proxy Bill Rodgers') honor.

Against what would normally have been better judgment, I decided to throw caution to the wind and I went out at a blistering pace. It was a pace that I knew I would not be able to maintain, but I was hoping that I would not actually have to.

I had a plan.

Because of the limited sight distances that the constant turns and hills and dense foliage on the course created, I was quickly able to break visual contact with him. I knew that it was harder to catch someone that you could not see.

I raced as though my life depended on it, imagining I was a colonial settler during the 17th century trying to escape the flying arrows of a pursuing Indian raid. My father had long told me stories of local farmers finding arrow heads in the ground, so it seemed like a fair enough thought to get my body to give that little bit extra.

There was no sign of John until I hit the final straightaway which led to a gathered crowd of onlookers ... and the finish line.

Trautmann came fast-charging out of the dense forest trail, and had with five yards to go, closed far enough to be able to reach out and touch my shoulder had he chosen to do so.

My stomach felt like it was being tied in knots.

We charged wildly across the finish line virtually nose to nose to a loud cacophony of high pitched yelling and screaming.

What a race!

John kept his word that day. He broke the existing course record, but so had I.

Decades later, many of my former high school teammates still remind me of the day that I held off 'the great John Trautmann'.

And to his credit, he was decent enough to extend his hand in a goodwill gesture of congratulations afterwards. That simple but gracious gesture, even if he had beaten me, was more than enough to allow me to hope for his success some ten years later while watching portions of the Olympics, with my young daughter sitting atop my shoulders. I recall glancing up at her three-year-old face and seeing the reflection of the flickering light from the television in her intense green eyes.

There were medals and trophies, and then there was life. In that prescient moment I realized that I wouldn't want to change my past, even if I were somehow able to.

John had what he wanted, he was an Olympian. And I had what I wanted: a family. I decided that it was a good time to start thanking God for some of my unanswered prayers.

...

Still, Marist College was a quick 40 minute car ride from my parents' driveway, which was a negligible distance when you consider that I would run for over an hour on most days anyway. It was a well-known and reputable school, and I thought that its mascot (The Red Fox) was as cool as the other side of the pillow. I even had the opportunity to work alongside someone who 'was' the Red Fox mascot a few years later, in 1987: Jim Norman. Still, that one inauspicious race stuck in my craw. It was the worst race of my high school career and I didn't want to have to wage a constant fight against a bad memory, a ghost from my past, every day. So, instead, I chose Geneseo.

I dutifully passed the college's three-year degree exam the spring of my senior year at high school, and I quickly chose Speech Communications as my major course of study.

And in spite of the tedious hours-long drive past trees and ... well, more trees ... Geneseo was a beautiful place. Once I had comfortably settled into Genesee Hall, a few hundred yards northwest of Erie Hall, I walked uptown.

**"[My father] had a name for the bottom of the sky--'the hem of heaven."
— Nancy Horan, *Loving Frank***

Main Street looked to me like something out of an Andy Griffith TV show; a Jimmy Stewart movie; or a Norman Rockwell painting. There were local 'mom and pop' stores, eateries, and elegant Victorian homes lining the thoroughfare. The Genesee Valley stretched out across the entire western horizon and the view from any of the college dormitories was simply breathtaking. I had been to the theme parks in Orlando, Florida; had walked the cultured sidewalks of Montreal; and run through the endless cornfields in Kansas – but never had I been to a more beautiful place than Geneseo, New York.

It felt like home.

In reality it was nothing at all like home. It was more like a non-stop carnival freak show to someone such as me who had lived a very regimented, 'proper', and isolated life growing up. Light blue and red neon beer signs in dormitory windows lit up the evening sky and served as beacons to legions of drunken co-eds staggering their way back home from *The Vital Spot* or *In Between*.

"Look at that party the other night. Everybody wanted to have a good time and tried real hard but we all woke up the next day feeling sorta sad and separate." — Jack Kerouac, *The Dharma Bums*

Blue hair, green hair, spiked hair, no hair, beer pong, dance parties, young couples making love on rugs out in the hallways … I had never seen – nor come close to even imagining – anything like it. Folks hanging off of light posts, singing 'off key' in the dorm lobby at 4AM wearing only one shoe, and impromptu musical jam sessions in someone's bedroom were all experiences that I marveled at, and sometimes laughed at … but did my level best to keep my distance from.

I was a runner.

I had been taught that the effectiveness of any democracy lay almost exclusively with the will of the people, and while my contemporaries certainly could 'party hardy', as went the phrase, it seemed to me that they were also dangerous and irreverent risk-takers, irresponsible students, and unfaithful partners.

It was a foreign way of life to me, and one that flew in the face of the very efforts that had allowed me to get to college in the first place. Beyond people getting sick the following morning, I worried that the work ethic that had helped to build this country into a super power would one day be replaced by a society that wanted only to be shocked and entertained.

But, I was just eighteen, and eighteen year olds rarely knew much about life anyway. So I chose to put my initial worrying aside and focus instead on trying to enjoy the uniqueness of the college environment.

Besides, those glowing neon beer signs were pretty cool.

Back home my success in running on the roads and in cross country had made me something of a big fish in a small pond. Whenever I showed up for a race people knew me, and there was typically an expectation that I would win, or at least place in my age category. Having my name listed in the November 1981 issue of *Runner's World* for my performance at the Callicoon 9.4 mile road race was a major thrill as well, even if it was in the back portion of the magazine. I made sure that everyone knew about that.

College was different.

Suddenly everyone around me vying for a prized spot on the Varsity team had been the top runner in their hometown as well. Some people don't adjust well to this loss of dominance, but I discovered that I preferred it. Unlike in high school where participation in track was often encouraged simply to 'make one look better' when applying for colleges and where many teammates did not train all that seriously, there were no 'stragglers' at this level of competition.

In college, if you didn't run hard … you finished last.

Every long distance run soon became an 'international event' in my mind. I visualized myself running in the Olympic Marathon in Seoul, South Korea for the USA, a flag stitched across my singlet. My cross country teammates soon represented Japan, Brazil, Kenya, Great Britain, and Russia. And on those few days that I finished practice first, I would imagine myself standing atop the victory podium, a crowd of 50,000 roaring in approval, and announce: "My father once told me, 'I give you my name. What you do with it is up to you.'"

Support from the sidelines: Racing at Delaware Park in Buffalo, New York.

Cue the roaring crowd.

He actually *had* told me that – and on several occasions – but I think it was more or less a way to keep me out of trouble, and not meant exclusively for an audience of wildly-cheering, non-existent South Koreans. The phrase would, nonetheless, strongly connect with a lot of television viewers some twenty-eight years later.

I had the honor of training with some very talented Rochester-area runners like Paul Dodd, Steve Stellwagon and Steve Mack, and those from other parts of the state like Scott Ambrose, John Bousquet and Tom Olendorf. Under the effective coaching of the late Martin Kentner I even earned a trip to the NCAA regional meet.

If I had any lingering doubts about attending SUNY Geneseo, they were dispelled once I experienced the professional way in which Coach Kentner treated his runners. Even when a runner fell short of a particular time or goal, he would look for something positive – a silver lining – to share.

Once, during an over distance 12-mile training run on Groveland Station Road, I began to stagger a bit and found myself suddenly falling off the pace. Long distances were my forte, especially out on rolling hills where my strength could make up for a lack of blistering track speed, so this wasn't the norm.

Coach Kentner pulled alongside me in his four-door sedan. He was wearing a broad smile and what looked to me like a Paul "Bear" Bryant hat.

"What's wrong, Tiger?"

I shook my head and told him that I just wasn't feeling well; my energy level had dropped considerably. My legs were tiring.

"Well, don't push it too hard then," he replied. Then added, "Your form still looks great though, Chris. You have an excellent running form."

Considering his compliment, as he drove off down the road ahead to support the other runners, I thought to myself: *You know what? I do have excellent form. It was both efficient and consistent, I can do this.*

And as the course turned back towards the welcoming village of Geneseo, I recovered my stride and soon found myself back at the tail end of the lead pack. Coach Kentner was wise enough to understand that a few simple - but sincere – words of encouragement could go a long way, and he knew when to use them.

Bravo.

There were some great thrills running for Geneseo as well, such as running on courses and at colleges all across the state for the first time including the famed Delaware Park in Buffalo; competing in the NCAA Division Regional Championships; and chasing the recent winner of a Texas Marathon to the finish line during the September 23rd, Alumni run. It was likely (excepting future terrifying sprints out of my dorm room in the months ahead) my most memorable run in college.

I wrote in my running log that night:

... Tom Olendorf is about my size, an inch or so shorter. At 3.1 miles, he surged ahead. I responded quickly. As we hit 4 miles, the first alumnus, John Nodecker, who had recently won a marathon in Texas, caught us. Then he pulled ahead. Tom told me to go with him. I couldn't believe that he expected ME to go with John! But I did. I ran stride for stride with him until 6.1, then we dashed wildly for the finish chute. He won 36:16.4 to 36:16.6 ...

There was also a great sense of comradery. I recall one training run conversation in which my teammates were discussing the possibility of former Geneseo runner Dale Teed, naming his sons Garren and Warren.

Think about it.

After reflecting on the likelihood that those poor children would rue not only their names, but their parents as well, I vowed to myself to name my children with as 'normal' a set of names as was possible!

Members of the 1984 SUNY Geneseo Cross Country team gather around Coach Martin Kentner to pose for our college yearbook photo. I seem happy enough.

By the late fall of 1984, I had run my way into the 'top five' on the team and it seemed that life couldn't get any better. The entire country was in a good mood, people were quite simply proud to be American. The United States had only months before cruised to an impressive medal count victory in the Los Angeles Summer Olympic Games, highlighted by American Joan Benoit's victory in the first ever Women's Olympic Marathon. *Time* magazine did a cover story on America's upbeat mood entitled, "I ♥ U.S.", the same week that the college semester began, and it was not uncommon to see people walking on the sidewalks wearing t-shirts with flags on them, that or the *Ghostbusters* logo.

But if there was one primary source, one causal factor, for this national lifting of spirits you would have to look no further than President Ronald Wilson Reagan.

Reagan, a conservative Republican, had by virtue of a booming economy, unmatched oratory skills, and having survived an assassination attempt, become very close to a legend in his own time. By late-October *Newsweek*, and virtually every other print publication, began to suggest that we were about to witness one of the greatest political landslides in American Presidential history. Most of the national polls had the incumbent leading his opponent, former Vice President, Democrat Walter 'Fritz' Mondale, braced for a possible fifty-state sweep and there was talk of a political realignment.

Even on college campuses across the country, often bastions of liberalism and progressive thought, one could see a multitude of 'Reagan-Bush 84' buttons adorning backpacks, baseball caps and jackets.

1984: President Reagan makes a campaign stop in Rochester, New York

There was a magic to his delivery when he spoke, and a sense of shared purpose in his words, that could not be denied.   As a speech communications student, I felt compelled to analyze every word and every gesture. The only question, it seemed, was his advanced age. At 73, Reagan would not only be President if he won reelection, but the Western World's de facto leader against the Soviet Union and the still present threat of communist aggression during the Cold War.

I watched along with the rest of America as Reagan put the 'age issue' to rest with a clever "I am not going to exploit for political purposes my opponent's youth and inexperience."   And as Mondale smiled and laughed from across the stage, so too did the millions of Americans tuned into network television across the country. The question of who would win was now considered a rhetorical question.

After watching the debate, which had been held in Kansas City, Mo., I announced to my mildly unenthusiastic roommate in C2D1 that the election was effectively over.

"I wouldn't be so sure," he warned, "I think that Mondale could still take it."

I fidgeted with the circular metal 'Reagan-Bush 84' pin on my jacket for a quick moment, as I replayed the facts in my mind as I knew them.

There was no other possibility.

"Reagan is going to win, Paul."

He put down his pen and cast me a sideways glance from his desk chair, a slight smirk now on his tan face, "You want to bet on it?"

A pencil drawing that I made of President Reagan for my art class at Geneseo. Not bad for an amateur.

"Sure," I replied in a higher pitched voice than I preferred, "If Reagan wins you have to buy me lunch the next day with your meal card."

"Deal," he replied, now leaning towards me with interest, "and if Mondale wins?"

"Then I buy you lunch, with my meal card?" I offered with raised open palms.

"What?" He complained dramatically as if to question my integrity, "That's it? Reagan is supposed to win, right? I should get something better than that!"

He was absolutely right. There could be no second guessing, no doubt conveyed about my convictions or my skills of prognostication. I had no choice but to think of the most extreme, most repulsive, most outrageous offer possible. What act or gesture of recompense would be able to top all others? As I was 100% sure that Reagan would win, there would be no risk of being called on to carry it out.

I went for it.

"If Mondale wins," I said bravely, "You take a crap in my mouth."

A look of surprised disgust, tinged with a hint of amusement, crossed his face.

"Why the hell would I want to do *that*?"

"I don't know," I replied, realizing a bit too late that I might have overshot the mark on this one, "I was just trying to think of something that would prove to you how certain I am that Reagan will win. I've told you before; I'm just not good at betting!"

"OK, OK," he laughed while shaking his head back and forth, "you can buy me lunch if Mondale wins. I'd much prefer that."

Mercifully, on Wednesday, November 5th, Paul was smiling and with his meal card in hand, motioned toward the food line at the all-too-familiar Letchworth Dining Hall: "Go ahead, Mr. Reagan, get yourself some food. Nice win."

When the political dust had settled and all the votes were tallied, Reagan had won 49 of 50 states in his bid for re-election; a near sweep, with Mondale able to hold on to only his home state of Minnesota. Reagan's Electoral College victory over Mondale was a staggering 525-to-13, and that feeling of unity and patriotism continued to stretch itself out over a welcome nation.

When I had moved into room C2D1 with Paul, a naturally gifted athlete in his own right, I could have no idea how much my life would change in just a few short months. For barring the single annoyance of our residence director taping large 'Ghostbusters' logos on every door (I truly loathed that movie) it seemed as though everything was going my way.

"None so good that he has no faults, none so wicked that he is worth naught." –
Edith Hamilton, *Mythology*.

4. The Twins

Paul and I had met the previous spring, both of us circling around the indoor track above the college ice rink. He told me that he appreciated the fact that I yelled out "track!" each and every time I ran by the slower runners, so as not to risk an unintentional collision.

Naturally, I was somewhat pleased by his unexpectedly positive recognition of what I thought was a rather important, but seldom appreciated, practice. We found ourselves running lap after lap after lap talking about everything and anything under the sun as we did so.

He spoke of a local rock band that I had yet to hear of called 'Rush' and of his disdain for the quality of the college food, while I shared with him details of the various marathons courses I had run and of the importance of training with consistency.

After we had both completed our workouts, he asked me where on campus I lived; indicating that he thought it might be beneficial to run together again in the near future, that is, if I didn't mind.

I didn't.

In a matter of weeks a friendship was struck and his family invited me out to their home near Geneva, NY. It was late April and we hiked through some woods not far from the shore of one of the Finger Lakes. Paul's mother prepared an excellent home cooked meal, and as I left, I offered to have Paul come down my way as well.

That summer, just before the Olympic Games were held, Paul came down to visit my family. When he arrived, I invited several of my good friends from high school to come over and join us. We swam, played some backyard volleyball, and ate some hot food, fresh off the grill, thanks to my dad. It wasn't lost on me as we swam lap after lap in the pool, and as we hit the volleyball back and forth over the net, at times taking a face plant in the grass, that both Paul and I thrived on exercise. The mere act of movement was something that gave us both satisfaction and purpose.

Understanding by now, that we had a great many shared interests and habits, we made a mutual decision to room together in the fall.

There was, of course, the uncomfortable obligation to speak with our current roommates first, but neither of us felt that they would be horribly upset by the news. As I was deep into the summer road racing circuit (often racing four times a week) and would be busy training for another marathon in August, Paul agreed to contact the college on our behalf.

We were quickly assigned room C2D1 in Erie Hall. It looked to be a fresh new start for both of us.

On the day that we all moved in, September 3rd, 1984, Paul and his father brought with them a large wooden loft. I had never seen anything remotely like it. Once assembled, it reminded me of an indoor tree house. Never much of tree-climber as a youth, the thought of being perched (relatively) high above the ground with little to no danger or effort was tremendously appealing to me. More importantly, however, was that it provided some much-needed space in the compact college room.

By having our mattresses raised up five feet in the air, we now had increased our floor space quite considerably. This created the novel effect of having both an 'upstairs' and a 'downstairs', and it allowed for additional privacy should we need it.

The transition to Erie Hall, and with a new roommate, was both comfortable and stress free. I had never gotten along so well with anyone outside of my own circle of relatives. In fact, within a few weeks Paul and I had, perhaps unsurprisingly, been nicknamed 'The Twins' by the others on the floor. We were, after all, the same height, had similar builds and were nearly inseparable in the early weeks of the semester.

Paul with his matching brown eyes and hair – and slightly more serious demeanor – was labeled the 'Dark Twin'. I was, therefore, dubbed the 'Light Twin' owing to my complexion and more upbeat persona. Neither of us minded the names, and it could have been a lot worse. For my part, 'Light Twin' was still preferable to what I had been nicknamed in the past, everything from 'Goldilocks' to 'Blondie' to 'Stretch Armstrong' (don't ask) to 'Leprechaun'. I had heard about some pretty horrific nicknames in my day, but ours were born from the similarities which had helped to build our friendship in the first place, so we embraced them.

"Names and attributes must be accommodated to the essence of things, and not the essence to the names, since things come first and names afterwards."
— Galileo Galilei, *Discoveries and Opinions of Galileo*

Living with my previous roommate, in Genesee Hall, had proven challenging at times. I admired his sense of humor and got a big kick out of when he played the Barry Manilow song, *"Read 'em and Weep"*, so many times in a row that the girl upstairs went totally berserk and started screaming through the ceiling at us. But there were chafing differences.

He was an upper classman, while I was just three months removed from high school. He had a long-time steady girlfriend, and for all intents and purposes, my girlfriend was my running. I am sure it was only natural for some of the hazing that ensued to have occurred. But I didn't particularly enjoy having an entire bucket of ice cubes thrown on me in the shower at 6AM, or having my bed short-sheeted after a tiring 12-mile run. He was a very good person and a loyal friend but, for me at that time, not the perfect roommate. The 'kicker' turned out to be his involvement on the Geneseo Volunteer Emergency Squad. As an EMT he would get 'called' at all hours of the night to suit up and rush to an accident scene. It was a noble calling, but I was a light sleeper to begin with and the calls wreaked havoc on my body clock. I can't count the number of times that I meandered onto the bus, on the way to run against some of the best athletes in the northeast, having had only three hours sleep, or with a splitting headache.

I will always be thankful for the many rides home that he provided me, and for the opportunity to see my first music video (the Eurythmics' "Here Comes the Rain Again") on his old black and white TV set, but it was time for me to make a rooming change.

In Paul, my newfound 'twin', I saw a kindred spirit. He was a student dedicated to athletic achievement, had stellar hygiene, enjoyed a good joke, and was close with his family.

Above: American distance runner and 1976 Olympian Bill Rodgers winning the 1979 Boston Marathon in an American Record time of 2:09.27. It was his third of

four victories there. I was amazed to discover that Rodgers' own daughter, Erika, would later share information about the C2D1 Haunting with her famous dad, who graciously signed this poster for the filming of *Please, talk with me.*

He was also, to his eternal credit, one of a very limited number of people in my life who would actually listen to me when I droned on and on about the incredible consistency of four-time Boston Marathon winner Bill Rodgers, or about the value of 'drafting' behind the lead runners, or of my aspirations to someday qualify to run in the U.S. Olympic trials.

Without question, we were as close as two people ... who barely knew each other ... could be. What I lacked in 'streets smarts' was easily compensated for by Paul's expansive knowledge of the local social scene and its customs. And where Paul sometimes felt that he needed to push a bit too hard to win a girl's attention, I had them flocking to me in droves. So much so, that Paul began to regularly call me 'Romeo' instead of Chris.

> *So tell me Romeo, how many girlfriends are you seeing now? Have you gotten in touch with that cute girl from Seneca? I hope you get all the soft bodies you can, then I'll enter you in the book of records.*

Letter writing has become something of a dying art in the 21ˢᵗ Century, often replaced by quick digital media posts and 'emojis'. Paul and I, corresponded repeatedly over the summer of 1984.

How ironic it was that possibly the only guy in the dorm who had dedicated himself to celibacy during that time was the object of so much female affection. Looking back recently at an old running log I found with the following entry:

Diet Pepsi 10K Run, Newburgh. 80°, very hot day, but still ran well. Uh, oh, saw Jeannie M. from Cornwall, I hope that she doesn't like me!

What is particularly amusing is that no mention is even made of my race finishing time or place.

Making matters worse for me (as I saw it back then) was that I wasn't someone who was good at saying 'no'; at least not after Paula had lost her life.

Paula was a tiny little girl with a huge personality. We had been friends since junior high when we ran modified track together. When we reached high school, she wanted to be more than friends. Her best friend, Barbara, recalls to this day how she had a strong infatuation with me. Our friendship came to an end when she asked me out on the sports bus after practice.

I had become absolutely exasperated by her relentlessness and finally told her – raising both hands in front of me – I would not go out with her, no matter *how* many times she asked me, explaining to her that I wanted to focus on my running so that I could get a college scholarship.

The truth of the matter was that she already had a boyfriend, and I knew that. Secondly, I was raised not to lie – and in spite of her many positive qualities, I simply did not like her in the way that she wanted me to.

Paula grew visibly upset by my refusal and decided to walk off the sports bus. The last thing she said to me as she exited the dimly lit vehicle was: "You *should* have said 'yes'."

I was told that she was hitchhiking home. I never saw her again.

Youngsters: Paula Perrara points at me after I had set the 7th grade half mile school record of 2:30 in Middletown, N.Y. A few short years later, she was gone.

She would be found – battered, raped, strangled, and left for dead – in a swampy area off Rt. 211 in Montgomery, N.Y. ... on March 1st, 1982.

She was sixteen.

When I left for SUNY Geneseo a year and a half later, I brought with me a picture of Paula that she had given to me. I hid it behind a framed photograph of my goddaughter Kara that I kept on my desk so that no one would know.

You should have said 'yes'.

For almost twenty years her murder went unsolved. And during some of those days I couldn't help but wonder what would have happened, how her life might have changed, if I had just lied to her.

Michael Ross of Connecticut, nicknamed the "The Egg Man" as he grew up on an egg farm, was charged with her murder through collected DNA evidence. He had killed eight young women, ages 14 to 25, all via strangulation between 1981 and 1984. He was executed by lethal injection on May 13th, 2005, the first in that state in forty-five years.

Instead, I constantly found myself sitting on the edge of some girl's bed trying to keep things innocent, or trying to get myself out of escorting someone to a dance, or politely eating lunch with someone as they attempted to make a more personal connection.

The romantic attention I received escalated further after I inadvertently got pulled into a 'bubble bath fight' with a few girls from A-Quad. Paul was *seriously* amused by the whole situation and requested (on multiple occasions) to join me the next time I found myself surrounded by a bunch of "naked, jumping girls."

My father, no doubt understanding my social naiveté, had given me two points of advice when he dropped me off at college the year prior: "Don't do anything stupid" and "keep it in your pants."

I was clearly 0-for-2.

In fact, my favorite quote at the time was from an elite Japanese marathon runner named Toshihiko Seko. He said: "The marathon is my only girlfriend; I give her everything I have." Suffice to say, I found his level of dedication inspiring. It wasn't that I was opposed to the concept of a serious relationship; in truth I wanted *nothing* more than to get married and have a family someday. Just not quite yet.

I knew that steady relationships demanded large quantities of time if they were going to have a chance to succeed. With my academic studies; my competitive running schedule; my work as Illustration editor for the college newspaper; my family back home … and the need for some sleep once in a while … I didn't feel that I had any.

Nor, for that matter, had I found a woman who I felt impulsively drawn to. The closest I had come to even the hint of a serious relationship was with a girl back home who I thought was physically attractive since the day I had kicked dirt in her hair (by mistake) on the playground in kindergarten. It turned out, when I did date her years later; we really had nothing in common. And at one point, I did approach Geneseo's top female runner at the time in order to see if there was any interest on her end in starting up a 'friendship'. It would be a friendship that – if projected out to the point of absurdity – might have led to us breeding an entire team of little "super runners."

I probably shouldn't have shared that part with her.

But I had no worries. I knew that 'Mrs. Right' was out there somewhere, and I wasn't about to 'whore myself around' in the meantime.

There was an inherent risk in such friendships though, as it inevitably came down to rejecting what would eventually become a string of successive marriage proposals.

At times I felt as though I might be living in 'Sadie Hawkins World'. I couldn't deny being flattered by the attention, and it was fun to watch the other guys in the dorm pull their hair out in jealous fits of frustration, but those moments were always overshadowed by my desire not to hurt anyone.

Besides, as much as I downplayed my own understanding or investment, it was clear to me that most of the girls were reacting to the purely temporal circumstance of me being 'cute' or 'cuddly', and not to any real emotional bond or tangible benefit that might lead to a lasting relationship. You can't build a meaningful relationship on 'cute'.

Like most roommates, Paul and I would have some very interesting conversations. He would share with me his difficulties in finding a girlfriend who would *not* add large amounts of drama to his life structure, and how he wondered if he might be setting his standards a bit too high in the pursuit of love.

I would wax philosophic about the troubling insignificance of the individual over the vast expanse of time and espouse the virtues of reverse splits during races. And although he claimed that he wasn't at all religious, or spiritual, he confided in me – and eventually Jeff – that he was being plagued by a series of 'prophetic dreams' and multiple incidents of déjà vu. By November 14th of that year, he had begun warning both Jeff and I that something "very bad," perhaps catastrophic, was going to happen.

I didn't know what to make of this. Nightmares were not uncommon to me, but mine were largely abstract and symbolic, hard to understand or interpret. They would contain vast expanses of gray sky, indistinguishable walking businessmen, dark caves, and glowing, spiked orbs humming in the distance. Certainly nothing specific enough that I felt could be applied.

But Paul claimed that his dreams were much more succinct, much clearer. Upon hearing all of this, Jeff decided that it would be best to write down some of the information Paul was sharing in his trusty notebook. I watched as Jeff, writing implement in hand, began to create a series of what looked to be 'decorative swishes' on the lined paper.

After a brief pause, Paul revealed to us that his dreams occurred "just between the wakeful and sleeping state" and although he seemed to be able to distinguish between which dreams would and would not come true, he often lacked specific details such as exactly when or who would be affected. But what now alarmed him the most was the certainty in his mind that if 'The Situation' (whatever it was) wasn't addressed properly that he – or somebody else – might end up in a casket, surrounded by their family: death.

"The possession of knowledge does not kill the sense of wonder and mystery. There is always more mystery." — Anaïs Nin

I glanced nervously over at Jeff, trying to get a read on his reaction because I myself was unsure as to how to respond to this, other than to rub my hands together nervously.

Just a week or two earlier I had spotted the latest issue of *Discover* magazine (November 1984) in the racks at the stationary store uptown. It contained a special report on 'The Hudson Valley UFO Mystery'. I stopped in my tracks when I saw it. It must be a different Hudson

Valley, I thought to myself, not *my* Hudson Valley.

But, as I paged through the issue, I was amazed to learn that the area I was born in, was raised in, was said by some to be a UFO hot spot. In spite of the fact that I figured there must be some more logical explanation about the phenomena that was being reported near Brewster, N.Y. and the surrounding areas like Pine Bush. The notion that there just *might* be alien craft flitting around in the skies near my home was disconcerting.

Now my roommate was talking – in a very convincing way – about prophetic dreams and fate.

Jeff, meanwhile, was betraying no emotion, other than the obvious: an interest in the information being shared with him.

I had noticed that Paul had been in a very serious mood the past few days, but I just figured it was due to the fact that his relationship with Beth – an energetic and attractive brunette – had recently gone sour. And I only knew this because she had been banging loudly on our door, in anger, looking for him the day prior. Even though Paul and I conversed on a daily basis, he remained typically tight-lipped about his relationships.

Shifting in my chair a bit, I tried to – nonchalantly – take a look at what it was that Jeff was drawing. But there was no drawing. Rather, what I mistook for the beginnings of a sketch was simply the artistic flourish with which Jeff wrote his words. It was a style of writing that would eventually be used to capture events that would change my *own* life forever. I just didn't know it yet. I smiled.

A sample of John Jeff Ungar's writing style excerpted from his journal notes.

Apparently, my investment in what Jeff was writing must have allowed Paul to feel comfortable enough to bring me into the conversation in a more active way:

"Romeo, you remember what happened the other day, right?"

My heart raced with an intensity normally reserved for my speed workouts on the track. I truly had no desire to recall what he was referring to. As soon as he had said it, my mind raced to a place where the memory had been stored. I cleared my throat a couple of times, as all ears would be on me, and pulled my shoulders into a proper posture as though I were about to deliver a public address.

"It happened just the other night. I was talking with Paul about how I wasn't sure if I was going to run winter track this year, when all of a sudden this look of 'awe' came over his face. It definitely seemed spontaneous. Then after about fifteen seconds he blinked his eyes, and then he started to hold his head with his hands and said: 'Wow, I saw this, years ago.'"

"Saw *what* years ago?" asked Jeff with a marked intensity, "What did you see?"

Paul pursed his lips for a moment. He was obviously debating whether he wanted to say anything or not. He looked over at me, glanced toward the ceiling, turned to Jeff, and replied: "Let's just say that what Romeo … rather … Chris was talking about … that has something to do with it. That's what I'm worried about."

Paul stood up, clapped his hands together once, and then grabbed his bathroom supplies with his thick tan fingers, signaling that the discussion – as far as he was concerned – was over. But, while the actual discussion had come to an end, the lasting impact of the conversation was just beginning to take root. And less than three months later we were all going to pay a price.

"The world, that understandable and lawful world, was slipping away." –
William Golding, *Lord of the Flies.*

5. Wondering

The entire first floor lobby of the C-Building had been filled with partygoers. Initially it was meant for members of Erie Hall and their friends, but by the time the cacophony of dance music, drunken laughter, clanking beer glasses, and bad pickup lines had wafted up the staircase into C2D, it was overflowing with party crashers.

I was aware, in advance, that there was going to be a party on January 26th and that it was going to be 'themed' but I had not planned on going as the theme selected was 'The Toga Party'. I had only walked out of one movie in my entire life, *National Lampoon's Animal House*, and it seemed to me that this was precisely what we were going to be getting.

One of my suitemates, a talented guitar player named Luke F., (who looked to me a bit like Rick Ocasek, the lead singer of The Cars), knocked on my half-opened door as he was passing by. He was wearing only a bed sheet ... and an expensive red neck tie. Paul had gone home for the weekend for some family function, so I was sitting alone atop the loft in a pair of red running shorts while reading about Italy's Orlando Pizzolato's recent victory in the New York Marathon on a steaming hot day. It was lost on no one that his name sounded like a derivation of 'lots of pizza' and being that he hailed from Italy, he had become an overnight world sensation.

"You're going to the party, right?" he asked in a manner that suggested that I would regret it if I did not.

"I dunno', Paul isn't here so … " I answered raising my palms to the ceiling. I had absolutely no clue why Paul not being there might have been an appropriate reply, but that's what I said.

Luke didn't seem to dwell on the weakness of my pathetic knee jerk excuse, and simply said: "I think Jeff is going." He was gone from my doorway, and headed off to the party, before he had the chance to watch my mouth drop open in overdramatized shock.

Jeff was going? Jeff? Jeff didn't even like it when the 'yahoos', as he called them, threw down a few beers over a quick game of poker. I just had to verify this information for myself. 'Yahoo' was a term used to describe the brutes in *Gulliver's Travels* that Jeff had been quick to employ.

I hopped down the loft's ladder and scurried quickly out my door. His door was a mere two feet beyond mine.

There he was.

The man who never seemed to go anywhere without accessorizing two or three layers of clothing, was now standing in his room and wearing only a sheet and holding aloft his trusty 35mm camera. I realized that it was the first time I'd ever seen his feet.

"Jeff, you're going to the toga party?" I asked in near shock, "With all of the drinking and cursing … and the *yahoos*?"

He gave me a sheepish smile and admitted, "I think I can capture some interesting photos."

Ah, now I understood! Jeff wasn't going down to the party to participate in it; he was going down to the party to *observe* it, to record it.

I let out a healthy laugh.

There could be no arguing: John Jeff Ungar truly was the eyes and the ears of the campus. Jeff was an extraordinary photographer, and he was probably correct in his point that, if he went, he would certainly get some memorable shots; shots memorable enough to overcome even his well-established disdain for all things 'unaesthetic'.

Without skipping a beat, I made a beeline back to my room. After all, if Jeff was going …

I was pleasantly surprised when Jeff and I emerged from the staircase and gazed out upon the undulating mass of smiling bodies moving to

"Two Tribes", by the band Frankie Goes to Hollywood. Everyone seemed so full of life, so happy and energized. Jeff set himself up in a corner not far from the main lobby entrance, his camera poised.

Corners are important.

"Youth is happy because it has the capacity to see beauty. Anyone who keeps the ability to see beauty never grows old." — Franz Kafka

As I waded into the energetic crowd I realized that I knew very few of the young revelers. Perhaps expecting this, the party organizers were distributing name tags to help break the ice. Jeff politely refused to take one, he informed the confused organizer that he preferred to remain 'anonymous'. I too, would have foregone the nametag, but I didn't want her to feel as though she – or her efforts – were being marginalized. I reached out with an open palm, and she smiled wide and provided me one.

Reaching into one of the many large glass bowls of chips, I looked about for a friendly face in the busy throng. There were a few, but most of them were across the large room and they were obviously making their moves on their select persons of interest.

Three is a crowd.

In any event, the reflections of the dancers in the windows soon caught my eye. The pitch black of the night sky created a strong contrast to the reflections of the flashing colored lights, the honey-colored drinks and the shining white togas.

"There is nothing in the world so irresistibly contagious as laughter and good humor." — Charles Dickens, *A Christmas Carol*

Normally parties tend to spill outdoors, onto sidewalks or into a bush or two. But on this night I can make out just one lone person on the outside looking in. It is difficult to make him out, but I can see him with my acute runner's eyes. He is standing about twenty feet from the southernmost windows – at the edge of the darkness – and standing very still.

I am not sure what he is watching.

"Chris?"

I turn to see one of the girls from my communications class standing behind me, beer-filled cup in hand, looking resplendent in her makeshift toga. I instantly feel bad that I can't remember her name, but the fact that I see her on a daily basis makes it far too awkward to ask her. I should know it, so I act as though I do.

"What are you looking at?"

"Nothing, just some guy out there, he's staring in. I hope he's OK. Do you see him?"

I point to where he is standing.

The girl pushes her long, healthy, sandy brown, hair back and presses her face against the window, "I don't see anyone," she whispers to me, "is he still there?"

"He's right ..."

I don't see him.

"Hnnnh. He must have gone. Oh well. Sorry."

At that precise moment there is a loud 'bang' on the window just inches in front of us, and it trembles from the surprisingly powerful impact. The girl screams in abject terror, her beer pouring out onto her shirt front, and she nervously grabs my arm.

On the other side of the window there is now a tall, thin, dark-haired college student, completely stripped, and being pressed up against the glass. He is being held there against his will by two massively built guys who restrain him from behind. They are laughing, and he is laughing too, even as he struggles to break free of their collective grasp. Soon most of the hundred-plus partygoers are laughing as they too watch the somewhat humorous scene play out.

"Holy crap, that was scary! Was that him? Was that the guy you saw outside?" my unnamed acquaintance asks.

Her look suggests she is still a bit startled by the strange event. She continues to hang on my arm, but is now pushing a soft hip up against one of my thighs. I know it is being done with a purpose; she has adroitly turned the uncertainty of the moment into an opportunity.

I can respect that.

"No." I respond, doing my very best to recall the characteristics of the unusual person that I had seen. "He wasn't as tall or thin as the guy up against the window. He was definitely wearing clothes too, darkish clothes."

His clothing was so strange and his demeanor so intense, that he looked to me a bit like some meandering, unbalanced, stalker ... or perhaps someone who had suffered so much that he resented seeing such unabashed happiness in others. He glared with a palpable intensity as if they were dancing upon his grave.

There is a slight tingling sensation in my extremities, but not the kind that would have been brought on by the young woman's affection. Rather the kind you get when you are home alone and the family pet begins to react strongly to something that you cannot discern.

"I know that this is going to make me sound very weird, but I really don't think that he wanted to be seen."

"You don't sound weird at all," the girl says, looking into my eyes with an unmasked desire. Her teeth are white and straight when she smiles and she smells like fresh spring flowers. Her eyeglasses do little to conceal the blue and green hues of her irises.

I feel an unfortunate personal test arriving, but before I have to deal with it the two boisterous, muscular dudes carry the cold, bare-skinned kid inside on their shoulders. A large majority of the crowd erupts with a drunken cheer, alcohol cups and containers being raised at varying heights in the air.

The shivering student is given a towel (which now leads me to believe that they had planned on embarrassing him) and begins walking over to an area near where the girl and I are currently standing. I recognize him now, under the bright lights of the main lounge. He is an Erie Hall resident, an Irish kid from Long Island ... Thomas something. O'Sullivan, O'Connell ... I'm not able to recall his full name either and it occurs to me that I really should work on that skill in the future.

A short, fat, thoroughly unattractive, bearded guy, with a pony tail wearing a red, plaid, wool shirt over his wrinkled toga, tells him that his dick is really small, and for some reason the Irish kid thinks that I say it.

He tells me to "Shut the F*** up."

No one has ever used the f-bomb on me before. I won't allow it. In fact, until this moment, I have only heard it used three times in my entire life, and I was able to list the frustrating details of each offense.

Such terminology represented an obvious disrespect or callousness towards those around you ... like blowing cigarette smoke ... into someone's face.

In this instance it's my face. I don't like it.

"Don't curse at me," I yell, stepping forward into his personal space, "I didn't say anything to you."

I'm not as brave as I might seem.

Although the Long Islander's reach is significantly longer than mine, he is thin and bony. I have seen him without his clothing and I now know that he will break much faster than I will.

I also know that if we fight, it will probably hurt just like the day after a marathon does.

My first fight happened in the 4th grade, against another student who also happened to be named Chris. Go figure. One of my friends had made up some sort of 'club' for the cool kids, but would only allow five members in it. I was the fifth.

Well, the other Chris wanted to join the club, and much to my dismay, was told that he would have to fight me to do so. I didn't want to fight, but a swift, if soft, punch to my mouth quickly created the need.

Being such a short, little, kid I must have seemed like an easy target.

Everyone said that it was a 'draw', but I think that I was losing when the teacher broke it up, because my mouth was still bleeding and all he had was a slightly swollen and reddened nose.

A month or so later, a kid named Mark (jealous because the girl that he claimed to be in love with had told her friends that she liked me instead) decided he needed to teach me some kind of 'lesson'.

I had no clue that the girl even liked me, nor was I aware that he was barreling across the school yard to kick my ass as I played kickball. All I knew was that my shoelace had come undone, and just as he began his assault, I had bent over to tie it.

This resulted in him soaring, off balance, over me. Unnerved by the giant shadow that was now covering me, I reached my hands up to cover my head, and inadvertently caught hold of one of his ankles, whereupon he fell, face first, onto the dirt base path.

There was total silence.

I did absolutely nothing to dispel the rumors that I knew karate, and no one again challenged me to a fight all the way up through high school graduation.

But maybe now was the time.

Perhaps he notices the look in my eyes, maybe he has seen my picture in the sports section of the college paper, or maybe (like me) he really isn't much of a fighter. Whatever the causal factor, he steps back and in a soft tone apologizes to me.

People are already beginning to stagger over to 'congratulate' him for having survived his stripping with a good spirited cheer.

I unclench my fists and let out a sincere sigh of relief. His friends were all around us by now, and even if I had succeeded in taking him down, they might not have let that act go unanswered.

Now I just have to figure out a way to rid myself of my hovering admirer.

The near altercation has done nothing to dull her interest in me, in fact, the opposite seems true. She grabs hold of one of my hands, the skin on her arms is very soft, her smile is genuine and her figure is temptingly full.

This is going to be tough.

But the facts are clear: she is going to marry someone someday, and it's not going to be me. I don't want to risk being the guy that her husband will ask her about years later, 'the one that got away'. Nor do I want to use her, or be used by her.

She is also borderline drunk.

A sobering thought crosses my mind: that somewhere the parents who raised her might be wondering if she is safe, being so far away from home. I will do my best, at least on this night, to make sure that she is.

"I have to go now," I offer, raising a brow and lifting both shoulders to suggest that I really have no choice in the matter, "I have to get ready for a big track meet."

I neglect to tell her that it is several weeks off.

She looks a bit saddened, but I am confident that she understands this is not a rejection of her; it is simply an inopportune time.

We kiss each other on the cheek, and I begin my slow serpentine through the noisy throng back to safety. Looking around at the vast clutter of inebriated young adults, I understand that others will not be so careful. What crosses my mind is that apathetic and desperate song line: "If you can't be with the one you love, love the one you're with". I wonder how many unwanted pregnancies will result from what is about to occur in multiple dorm rooms and fraternity houses in Geneseo over the next few hours, and what the response to that will be? I wonder how many of my peers will wake up in the morning vomiting in the toilet bowl, their skulls pounding with aches from a wild night of unbridled reverie.

Jeff for his part is keeping a watchful eye out for what he hopes will be some notable photos. His initial take on the evening's catch is somewhat cursory and tepid:

"The lighting isn't that good in here, so I'm hoping that I've got the exposure timed properly. At least my flash seems to be working right now. How about you? How are you doing?"

I observe that at some point over the last half hour he had acquiesced and was now wearing a name tag of his own, just like the rest of the 'yahoos'. Recalling the reaction of the girl when he initially refused, I like that he is now wearing one. He notices my approval and he affords himself a slight smile. A quick Reagan-like 'thumbs up' later, and I am heading back up to the friendly confines of room C2D1.

I pull off my sneakers, and eagerly throw myself onto the old, soft, couch, and gaze up at the underside of the loft. It is adorned with multiple strands of large, colorful, Christmas lights around its perimeter and has a large, decorative fishing net hanging down from its center.

The bottoms of the medium brown window curtains rest calmly on the couch back beside me.

My ears are still a bit desensitized from the loud music blasting at the wild party. As my body begins to relax I wonder where the factories that made the lights, the net, and the curtains, all of these things are located. And how was it that all these objects had, to the proper effect, come together here and now?

I feel lonely.

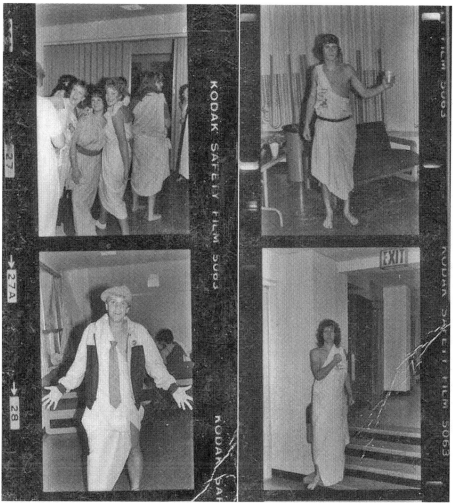

A block of photographs taken with John Jeff Ungar's 35mm camera during the Erie Hall Toga Party: Craig Norris (top right), Jeff (bottom right) and I (bottom left).

It would be a lie trying to convince myself that I didn't have the very same sensual urges and impulses that the revelers down at the party had. In fact, a part of me wanted to lay down with that soft-skinned girl under these colorful lights that were now suspended, almost watchfully, above me. Aware of the many potential consequences, as I was, I knew that it would be a fool's errand. It would be an error akin to sprinting the first mile of a 26.2 mile marathon in order to feel the temporary thrill of being ahead of the other runners. Those runners rarely completed the race.

Since the age of eleven, under my father's guidance, I had done the difficult yeoman's work. My arduous running training had already afforded me success, health and heaps of admiration and I was not yet twenty. The thousands of difficult hours of preparation, miles run under sun and stars, through rain and snow, had made racing competitively both satisfying and worthwhile. My fervent hope, right now though, was that my dedication to wait for my 'true love' would someday prove as fruitful.

It is then that I remember: 'Genesee Hall'.

The pretty girl from the party lives in Genesee Hall. It would be a simple thing to go over to talk to her for a while. We could just be friends.

Then, the thought of the strange-looking person that had been staring into the party from the darkness somehow creeps back into my mind. There was definitely something 'wrong' and unbalanced about him. Not wanting to risk a chance encounter with him, I decide that it might be best for me to get some much needed rest instead.

When Jeff develops the film there are a few memorable shots. In spite of my many misgivings, they bring a welcome smile to my face.

There is a photo that I had taken of Jeff where he is standing like the great Roman orator Cicero. I can imagine him standing amongst the patrician senators declaring: "The life given us, by nature is short; but the memory of a well-spent life is eternal."

Craig looks like a living, breathing, replica of the marble statue of Augustus Caesar in Prima Porta, albeit with a cup of alcohol replacing the consular baton.

I laugh out loud when I see the photo Jeff has taken of me. Had I just climbed out of a Salvation Army dumpster?

At some point early on in the party Jeff had succeeded in convincing me to add additional layers of clothing (a cap, coat, clip-on tie, sneakers, etc.) after several girls had cornered me and were trying to forcibly tear my toga off in an attempt to verify whether or not 'the curtains matched the carpet' as they so tactfully put it.

"You know what always happens when they get around you," he had sternly warned me, "you don't want to take any chances, Chris."

He understood my goals, so I dutifully complied with his request.

Eventually all of the images will become notable because of what they would represent: they are the last images of any of us ... before the ghost.

Oh. Now I remember.

Her name was Sally.

"Do not leave my hand without light." – Marc Chagall (Interview, 1977)

6. Piercing the Veil

I had never heard of the Warrens. Apparently Jeff *had* ... and now they were here on some type of 'barnstorming tour' in Geneseo, tonight ... January 30th, 1985.

Jeff and I approach the double wooden doors of the towering, ivy-covered, brick structure where the presentation will be held. It is the kind of clear, chilled, night that calls to you to look up at the shining lights in the heavens above. I glance around through the steam of my own breath at the high level of enthusiasm etched onto the faces of the crowd that is entering around me.

Jeff leads the way to a set of seats on the left side of the large room. About halfway down, he stops, assesses, and then sits us right next to the aisle. I settle into my red-cloth theater seat, and as Jeff deftly twirls his pencil through his fingers, I study the growing crowd.

The Alan Parson Project's "Eye in the Sky" is cleverly playing itself in my head.

Most of the gathered are college students, but it is evident that there has also been advertising in the local papers as the high percentage of middle-aged women; men in business attire; and youngsters in brand new *Ghostbusters* t-shirts give it away.

I notice that many of the students sitting in the Wadsworth Auditorium are still abuzz, reflecting on and laughing about the wild toga party held in our dorm just a few nights prior:

As the auditorium rings with the sounds of excited voices and people exchanging greetings, Jeff jots down some thoughts.

I nod my head, and he shows me his writing: *In gliders they came, the twelve … offspring of the Pleiades, there silver ships.*

In gliders they came ... The 12 , offspring of
the Pleides , there silver ships

Contemporary Forum Presents: 1/30/85.
The Warrens

psychokinesis — ghosts draw peoples/rooms
heat and appear — on infrared film.
smoke
laws of attraction—ghosts attracted to
ex president
on stage compassionate or sympathetic people.

— mother-in-law — 2 wrecks died in back of car
— Boy/dog — elderly woman staring at puppy
curtains in windows

— Man standing at bookcase — (color)   laws of
attraction

usually alone   — telepathic image explains
why some people see things while
others don't
3:00 witches hour — insult to trinity.

psychic energy drawn from you — beads of light
from you — shot about — basketball size
image forms

phantomania — weight ~ diet
psychic paralysis   cannot move

Nice.

Jeff and I had decided to collaborate on a science fiction based comic strip called "Operation Overlord" that was going to be submitted to the college paper. This was the initial concept for the third strip.

I offer a positive 'thumbs up' gesture, and he hands his journal and pencil over to me, perhaps expecting me to add my own creative thoughts to the mix. Instead I record what we are doing at that moment: *Contemporary Forum Presents, the Warrens,* and the date.

Jeff looks slightly disappointed with my lack of assistance, but I just smile.

The theater lights dim and some esoteric background music can be heard. A large screen hangs near the back of the stage that features the same image that Jeff showed me on a flyer at Letchworth Dining Hall just hours earlier.

A sense of uneasiness has me leaning forward in my seat; I am afraid to relax. There is something about this moment that seems like it might be irreversibly transformational. 'Forced change' was not always good, and this worries me now as I find myself part of a potentially 'larger' moment; a larger moment that can be at once enlightening and dangerous.

...

When I was eleven my father, with my Uncle Patrick, took me to see a major league baseball game in New York City. It was May of 1976, and the Yankees were facing the Cleveland Indians in their newly remodeled stadium. I gaped in awe at the colossal size of the sporting arena as my uncle made note of the hitting prowess of the Cleveland first baseman, John Wesley "Boog" Powell, and my father reminisced about his own baseball accomplishments as a youth.

In the seventh inning, Powell, a hulking right-handed hitter, clobbered a pitch from Jim "Catfish" Hunter well over the outfield wall.

I jumped up in celebratory fashion amongst the thousands of Yankees fans, my uncle had been right!

And as big ol' Boog rounded the bases he was showered with cat calls and boos, and I was met with glares of disgust and anger from many of the pinstriped denizens around us.

That was the first transformative moment I could recall, and I could recall it with great clarity. My youthful celebration was being tempered – shamed – into forced submission by the pack.

The pack frightened the hell out of me.

The crowd demanded that Powell's home run be met with contempt, and there would be no tolerating an eleven-year-old celebrating ... no matter what the reason.

Not more than five minutes later, Yankees' third baseman Graig Nettles lined a shot over the right field wall and the building shook around me as he went into his home run trot for the 152ⁿᵈ time in his career. I worried now that if I didn't cheer properly that my relatives and I might be in physical danger. So I forced a smile and quickly clapped once again becoming safely 'invisible', an unnoticed cog in a giant roaring machine. Yankees win 4-3!

Correction: WE win, 4-3.

On the ride home in the back seat of the car I imagined the Great Bambino, Babe Ruth himself, lighting up the pre-moon landing skies with a colossal blast that looked to touch the very bottom of heaven. I visualized the fans, wearing woolen caps and wide smiles, roaring wildly in approval at their modern day gladiator.

My sad guess was that all of those thrilled fans, save the very youngest, were dead now. Ruth was dead. The old Yankee Stadium was dead now, no more 'Ruthville'. My young chest ached in memory of all those now quieted smiles ... and dreams.

"Are you all right back there?"

"Yes. I'm good."

I wondered if somewhere, resting in a comfortable recliner, an old man was dozing off to memories of that May day in 1920s when his uncle and father brought him to see a major league baseball game in New York City ... when he was eleven. I wondered what his mind considered on his way back home. I put my child's hands on the cool, smooth car window as we drove past a large group of illuminated homes. I hoped that he was there ... somewhere, and that I lived long enough to someday be him.

...

"Have you ever heard of the Amityville Horror House?" asks Jeff.

I snap back into the present; the crowd all around me is starting to clap.

"Oh, sure," I say, "Who hasn't?"

The truth of the matter was that I actually knew very little about the story. Since I was a little child and cried at the sight of a green-skinned Herman Munster, I had tried to divorce myself from anything related to horror or the macabre. What I had heard was that a haunting had supposedly taken place somewhere in New York state and that a woman claimed to have seen some type of demonic eyes in a fireplace. Of course, my information might have been totally inaccurate, as I had heard it at the lunch table in high school, from the very same crowd who had asked me whether I was a lover or a fighter.

At least on that topic I had now concluded that I was neither ... I was a runner.

"These are the individuals who investigated that case."

I draw in my breath ... *here we go.* I rub my now full-grown hands up and down on the cool, smooth metal undersides of the theater seat.

The Warrens' Ain't Afra

by Susan Connelly
LAMRON Staff Writer

Excitement filled the air as the Real-life Ghostbusters Ed and Lorraine Warren, kept the crownd waiting in Wadsworth Auditorium. "Do you believe in ghosts?" was the most popular question being thrown back and forth amongst the members of the audience. This sweet, grandparent type couple, has been hunting ghosts for thirty-seven years; in that time-span they have dealt with approximately three thousand cases of exorcism.

Their interst began before the couple met. Ed Warren grew up in a house that was haunted, while his wife has been a psychic since her childhood. Ironically, both wre raised in strict Catholic settings.

The Warrens work closely with priest and ministers of all denominations. They are highly knowledgable on the power of God and the deceits of the devil. Although the Warrens firmly believe in all of this psychic phenomena, they admit that seeing and experiencing these occurences often depends on being in the right place at the right time.

The Warrens' goal was to prove, beyond a shadow of a doubt, that these things actually occur. They were very convincing. Slides,

ghost is seen only by an individual. Ghost syndromes are most commonly created because of tragedies. When a person dies, they refust to accept the fact that they have passed out of their physical

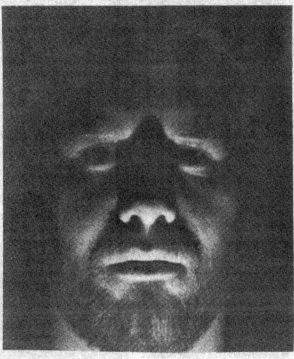

Douglas Dean - the incident from which the exorcist originated.

Other strange phenominon depicted ranged in a wide variety. Religious statues spouting ancient human blood and shedding genuine

The Warrens' presentation is rich with what is purported to be both photographic and audio evidence. Ed reminds me of a modern day P.T. Barnum, strong-voiced and direct. There is no hesitancy in his voice or his mannerisms as he facilitates the show, selling us dreams of spirits and mist. What impresses me about this is that it is not him, but his regal wife Lorraine, who claims to see behind the veil, the thin spiritual fabric that separates the living and the dead. They speak of the Jackson Homestead and the Brown Lady of Raynham Hall. They offer a chilling account of an old lady who was photographed sitting in the backseat of a car ... at her own funeral.

Lorraine has an air of sincerity as she relates her many experiences. I think that she is brave. I can never see myself being as brave as her, standing on a stage under the heat of the bright lights, speaking about something as controversial as ghosts. But I also know that life has a funny way of repeating itself. Mrs. Warren seems to look in my direction as she says:

"There is a Law of Attraction. Ghosts are attracted to compassionate or sympathetic people."

Nothing in any book I had ever read allows me to accept a thing that she or her husband have shared on this night ... but I cannot push away a voice in the back of my head that seems to be saying: *she is right.*

The normally boisterous college crowd remains unusually respectful, and is clearly drawn into the moment. I marvel at the human mind's (seemingly odd) desire to want to accept concepts and evidence simply because it seems the fun thing to do at that moment.

They are sheep.

This is not Yankee Stadium. I am not eleven years old. I am not going to accept any of this simply because they do.

I try to ignore the voice in my head that again says: *she is right.*

As the Warren presentation came to a close, audience members were invited to approach the stage and meet the two famed demonologists. A line formed immediately, and Jeff signaled that he wanted to speak briefly with Ed and Lorraine, maybe ask a few questions of them. Jeff was well read and somewhat of an esoteric enthusiast and the opportunity to speak with two paranormal icons was not to be passed up!

Initially Jeff was ahead of me in the greeting line, but in an effort to buy himself a few extra moments to compose his thoughts, he offered to let me move ahead of him. For my part I had absolutely no clue as to why I had even gotten on the line, except perhaps to accompany Jeff. The line moved faster than Jeff and I had anticipated and I suddenly found myself cautiously walking up the steps to the stage and face-to-face with 'The Amityville Horror' folks.

There is a Law of Attraction. Ghosts are attracted to compassionate or sympathetic people.

I made eye contact with Lorraine as my left foot lifted from the final step and I reached the stage. Then time seemed to slow.

...

I watch as her eyes focus on me, as she draws back her shoulders, as she glances nervously towards her husband, and as he begins to notice me approach.

When Ed moves in to block me, with the practiced ease and effectiveness I would associate with a veteran law enforcement officer, Lorraine says to me:

"I don't want to know my future."

"Oh, Jerry, don't ask for the moon. We have the stars." – Bette Davis, *Now Voyager (1942)*.

7. Bloodlines

I should never have happened as I did, the odds were against it. My parents grew up hours apart – separated by one hundred miles (the city of New York) and the deep waters of the Hudson River. Both defied expectation, and history, by becoming the first in their families to seek a higher education: college. Even before the passage of Roe v. Wade the odds of a woman keeping a child that might destroy the chance for a professional future, when it was oh-so close, were not good. My mother made the choice to forego her dreams so that I could exist. Without surprise I was recessive genes personified: male, blue eyed, left-handed, and blond.

I should never have happened as I did. I was writing poetry at the age of four but couldn't tie my own shoes until I was almost ten, preferring buckle shoes that, with my complexion, made it look like I had stepped out of some seventeenth century Dutch painting.

Yet, for all the obscurities and risks associated with my existence, I was given a name for the ages: Christopher Vito Di Cesare.

Christopher is Greek in its origin and means "bearer of Christ", Vito is the masculine form of vita, or "life", and Di Cesare breaks down from the Latin as "from Caesar".

I was reading a volume of the *New Book of Knowledge* encyclopedia (I had an entire set located in my bedroom's bookcase) during the summer break following sixth grade when I realized 'it': my name.

Now, if my Italian paternal relatives had their say, I would have been named differently. I would have been Vito Jr. Jr., or Vito III or some other variation. But my German/Irish mother liked the sound of 'Christopher' and in spite of the mounting opposition she basically decided: It's my baby, so I'm naming it.

Christopher Vito Di Cesare: The bearer of Christ's life from Caesar.

I was just a kid, but I knew both my history and my religion. Ultimately it was Augustus Caesar under whose authority Christ was hung for sedition against Rome. Claiming that you are the King of the Jews while Rome is occupying your country by force is not much different than being a signatory on the Declaration of Independence; it means war. If the Biblical accounts were true, Rome and Caesar had taken Jesus' life, and my name … my ridiculously impossible name … was suggesting that I (a bloodline descendant of the Caesars) might now need to somehow make up for it, or give it back.

I would have been much happier if my name had been something more tangibly achieved like Bobby Rodgers, or Billy Presley or Aaron Murcer.

I am sure my parents didn't plan it that way. But right or wrong, believer or apostate, Christopher Vito Di Cesare seemed like an awful lot of internal pressure for a quiet twelve-year-old who more often than not steadfastly refused to leave his room without being coerced to do so. My idea of risky behavior was whether or not I should add some pepper to my mashed potatoes; which, when push came to shove, I probably didn't.

And, I reasoned, Bill Rodgers the marathon runner and Will Rogers the actor and humorist ("The only difference between death and taxes is that death doesn't get worse every time Congress meets") had almost identical names and they weren't at all the same person. My name was likely just a coincidence; a fluke.

Still, on the off chance that life would demand something great of me one day, when I went to church, which I did with my family on a weekly basis, I would study the stained-glass windows. The south wall of Sacred Heart Church, situated in southernmost section of the city of Newburgh, was adorned with large and colorful stained glass windows. As the sun's bright rays moved across them, light beams of blue and gold, red and green, would cast reflections down onto the unaware and often praying parishioners.

There they were, the Saints: A select group of inspired humans who were remembered now for some two thousand years for their ostensible inspirational acts and sacrifices. In a world where the Vietnam War; urban blight; celebrity divorces; and Watergate dominated the headlines – and where drug-fueled performers like Jimi Hendrix and Janis Joplin were celebrated – *they* offered hope to a young boy who was trying to look outside the bustling human fish tank ... for a sign of God.

But I couldn't share all of that with Jeff right now.

I was beleaguered by what had just occurred at the conclusion of the Warren's presentation. Jeff should have gone on the campus ghost hunt with the rest of the crowd, but instead he sat with me trying to make some sense of what had just happened. As I wrung my hands together Jeff continued his investigation:

"Did you make any faces, any strange gestures?" he asks, his pencil scribbling furiously, trying to accurately record the events of the last half hour.

As he shifts a bit in Paul's desk chair, Jeff is mulling over the many possibilities in his mind. He speculates that I have a 'gift', something genetic perhaps ... or that maybe my brain is too big for my skull. I smile. It is funny stuff. Will Rogers kind of stuff.

But Jeff is not smiling. His eyes glance about the room as his brain searches for answers. He asks if any of my family members had spoken about strange or amazing events in their lives.

My grandmother Grace would tell me about how her grandmother (my great-great-grandmother Maria Antoinette Ricciuti Fracasse) had been a seer, a fortune teller. She had brought with her – from Limosano, Italy – a set of very large, ornate reading (tarot) cards.

She shared with me:

"I was living with my grandmother when I was around 7 or 8 years old. People would come, from all over, to talk to my grandmother. They came from New York City, from New Jersey, from Chicago even ... How they knew about her, I had no clue. It was all kept very quiet. She would tell me to go out and play."

Well, like any curious child, one day my grandmother Grace found a 'door' in the headboard of her grandmother's bed. Inside she found all sorts of items from the reading cards to lobster eyes. Grace wondered about these things and claimed that she would eventually do some readings herself once she got a little older.

Above: Standing with my grandmother, Grace Di Cesare, at the age of nine in Cronomer Hill Park, Newburgh, NY. Her own grandmother, Maria Antoinette Ricciuti Fracasse, was reportedly a seer.

Eventually her grandmother became gravely ill. She lay in her bed in a coma-like state. The doctor advised the family that she would soon pass on. Friends and relatives gathered by her bed to pay their last respects. But one day became two, and then three, and then four.

"We tried everything to make her comfortable, opening windows, adjusting her covers. Then, I said to my Aunt Margie, 'I know what to do!'"

When she had the opportunity, Grace retrieved the reading cards, and with her worried Aunt by her side, threw the entire deck into the furnace.

"And wouldn't you know it, Christopher," she had said ... "the death card turned face up! Aunt Margie could verify this, too, but she's gone now."

Grace and Margie went back upstairs, and at midnight – just two hours after the cards were burned – her grandmother was gone.

"Some people believe, and some don't," she offered, "but you know the flash of information when it comes to you. I don't know where it comes from, maybe God ... but I've felt it."

I would certainly have shared this information with Jeff when he asked, as it was exactly what he was looking for ... if I could have. The difficulty, though, was that I would not be told this story for another twenty-eight years.

But, I did have one story to share. It had occurred on January 29th, 1983 ... almost exactly two years to the day earlier.

My family and I had arrived at church about ten minutes late (which seemed to have been our unintentional custom) and were forced to stand in the back of the church so as not to interrupt the priest while he shared his homily with the congregation.

The sole benefit of this inconvenience, to a young boy, was that since we were close to the church doors, when the mass was completed we were among the first to be able to make it out the front doors.

To my dismay, on this particular day my father mentioned that he had seen some relatives during the mass that he wanted to wait and say 'hello' to before we left.

So we waited.

Among the last to straggle out of the church was my great-great-uncle Johnny and his wife. When he saw me, Uncle Johnny walked over and began to shake my hand in an unusually energetic manner.

"It's great to see you, Chris," he smiled.

While I appreciated his kindness, I was perplexed by the intensity of it. He was acting as though he hadn't seen me for several years, when in fact I had just seen him just two weeks prior.

Then, it happened.

A look came into his eyes, the kind of look that says: I know something that you don't. Around his head I thought I saw a white mist swirling, looking almost like the gold circles painted in the old religious paintings.

Then, everything slowed.

"Howwww arrrre youuuu" rolled slowly out of his mouth as the world came to a stop around us, and then kicked back into gear.

I am sure that my eyes must have been opened comically wide, because it seemed to me like my uncle – or someone – had stopped time.

He then moved to greet other members of my family as I looked around to see if anyone else was reacting to what I was. No one gave any indication that something was amiss, and five minutes later as we walked to our parked car, I asked aloud:

"Did anyone see what happened with Uncle Johnny on the church steps? You know the whole 'mist around his head' and the slow motion way in which he was talking?"

Their dumfounded expressions told me all that I needed to know.

My father laughed a bit and suggested that I might be reading too many comic books. My mom looked worried, and my two sisters were staring at me – waiting for me to turn the statement into some kind of joke, or an opportunity to tease them; which I probably should have done just because.

Eighteen days later, on Ash Wednesday, my uncle was dead.

"Behold. I stand at the door, and knock." – *The Revelation of St. John the Divine, 3:20.*

8. "Now it's Happened!"

That's the way John Jeff Ungar began his journal notes.

It was just two weeks after the Warrens had made their way to Geneseo and – possibly – into my psyche.

It was Monday, February 11th, 1985, and I was walking back to Erie Hall in an aggravated mood. It was 26°F and my nose was frozen on the inside – a thin layer of crystallized ice forming underneath my jogging suit; sweat from an intense track workout freezing as I trudged across the windy campus.

Normally, after the team workout, we would hit the showers and clean ourselves up. The concept of the group, or communal, shower was fairly new to me. In high school most of us just washed our faces, threw our clothes on over top of our running attire, and jumped on the sports bus after a tough practice, acne be damned.

College was a different beast altogether.

In fact, I found we were *expected* to shower, especially after races when we were required to dress in a way that well represented the school on our trips across the state: formally. Walking into a fine restaurant wearing muddy shoes with obvious salt residue on one's face was just not going to fly!

Excepting one time in a friend's pool, I hadn't ever stood elbow-to-elbow with a naked person. Yet adjusting to showering in close proximity with my teammates was not as difficult as I imagined it would be. The rejuvenating effect of the warm water on tired, aching, muscles, and the fact that I was in my top shape, was enough to offset any initial discomfort on my part. Most athletes build up a tolerance for what they are seeing as they become part of the competitive athletic team culture anyway, which amounts to every possible, often unexpected, variation under the sun.

For me, the experience was not much different than the contrast between the shock of changing a baby's diaper for the very first time, and then raising several children: you quickly get used to it.

Now that I was accustomed to the luxury of using the showers in the Athletic Center, they had stopped working. A neighborly hockey player (with the sounds of a worker banging on some pipes behind him) informed me that the showers were not working as I was getting undressed. Apparently some of the pipes had frozen.

That is why I was walking back to Erie Hall … freezing, tired, and angry.

The large brown 'care package' that my parents had sent me for Valentine's Day was sitting quietly at the foot of my desk, unopened.

C2D1 was dark and quiet.

As I flicked on the standing floor lamp beside the window, the heavy wooden loft above me creaked loudly. I had never heard it make a loud sound like that, and my first reaction was to bolt out from under the loft so that it would not collapse on top of me.

I watched the objects on my desk for movement, and looked for evidence, perhaps, of a minor earthquake. They were uncommon on the east coast but did occur from time to time. I quickly ruled that possibility out as there were no screams or yells or sounds of a commotion echoing through the dormitory as an earthquake no doubt would have caused.

Paul and I, combined, weighed almost 300 pounds, and the loft had never so much as 'squeaked' or even 'clicked' before now.

This was unusual.

I glanced up into the darkened area by the ceiling that contained our mattresses. Seeing no movement, I called out: "Paul?"

There was no motion, no sound. I walked over to one of the support beams and gave it a good shake. It did not budge. Inspecting the underside of the wooden supports, there were no signs of cracked wood or chipped paint.

Perplexed, I took a tentative seat on the couch's edge. The final possibility could have been that there had been some type of loud tumult outside, perhaps the sound of building repair construction further on down the campus property, which gave the impression that it had been inside the room.

As I pushed the curtain aside in an attempt to verify this theory – and squinted out into the bright, icy, winter day – the loft made another loud "Crrrreak!" This time it was followed by the sound of someone crawling or moving on top of it.

My only guess now was that Paul was playing some type joke on me. There was no precedent for this, he had never done anything like this before, but the experiences from the prior year (ice buckets et al) were still fresh in my memory.

Well, *two* can play that game!

I carefully slid off my running sneakers, in order to reduce the sound any walking might make, and as silently as I could, I crept out the door and crossed into the quad bathroom. Quietly, I filled a glass with ice cold water and then crept back to the room. My plan was a simple one: slide up the ladder, locate Paul, and then douse him with the water and a taste of his own medicine.

Everything proceeded effortlessly according to plan with one minor exception … when I climbed up the loft's ladder and gazed over at Paul's mattress, and then over to my mattress … no one was there! What the …?

I squished up my face in confusion, decided to drink the refreshing water, and then climbed back 'downstairs'.

This must be some type of brain freeze, I thought.

But now I was *very* wary because earlier in the day something even more bizarre, and absolutely unexplainable, had occurred. It took little to no effort to recall the events in my mind.

The light blue, 5-subject, spiral notebook that my mother had purchased for me at Lloyds Department Store back in September had been sitting on my desk, crammed with notes and handouts from my professors. Alongside it were the type-written instructions pertaining to a 15-20 page paper that would soon be due for my Ethno Cultural Non-Verbal Communications class, Dr. Harold Battersby's class.

Born in Surrey, England, Dr. Battersby had a Ph.D., in linguistics was fluent in over a dozen languages, and had worked for four national governments as a translator. The college would go on to create an Anthropology scholarship in his name after his passing in the summer of 2011. He was an impressive and entertaining man and, as such, I wanted to create an impressive and entertaining paper.

I fed the thick typing paper into my *Brother* word processor, having already done my research and planned the rough outline in my head.

The topic of the paper was a fascinating one: *Somatotypes* and their effect on communication and culture. The study of Somatotypes, or physical body structures, was derived from ancient Chinese science of physiognomy which separated the human body into five main types:

- *Endomorph – very heavy*
- *Mesoendomorph – stout*
- *Mesomorph – muscular*
- *Mesoectomorph – slender*
- *Ectomorph – very thin*

My paper was meant to examine the varied perceptions of such somatotypes in society, as well as body language and its effect on interpersonal communication.

As my hard-working fingers typed away in synchronized fashion, decent progress all but assured, someone nearby called out my name: *"Chrissss!"*

Not wanting to have my workflow impeded, and without looking up from my papers, I casually replied, "Come in."

There was no answer, nor did anyone enter the room.

Fair enough. I preferred that, whoever they were, they moved on and bothered someone else anyway. I was busy.

A minute or two later (I was far too focused on my assignment to carefully gauge the time interval) I heard the voice again: *"Chrissss!"*

It was a male voice. And this time the voice sounded louder, closer, and stronger. Not wanting to be bothered for a third time, I decided to get up out of my chair and see who it was. It shouldn't be too difficult a task to let the person know that I was too busy for a conversation right now. I opened the door of C2D1 and glanced out in the hallway.

"Hello?"

No one was in sight, in either direction.

I closed the door and then, ducking under the loft, made my way over to the window and looked down from my second floor location.

No one was down there either. Not a single soul.

This must be some type of practical joke, I concluded. What else could it have been? And as funny or entertaining as it might be to someone else right now, I was not about to be part of it. I had an important deadline to keep.

In order to rid myself of any bother, I powered up Paul's stereo and cranked up his Sammy Hagar's *Voice of America* CD. The first song that played was "I Can't Drive 55". This was ideal for my purposes in that the loud rock and roll song would easily be able to drown out the sounds of anyone who might try to continue to pester me ... especially with me now wearing Paul's headphones.

Barely a minute into the song, it came like the rush of wind that a speeding train makes as it passes, and I heard *in* the headphones ... *over* the music ... *"Chrissss!"*

In a state of severe temporary panic, I had thrown the headphones on the floor, turned the stereo off and quickly fled the room; eventually making my way to track practice.

That was three hours ago.

Now confronted by the addition of the broken gym showers and the strangely creaking loft, I just want the madness to stop so that I can finally take my shower.

This clearly wasn't my day.

The sweat that had frozen on my body while outside, is now warming into cold droplets of water that, at uncomfortable and unpredictable intervals, gradually make their way down my back and into the waistband of my running shorts, giving me the shivers.

When I open my closet door to get my shower supplies I am startled by a frigid blast of air that pushes by me and out into the room.

Things have become downright eerie in Erie Hall.

I move my hands around the darkened closet space in search of a used ice pack, or anything else that might have caused this intense drop in room temperature. A sleeve from one of the running shirts hanging in the closet drops lightly onto the back of my neck, and I jump up and leap back from the closet. Taking a moment to catch my breath, my eyes note the gently swaying garment, and I laugh; "Stupid shirt."

I decide to close my closet door.

Turning towards my dresser; I feel a sharp tug on my right sweat pant leg. This was odd, because there was nothing currently near me that I could have gotten caught it on. Looking down, I notice that the ankle snap is now 'popped' open.

On any other day, in any other place, I would not have noticed this. But on *this* day ... it is all I can concentrate on.

I bend at the knees and work the snap with my fingers: snap – unsnap – snap – unsnap.

The structure is sound.

I rally around the notions that I simply had not completely snapped it closed before my run, or, perhaps that I had partially loosened it prior to being told that the gym showers were not functioning. Amid all the other chaos, it was certainly possible.

The left ankle snap opens.

Still, I *was* bending forward, and the flexing of my calf muscle might be putting added pressure on the fabric around the metal clasp. This is logical enough.

I stand back up, and I can feel a few microscopic hairs on the back of my neck rise in fear as I watch my latched closet door slowly open. There is now a two inch opening between the door's edge and the door frame.

Letting loose a much needed audible and nervous laugh, I counsel myself, *just stay calm, Chris.*

The air is dry and cool and the latch might not have caught properly. Reaching over, I make sure that I latch the closet door properly this time. I give it a quick tug. It remains latched.

I notice that there is a slight ringing in my ears that I want to go away, and rubbing my right hand across my forehead, I feel a little of the pressure leave my eyes. The dried particles of salt on my fingertips remind me that I need to shower ... badly.

I strip off my wet, soggy, clothes and my skin – although chilled by the suddenness of the winter air – is happily liberated. I stretch out up onto my toes, reaching up with arms extended towards the roughly textured, spackled ceiling. My arches, my calves, my shoulders, and my biceps are now warmed by the flow of blood into them as they expand. Letting my head drop back a bit, allows my neck to release some additional tension. I close my eyes.

Relax.

My body lets out a tired yawn and I return to a flat standing position. I take a few moments to knead my wrists and palms and fingers to reduce the tenseness in them. I lower myself into a sitting position and extend my well-defined legs out in front of me. The back of my knees feel the calming pull and leaning forward, I grab my feet and begin to pull them back towards me. This was a pre-workout exercise that the entire cross country team completed at the start of each workout. I was never a big fan of stretching before a run, allowing that my legs would gradually 'kick into gear' by themselves, but I was now fearing some type of nervous breakdown might be occurring. I had seen some athletes fall to pieces (crying, yelling, throwing things) as a big race was about to start because of too much stress, and even though I can't place my finger on what is causing my present difficulty, I know enough to realize that seeing and hearing things that are not really there is a problem; a major problem.

My hands pull with a constant pressure until my toes can bend upwards no more. A few runners that I know have elongated, bony toes that can be pulled back, almost to the top of their foot. But my toes are stubbornly short and I cringe at the prospect of having them forced upward to that degree. 4:27 mile or not, I would more than likely pass out from the pain if that were ever to happen to me.

Turning my head I notice that Paul's silver and black headphones are still lying on the floor (I had thrown them off of my head earlier in the day). They sit there in silence, not far from me. Picking myself up off the rug, I place them carefully atop his stereo. I am hoping that they are not damaged.

On a refreshingly positive note, whoever was making those sounds, calling my name, had apparently moved on to bother someone else. When I find some free time I'm going to carefully inspect the room for any extraneous wires, or for miniscule holes drilled in the walls that would have aided the morons in their attempts to frighten me. They had been successful, but I was now back in command of my senses and fairly certain I would discover who they were. I did a cursory rundown, since my thoughts were not focused on the matter, of the potential culprits.

As I am not pledged to any fraternity an 'outside group' is an unlikely scenario.

To an unbiased mind, the most likely suspects at the moment would be either Jeff or Ed as they live on the other side of the wall in C2D2, and they had also lived in the dorm the prior year. They know the layout of the building, its caveats, and have a near perfect location from which to launch their assault on my senses.

The problem with this theory, conversely, is that neither of them was prone to frat boy hijinks. Jeff, in fact, loathes such behavior and considers it a sign of an infantile intellect and Ed expends little energy on interactions with his suitemates.

Brian and Luke, one room further down at the end of the quad in C2D3, were most certainly capable of pulling off an elaborate hoax, but getting Ed and Jeff to grant them considerable access to their room – and for that vapid reason – seemed more than a bit unlikely. Besides, I reasoned, between Luke's jam sessions as a guitarist with the Rolling Gumbys (a popular college band) and Brian's active social life, the two of them taking large amounts of time – in an attempt to torment me – made absolutely no sense at all.

That left two possibilities: my roommate Paul, or some stranger with seemingly unlimited time and resources, who has singled me out for reasons of which I am currently unaware.

Paul was the only person (aside from me) that had continuous access to the room which would allow him to somehow alter the effectiveness of the closet door latch. It is his stereo, his CD, and his headphones that I had been using when I heard the 'voice' that called my name that third time. It was he and his father who had supplied the, now-creaking, loft with them, and there's no reason why he couldn't have found the time to loosen a few of the snaps on my sweat suit.

Still, this scenario also seemed highly improbable.

Why would he want to damage his own loft, or my closet door? Even when I consider the disconcerting 'dream' that he mentioned to Jeff and I, regarding something awful that was almost upon us (this situation *was* awful) how would he have even known to rig his stereo? I never used it without his permission.

No. It wasn't Paul.

I would need more time to solve this.

Turning away from the stereo I am alarmed by the fact that the closet door has opened again. I remain standing, absolutely motionless.

There is something very, very *wrong* about all of this.

An unfamiliar, but seemingly primal, fear washes over me. Unseen waves of cold, like tendrils of chilled wind; move in and around my uncovered thighs. My body parts tighten and I squeeze my hands into fists. It feels as though I am being molested.

Some*thing* is in that dark closet.

I am unable to explain how this happens, but my mind 'picks up' the alarming image of a deformed, broken man. He cannot move without great pain or effort. He was lying in wait inside the murky shadows, and I could just barely make out the shapes of his unblinking eyes. Certain that he is carefully reviewing my bare form; I cover my privates with the towel. There is some type of shared understanding that I cannot make sense of. The creature, peering in from the darkness, wants to be young like me, to be able to run effortlessly across the land like me.

Oh my god, he wants to *be* me.

The deformed man, who is whispering words that I cannot properly hear inside my head, begins to slowly open his jaw ...

Total and absolute panic now sets in.

I sprint past the partially open closet, casting my towel back behind my head and over my back so that he cannot see any more of me, as I scamper into the bathroom like a young child afraid of the sound of thunder.

My arm muscles flex with extreme effort as I feverishly slide the heavy wood door back across its track in order to close it; to keep that thing from following me in.

Leaning my full body weight up against the door in order to keep it closed, I look at my heaving, frightened reflection in the mirror. I am not looking very happy right now, more like a six point buck draped over a hunter's roof rack.

I have absolutely no idea what the *hell* is going on, but I am going to take my shower!

I can't.

Tremors of fear shoot through my body from the 'imagined' terror, and as I stand under the shower head, I cannot bring myself to turn the water on.

Whatever has gotten into my mind has become dangerous. I am still confident that, with the passage of enough time, the creaking loft, the disembodied voice, and the unlatched closet door would be logically explained away. But that unknown length of time certainly has not yet passed, and for me to cover my eyes and ears with running water would be nothing less than foolish. How would I hear it, or see it, if it decided to come after me?

A part of me, the disciplined and organized runner, is now actively and forcefully judging my fear: *Are you kidding me,* seriously? *Do you actually believe that there is some* boogey man *in the closet? Turn the damn water on!*

Fear wins out.

I have been standing here, in this shower stall, for at least twenty minutes; possibly as many as forty. For the life of me, I can't ever remember being this cold. The air temperature in the building is at least 65°F, yet my finger nails, my lips, and any other place that does not produce melanin now retains a slight blue tint.

'I'm a blue blood, I'm royalty," I joke to myself, but nothing about this situation is remotely funny. I cross my arms to try and reduce the aggravating shivering, to hold myself still.

If the *thing* should come for me, I need a plan, and that plan requires a body guard; there was safety in numbers

One arrives.

Paul enters the quad. He is whistling a familiar tune, and I can hear him as he walks past the heavy wood bathroom door and into C2D1.

This is amazing luck!

After he has a few moments to 'settle in' from his long day of classes, I will call him into the bathroom and then create a conversation – about anything – in order to keep him nearby; just in case.

This does not happen.

For as I formulate my plan, one that would involve me running towards the right into the main hall area, and not to the left into a dead end, I hear Paul screaming in what sounds like abject fear: "Holy shit! Holy *shit*!"

Before I have the opportunity to call out to him, the wooden door to the bathroom screeches open, and Paul – looking like he has just been told he has an incurable disease – is gasping for air, bent over slightly, with both hands on his knees. He looks terrified.

I decide that I might have to cross Paul off of my list of suspects, for not even the legendary stage performer Lawrence Olivier could have acted this convincingly.

"Paul?"

Against my intent, I scare the hell out him, and he jumps back with a look of sheer fright etched on his young face. He had not been aware that I was in here, as I had been hiding, silently, behind the flimsy shower curtain.

"What's the matter with you?!" he yells while trying to catch his breath. "Why are you trying to scare the crap out me?"

"Sorry," I replied in mock complaint, "I was about to take a shower, what's the matter?"

His big brown eyes are still wide with fear, and I can tell that he is deliberating whether or not he should tell me. Given this day's events, I can certainly empathize with him.

"You won't believe me," he says, between pained and apprehensive glances over his shoulder into our room.

"Tell you what," I offer with my hand literally extended outward for effect, "Why don't you just hang here for a bit. When I'm done showering we can both go back to the room together, and you can decide if you want to tell me then."

He glances once more over his shoulder, and then looks directly into my eyes. There is a moment's hesitation. Like me, he is in uncharted territory. He slowly nods his head in the affirmative.

I have my guard.

"Never confuse movement with action." – Ernest Hemingway

9. Land of Confusion

Some conversations are hard to start. The 'I'm only interested in you as a friend' conversation; the 'I really don't want your *Watchtower* pamphlet' conversation; and the 'I think it's time we bring [insert pet's name] to the vet one last time' conversation are all prime examples of this. They are difficult to enter into with any comfort because you know that the conversation – no matter how necessary – will be bringing a measure of sadness to the person that you are addressing ... someone who you have no ill will towards.

I can only imagine what thoughts are running wildly through Paul's mind as we walk into C2D1. He gives me a minute to get dressed and then, in the most honest face I can imagine says:

"There is something in here!"

I shoot a quick glimpse over at my closet door, which remains open a few inches, and I hope that Paul doesn't notice.

"What do you mean?" I ask trying my best to calm the queasiness that is growing in my stomach.

Paul blinks his eyes a few times, almost as if he was holding back tears, and says, "You aren't going to believe this. I know this is some crazy shit, but ..."

He takes a few steps over to his desk and then with his back turned to me, he begins to recreate the events that led up to his frantic sprint into the bathroom area.

"I came into the room," he says retracing his steps, "put my books and my room key down, and then I heard someone say your name: 'Chrissss!'"

His eyes look worried as he turns to me, "But no one was here. The voice was *this* close," he adds putting about a foot between his ear and his extended hand. "I'm telling you, I swear, there was no one in here! It called your name, twice! I freaked!"

Paul paces back and forth a few times, and then repeats his words and his actions: "The voice was *this* close!"

There is not much that I can say right now. I am wrestling with my own doubts and fears. I still haven't ruled out that this is one elaborate … and epic … prank.

But the threads of my courage have already starting to fray. That Paul had heard the 'bodiless voice' is at once frightening and comforting to me. Frightening in that something freaky is going on in the place where we work, talk, and sleep – comforting in that I can now be more confident in the likelihood that I am not actually losing my mind.

But overriding all of this was a growing dread of the realization: this was all aimed at me.

Photograph of the loft in room C2D1 in late September, 1984. 'Upstairs': Paul's mattress is on the left, mine (partially obscured) is on the right. By the time the haunting began, I had replaced the generic hot air balloon poster with one of U.S. marathon runner Bill Rodgers, and Super Pickle was hanging from the ceiling.

After all, Paul may have been terrified by the unexplained phenomena, but he hadn't heard *his* name called. He had heard *mine!* And if this were a practical joke, the hoaxers would have called *his* name when he had entered, not *mine*. We had both heard: "Chrissss!"

I feel a bit light-headed, and my ears feel icy cold. There is no way that I am going to share what had happened to me, not right now anyway. I don't want to add any element of hysteria. Feeling a bit deceptive, all I say to Paul is: "That *is* pretty weird."

He looks at me; I know that he expects more of a response, that he *needs* more of a response. I just can't give it to him right now. I'm so sorry.

"Let's get out of here," he says, "I don't want to talk about this anymore. It's over, it's done."

The Letchworth Dining Hall is one of just a few social hubs for Geneseo students. It is located in the northwest corner of the college grounds. I have eaten here since I arrived at Geneseo one year earlier.

A young student named Eileen works here; she is one of the nicest people I have met since attending college, even though we hadn't actually formally met (although I did see her having a fairly decent time at the toga party). She looks you in the eye each time she speaks with you, and she smiles, and she treats everyone with respect; 'old school' manners.

As I watch her preparing and serving the food, I am hoping that she finds happiness one day and that it is with somebody who is as nice as she is. For even on this terrible day, her friendly demeanor has a positive and calming effect on both Paul and me. I make sure that she sees me wave my 'thank you'.

Making our way to the first empty table, I am careful to observe as many of the eating faces as I can. No one stands out to me as looking like they might be gloating over a well-played prank. This disappoints, and unnerves, me. I needed this all to be one big joke.

We do not utter one word about the impossible voice in our room, instead we eat our sandwiches quietly as the overhead speakers share "Eyes Without a Face", by Billy Idol; of course.

By 8PM, Paul and I are settled into our nightly homework routines, both of us are sitting at our desks, quietly working … Paul has his headphones on.

I work on my assignment for about 40 minutes, and then allow myself a break. The October 1984 issue of *Runner* magazine, which covers the prior summer's L.A. Olympics results, is my choice for the evening. There is an article in there by Eric Olson entitled: "A Race Hot with Mystery" that provides a detailed review of the men's Marathon.

There were two pre-race favorites, world record holder Rob DeCastella (2:08:18) of Australia and Japan's Toshihiko Seko (2:08:38) who had won six of the seven international marathons that he had run. Aside from the now-aging American distance running great, Bill Rodgers, these were my two favorite marathoners. DeCastella had massive and powerful legs that allowed him to power across the finish line, and Seko (who was my approximate height and weight) applied an unmatched determination to the sport. In these two great runners I saw some minor aspect of myself. Neither of them medaled on that hot Los Angeles evening, with the Australian finishing 'just out of the money' in fifth following a late race charge, and the modern day Samurai finishing 14th, just ahead of American record holder Alberto Salazar. Salazar, boo.

I am poring over the article – and its many photographs – looking for quiet clues as to how the race was won and lost by the world's eighty-four fastest runners.

This is when Paul commands me to: "Stop it!" I smile as I look up, assuming that he is simply trying to get a rise out of me, but he hasn't even lifted his head from his studies. As it was just as likely that he was complaining because an annoying radio announcer was talking through the intro of a song, as he was me, I quickly return myself to my magazine:

I find the large photo on page 145 compelling. It shows the eventual winner, Carlos Lopes of Portugal, looking back at both DeCastella and Seko, just prior to making his decisive move.

He must be seeing something in them – at that precise moment – something that tells him that the time to move is 'now'. Was it that Seko had just tossed his hat off onto the road's shoulder which suggested he was overheating? Was it DeCastella's decision to slow for water at the last water stop that was suggesting he was dehydrating?

The higher the level of competition, the more the mental aspect comes into play. One single split-second decision can have a lasting effect on a two hour race.

That is what I loved most about running. I didn't like the rigors of training any more than anyone else did, but I recognized that effective training might place me into a situation where my mind will be able to strategize me to a victory.

My 'smartest' race took place in my hometown, on the day before Thanksgiving, in 1983. It was during my first visit home from college. I wrote:

Yes! I had the good fortune to win the Town of Newburgh 10K (6.2 miles) Turkey Trot in front of a hometown crowd! It was freezing out but in spite of some initial muscle tightness and the fact that my feet were so numb that I could hardly feel the ground when I ran my first mile was in 5:30. Perfect! I was able to break free of the lead pack - that included Daniel Leahy and Lynn Warren from Newburgh Free Academy - by 3.5 miles. My mom and sisters were there, and happy to see I was in first by a few feet. I heard Dan say to my sister, "Don't worry, I'll catch him." "No, you won't!" she yelled, "That's my brother!" I thought that was funny. A mile later we ran by my grandparents' house. Grandma and grandpa, Jesse, Dylan, and my Aunt Nancy were all cheering loudly for me by the edge of the road when I ran by in first place! Great-grandma was holding Stacey in her arms and standing in the big picture window and smiling at me from the house. Super!

It was the vital combination of an effective strategy and fierce determination that led me to sweet victory in my hometown 10K in 1983. Success in dealing with the happenings in room C2D1 didn't seem as clear.

Dan Leahy, who was wearing all red (like a Russian) began moving up on me when we hit the long hill just before the mile 5 mark. The smells from Pizza Hut and McDonalds on Rt. 300 made me hungry! I let him work the hill hard to close the gap while I coasted, a bit like a runner's version of Mohammed Ali's rope-a-dope (even though he is very arrogant). When I slowed down, Danny thought that I was fading fast. I could see from his closing shadow that he was pumping his arms and legs to catch me. He wanted to pass me on the hill and take the lead. But by the time that he closed to within a few feet of me halfway up the hill, I could tell he was exhausted. Having slowed my pace for a while, my legs were now fresher than his. I kept repeating "Today, not tomorrow" over and over inside my head. It would have been very easy to give in to the pain and slow down and settle to finish in the top three. But I knew that if I could run a bit faster, no matter how much it hurt, that I could say that I won this race forever. A course record can always be broken, but they can never take a victory away. As I crested the 3/4 mile-long hill, I 'put the hammer down' (like my dad says). When Dan saw how quickly I was pulling away from him, he just let me go.

The race for first was over. The only hard part was breathing in the fumes from the tailpipe of the police car that was the lead vehicle. Each time I tried to change the side of the road I was running on to get some fresh air, he quickly went to the same side! Oh well. It felt like a dream running down the final stretch of the race course, all alone with no one near me. I ran through the finish chute and after I crossed the line I literally fell on my knees and kissed the ground like the Pope does when he lands in a country. I won in 35:51 on a very difficult course. Leahy crossed the line 36 seconds behind me in 36:27 and Lynn Warren finished third in 37:56. My dad finished 14th with a time of 41:04. It was one of the toughest and hilliest 10Ks that I ever ran. My dad said I would have run a 33:51 on a flat course. Winning this race in my hometown is now my greatest accomplishment, even better than when I ran the Montreal Marathon when I was 14! After the race I got TWO trophies, a small one for winning my age category (16-20) and a giant one that is almost three feet tall! for the winning the entire race! My sister Nicole gave me a fuzzy brown 'good luck monkey' doll after the race? She was being nice, so I'll keep it.

10 THE EVENING NEWS Tuesday, November 22, 1983

DiCesare first in Trot

Christopher DiCesare registered a time of 35:51 to finish first overall Sunday in the Town of Newburgh 10-kilometer Turkey Trot.

DiCesare competed in the 16 to 20-year-old division, while Laura Meier, who was the first female runner across the line with a time of 46:26, also won the women's 16 to 20-year-old division.

A stuffed good luck monkey doll, I'm not even sure what I did with it after she gave it to me. Did I leave it on my …

"CUT THE SHIT! I don't want to play these games!"

I am harshly rattled back into the present. Paul has yelled a second time, and I am fairly sure now that he is directing his comments towards me. I decide to put my magazine away, and watch him. He is flailing his arms – almost wildly – above his head. This is no joke.

"Stop, I told you to stop!"

It was common knowledge that you are not supposed to wake a sleepwalker, but I have no idea what this is all about.

Still, this is my friend and something is clearly not right. I decide to intervene.

"Paul!"

I yell loudly enough so that he would be able to hear my voice over his headphones.

It works.

He turns, with an angry expression, and pulls his headphones above his ears. It looks as though he is about to yell back, when a look of pure confusion washes across his face. He asks: "How did you get back to your desk so fast?"

"What are you *talking* about," I reply with an annoyed expression, "I've been sitting here reading, I haven't left my chair!"

I don't like being yelled at, not by that drunk Irish kid, not by a roommate, not by anyone. Civilized and educated people should be able to talk things out without having to scream or curse. My take on it was that if you had to yell or curse, you were probably already losing the argument.

"You keep blocking my light," he fires back, "You keep making shadows across my desk; it's blocking my light!"

In an attempt to tone down the conversation, I ask Paul: "And just how exactly can I do that if I am ten feet away from you? It's not like I am Mr. Fantastic (of Marvel Comics' *Fantastic Four*) where I can stretch my arms across the room. Am I right?"

Paul is now considering my statement. I can tell that he thinks it is reasonable enough. The problem was though, if it wasn't me, then it was someone ... or some*thing* ... else.

I see it in his face as his mood darkens. This is just too much. I can't blame him; it is too much for me too. But where I am a trained athlete, who has won races by masking restlessness and fear, Paul, for all of his many strengths and talents ... is not.

"That's it!" he yells as he stands up and throws his head phones down onto his book-covered desk, "I'm going out for a while. This place is getting f***ing crazy!"

Number five, and twice in one month, I lament silently. I know that it won't happen, but I am still hoping that the world will someday become enlightened, and the word will just fade away.

Paul pushes out of the room at a brisk pace and I get up from my chair to close, and lock, the door behind him.

I need some quiet time to help me figure out just what the heck is scrambling the structure of my life. Maybe someone put some type of drug in our food?

But that doesn't make any sense because I didn't eat lunch with Paul this afternoon, and we ate different meals at dinner.

It might be a gas leak that is causing the hallucinations in Paul and me, but I can smell no gas, and the college has carbon monoxide alarms that would alert us if that were the case.

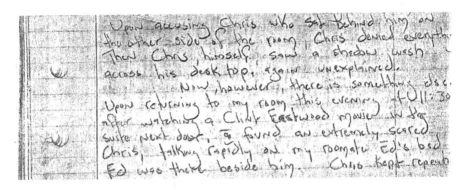

When I had lived in Genesee Hall, I watched as a hypnotist appeared to 'control' the minds of some of the students. Was it possible that I had been hypnotized then and that the trigger word had inadvertently been uttered? Eh. More nonsense, it wouldn't be affecting Paul at all if that was the case; he wasn't there.

In any event, I am not going to let one freakish day shake my foundations like this. The care package that my mother had sent is still sitting on the floor close to my desk. Written very neatly on the outside of the parcel are the words: "Do not open until Valentine's Day."

I double check my calendar, it is still days away, but I am in dire need of something to ground me, and a care package from my family seems the perfect remedy.

Using a pair of scissors, I slice a neat opening in the box. A hand-written letter from my 82-year-old great-grandmother is carefully placed atop the assorted goodies. She wants me to stay warm. I love her.

There is a red and white sweater that she knitted for me just under the letter. I lift it up into the air. Even though I would have been too big for it when I was ten, I appreciate her effort. I chuckle.

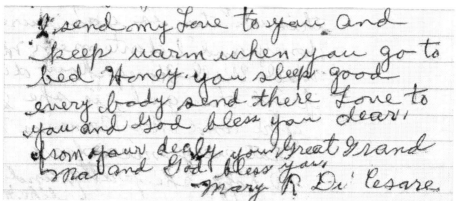

A cropped section of the actual letter from my great-grandmother that I was reading on the night of February 12th, 1985,

There are humorous individual letters from my two sisters, Nicole and Melissa; a full-length letter from my mom; and some money from my dad with the latest dartball stats on green and white striped computer paper as well. At the very bottom of the carton is a thin red box of *Hot Tamales*, chewy, hot, cinnamon candies.

I hold the box up into the air over my desk with perhaps as much reverence as I've ever seen a priest hold the communion wafers above the altar. I'm not comparing them; mind you, just my actions.

The box is difficult to open, and I am forced to open it on the 'wrong end'. Nonetheless, the thin, red, cylindrical, cinnamon treats make my mouth burn with happiness.

Pouring several of the candies into my mouth, in order to maximize the excellent flavor, I re-read the letter from my great-grandmother. I know that she will not be 'with us' all that much longer, just by doing the math, and I want to take in every word that she has written to me.

When she was born there were no automobiles, no televisions, and no air conditioners. Women could not vote. I wonder what it must have been like to have lived through the beginnings of the communication age. She witnessed the 'Roaring Twenties', survived the Great Depression and then cried as her son, my grandfather, went off to fight World War II. I wonder what she was thinking when Neil Armstrong stepped onto the moon – or what thoughts went through her mind when President John F. Kennedy (the son of the man who almost had her husband killed bootlegging alcohol during prohibition) was shot.

Without her, there would be no me, and even though I had seen her almost every week from the time I was born until the time I left for college, there was so much more that I wanted to know.

My great-grandfather, who she was married to for over 50 years, once told me that life was quieter back in the 'old days', that there was less noise, fewer people, and the skies weren't crowded with wires or cables or airplanes. He said that people were much more polite; everyone said 'hello' to one another on the street. That when the actor from the movie *Gone with the Wind* said: "Frankly Scarlett, I don't give a damn!" many folks considered that profane.

He had seen Babe Ruth, Lou Gehrig, Mel Ott, and Ty Cobb all play baseball, and said that it was expected that you 'dressed up' when you went to a ball game, as it was a special event.

I lean back into the support that my brown, sturdy, wooden chair provides. I miss my great-grandfather. He had passed away over seven years ago. My heart is still sad that the last time I 'saw' him I did not express my respect or love.

He was eighty years old and had collapsed in his home. He was lying in a bed at St. Luke's Hospital, tubes in his arm, a black patch over one eye. The man who once had the strength to swim across the Hudson River was now tired and fading.

My intentions were simple: to let him know that I loved him, and that I was proud that he was my great-grandfather.

But there was a sickly smell in the entire ward, and as he made a determined effort to look over at me – for the last time – I was wrinkling up my nose, sticking my tongue out, and saying "Uh, what's that smell?"

My dad nudged me and said: "Stop that."

My great-grandfather looked sad.

Shame.

I walked away a few feet and leaned against the shiny beige wall that held a fire extinguisher. On the way home in the darkness, as the pattern of the streetlights intermittently lit my face, I silently cried, my mouth moving to the words, "I'm sorry grandpa. I'm so sorry."

I can't remember his funeral.

I place the letter back down onto my desk. My eyes are wet. I am relieved that Paul has left the room and that my door is locked, I don't want anyone to see that I have been crying.

Tossing a few more pieces of candy into my mouth, I decide to offer some to whoever it is standing behind me, near my right shoulder ...

"Reading is one form of escape. Running for your life is another." – Lemony Snicket (Daniel Handler)

10. Counting to Ten

The sky was a spectacular soft blue as we flew in the direction of the sun. I stretched my neck so that I could look through the dirt-spotted window and see the brown and green patchwork far below us.

My dad, sporting a new pair of dark-rimmed glasses and with thick dark hair still on his head, pointed out the location of the Newburgh-Beacon Bridge, the Mid-Valley Mall and Algonquin Park below us. The small piper cub airplane ride was a revelation, and a far cry from lying on the warm sidewalk watching the blue and red dotted gypsy moth caterpillars inch across it.

It was such a liberating feeling, that soaring through the heavens.

Landing on the stationary and constricting ground was something of a letdown, and I stared at the small flying machine as we drove away from the airport. But when I was joyfully riding in the 'chariot of the gods', there was one moment – one unforgettable moment – of sheer panic: the tiny plane had hit a strong wind current called 'turbulence', which had thrown my entire frame well up into the air.

My stomach felt like it had jumped into my throat, and I was unable to get a grasp onto anything in spite of the fact that I had been reaching out wildly with both arms. My eyes darted rapidly about the compact cabin as they looked for some type of hand hold. I remember closing my eyes when I realized that I was unable to regain control of my balance, to resolve the situation. A second later, my rump landed back onto the soft fabric seat, and I was safely staring down at the dark sparkling water of the Hudson River.

That had been the scariest moment of my life ... until now.

I am sitting as still as I can. Muscles that have spent thousands upon thousands of hours making my body move as fast and as far as they could, were now being called upon to keep it perfectly and absolutely still. For, if my senses are functioning properly, the impossible is occurring: *something* is standing behind me.

There is no doubt that whatever 'it' is; it's shaped like a person. My peripheral vision – whether through slight changes in light or color - holds it in place, and even as an out-of-focus mass, standing by the stereo, it resembles a human figure.

Here is the problem with that: only Paul and I had been in the room all night; only Paul and I had been given keys to the room; and when Paul stormed out, complaining of shadows circling around him while he tried to work, I had immediately locked the door behind him.

The only other entrance into the room is through the second story window, which is a good eighteen to twenty feet from the ground ... and was also locked.

Unless some manner of Navy Seal had reason to scale the exterior wall of my college dormitory, use a glass cutter to carve a hole in the window, and then slip into the room to conduct a reconnaissance mission on me ... absurd.

I close my eyes, just like I had on that airplane, when I had lost full control of my environment. There is no captain to guide me gently to the ground this time; it will be entirely up to me.

I will do it myself. I will count.

Tossing two more tamales into my mouth, I clear my mind, and as my grandmother had demonstrated on my sister ten years prior – and as I had applied successfully in race after race ... I started counting.

One.

My brain is working hard to understand.

Two.

My breathing rate has increased.

Three.

I can now feel the pulse in my neck.

Four.

Every part of my body begins to tighten.

Five.

There is a ringing in my ears.

Six.

I think I might vomit.

Seven.

I need to look ... just to make sure. I'm not sure that I can trust my senses anymore.

There is no eight.

At 'seven' I turn my head slowly to the right. I am now looking at Paul's desk. The quiet familiarity of his headphones on its flat surface, the wolf poster on the wall, and the sports drawing that hangs just above it allow my entire body to breathe a sigh of relief ...

Until I see the pale, bluish face ... the slightly opened mouth ... and a tilting head about a foot to the right of them.

My chest heaves.

The head and face, almost as if they are only loosely connected to the body, float an inch or two closer my way. It wants to see me up close.

My neck muscles twitch and it is hard to swallow my saliva. I try to say "no," but I cannot speak a word.

There is no *way that this is actually happening*, I am thinking.

As quietly and steadily as I can, I stand up. I am not sure if I am breathing right now, and my legs have a slight tremble. The almost holographic head shifts/glides back into its original location, atop the blue and yellow striped shirt.

I think it is a shirt, it looks like a shirt.

Next, its torso slides unnaturally forward from its hips; the dark blue-covered legs are half in front of, and half *inside* of Paul's stereo! I *literally* pinch the side of my own left thigh with my thumb and forefinger in order to make sure that I am awake.

I hope, dearly, that I am not.

I attempt to concentrate on what exactly it is that I am seeing in order to make some kind of sense out of it all. My visual and mental focuses are now working together in the attempt to define this absolutely impossible object.

The thing's eyes, uniformly light gray – with the barest hint of blue, like a pinhead – in their centers, seem to be moving around unnaturally, in their sockets. It is looking at me with a unique intensity that is incomparable.

I am very afraid.

My mind is still telling me that I am not supposed to be seeing this, that I should not be seeing this; that it simply cannot be happening.

Its mouth seems to make a slight smile, the loose corners lifting slightly. Or maybe it is a pained expression.

The thing looks 'wicked' to me … wicked and terrifying.

I know, more than anything I've ever known, that I will never be the same.

My entire torso convulses from an intense and unexpected chill that runs its way up my spine, causing both of my arms to fly momentarily upward, the box of candy flying out of my useless right hand into the now chilled air of C2D1.

I scream.

I scream loudly.

I continue to scream as I bang my knee against the sharp, hard, edge of my desk and make a mad dash for the door, for safety.

"Help, please, help me!"

I am banging on Jeff's door.

He is not there.

"In Xanadu did Kubla Khan
A stately pleasure-dome decree:
Where Alph, the sacred river, ran
Through caverns measureless to man
Down to a sunless sea."
- Samuel Taylor Coleridge, *The Complete Poems*

11. No Time for the Madness

Looking back, there was precious little to suggest that this traumatic experience was about to happen. Unlike today, where the social reach and societal impact of the many paranormal television shows, and thousands of paranormal groups can easily be registered, this lengthy Reagan Era extreme haunting literally came out of the blue (of my college dorm room walls).

I had no particular interest in the occult, as it was labeled then, nor would I watch *any* type of horror film. I had no idea who George A. Romero was, and for me a 'zombie' was simply a marathon runner who was staggering to the finish line due to extreme dehydration. No one in my circle of friends possessed a Ouija board, nor would I have deigned to use one if the opportunity had presented itself. For me, my cousin's 'Magic 8 Ball' novelty toy was the posted speed limit when it came to any external predictors. I was an upbeat, popular, and successful student-athlete who had no need for the increased attention – and likely derision – that claims of the 'undead' would no doubt generate.

While I did have an extremely inquisitive mind, I never was a huge risk taker. My alcohol consumption over the three years I spent at Geneseo consisted of one glass of vodka in September of my freshman year and a half-finished can of Molson's Ale over two years later. While more than a few of my college mates would apparently smoke the 'hippie cabbage' (marijuana) when they were able to, I never had so much as a single cigarette.

I rode on a motorcycle only once (and burned my leg); I never skipped a class in high school; and I waited the full thirty minutes before going into a pool after eating.

As I grew, I began to take greater joy from life's natural euphoria, and I never needed nicotine or coffee or alcohol to start my day or to survive the grind of life. Rather, I reveled in feeling the summer sunrise as it slowly warmed the surface of my skin; gazing up through clouds of my breath at a winter's deep starlit sky; feeling the cool wetness of spring morning dewdrops on my ankles; and making a color chart of reds and yellows, oranges and browns with autumn leaves in my outstretched palm. These were my quiet, isolated joys.

I also loved baseball.

My love affair with the Nation's pastime began, fittingly, on our Nation's 197th birthday: July 4th, 1973.

I was eight years old and bored out of my noggin. The large family gathering grew old for me after three hours of sitting in the intense midday heat, staring at the dragonfly-infested motionless lake.

After making a quick tour of the happenings outside the house (the trading of real estate tips and sharing of gossip by the macaroni salad), I found that my Uncle Patrick was, smartly, hidden away inside the large air-conditioned home. Walking in quietly, I stood beside him as he watched a baseball game on a large color television.

"Hey, buddy," he smiled "take a seat. Why don't you watch the ballgame with me? It's the Yankees vs. the Red Sox."

'Who would wear red socks', I wondered to myself as I complied.

One of the announcers used the word 'huckleberry' and I found that amusing, mostly because it reminded me of that blue Saturday morning cartoon dog who sang "Oh, my darling." I must have been smiling, because my uncle asked me if I liked baseball.

"Sure."

"Oh yeah? That's good. Who is your favorite player?"

...

I was saved by a smallish-looking left-handed batter with the number '1' sewn onto the back of his pinstriped jersey.

"Him!" I pointed, nervously, towards the television screen.

"Oh. Bobby Murcer? He's a good ballplayer, Chris. They say he's supposed to be the next Mickey Mantle."

When the baseball settled into the right field bleachers (for Murcer's 15th home run of the season) less than a minute later, I had decided that baseball was pretty darn cool. In my young mind: it 'worked the way it was supposed to.'

Halloween: Dressed up as New York Yankees' star Bobby Murcer in 1974.

Six months later, with my allowance money in hand, I walk the quarter mile down the road to Charlie's Farm Market to purchase my first pack of baseball cards. There are seven red card-shaped packs sitting inside of a thin cardboard display box. This will be the very first time that I make a purchase — of anything — on my own. There will be no mom to ask me if I am sure that I want that, no dad to tell me to make sure I count my change. As a moth to the flame, I walk slowly towards the counter where the box rests. The outside of the box seems to be adorned with images of some of the cards that might be found inside the sealed individual packages. A slight anxiety runs through me when I don't recognize any of the names that I see on the box top: Bob Boone, George Scott, Nolan (something) ... but I am here with a purpose. I pick up all seven tightly sealed packs. I carefully move my soft fingertips around the edges, front and back of the packs. Each of the packs look identical, the image of a baseball placed, appropriately, in the center.

"BONUS team checklist inside!" reads a yellow block below the baseball logo. I don't know what that is, but it seems like it might be a good thing due to the exclamation point. Further below, in small print: "with one stick bubble gum."

I let two of the packs fall out of my hands, then two more. Three packs (only one of which I can afford to purchase) now look up at me. After careful consideration, and a few more 'finger runs' to see if I can glean the 'lucky' pack, I choose the pack on the left.

The center pack had been tempting as it was balanced and sat safely in the middle away from harm, and the 'right' pack had the distinct advantage of sounding like the correct choice by virtue of its name, a coincidence? But I am left-handed, and he is left-handed, so the pack on the left it is. Smiling a hopeful smile, I have joined the ranks of those who have purchased things!

Opening the pack from the back, I see the white-powdered, cardboard-textured pink stick of gum. It is promptly tossed into my mouth. Worried now that the sharp corners might cut my gums, I produce some warm saliva to soften it.

As I slowly make my way back down Rt. 17K, almost incidentally, I glance down at the opened pack of Topps baseball cards and see the name 'Bobby Ray Murcer' on the green, white and black card back! My eyes bug out, 'Murcer is my favorite player for sure!'

I run home to tell my confused parents that some ballplayer from Oklahoma – that I had never mentioned before – is my hero.

He had connected the lines of possibility and probability for me.

...

By the time that January 1985 had arrived – and just one month before the haunting would begin – I was very comfortable with the transition made from high school to college.

Some have, very fairly, raised the issue of me potentially suffering from Seasonal Affective Disorder (SAD) as a possible explanation for the haunting. Western New York is, after all, known for its brutal winters, with lake effect snow (from Lake Ontario which separates sections of New York from Canada), fierce westerly winds and freezing temperatures. Such conditions do lend themselves to spending large amounts of time indoors. There were no smart phones, no laptops, no *YouTube*, no *Facebook* to keep oneself occupied and better connected to the events and the people in the 'outside' world.

Having no vehicle by which to get around with would also have been an isolating factor.

However, I had already gone through the long winter months (away from home) the year prior and suffered no ill effects. I was still running outdoors on the roads every day; and I was constantly surrounded by a great group of friends that included Paul, Jeff, Beth, Linda, Ed, Judy, and many others.

There were movies to watch, comics to draw, concerts to go to, and some hellacious games of ping pong.

"A friend is a gift you give yourself." — Robert Louis Stevenson

The truth was that I was having a blast!

My favorite facet of college was being exposed to new things.

Late in the fall semester Jeff began to share with me a whole new world of music: the European world. Or as Jeff would call it: 'Early 80s New Wave synth-pop', sometimes cleverly referred to as the second 'British Invasion'.

Peter Gabriel's thought-provoking and iconic "Lay Your Hands on Me" made Stevie Wonder's repetitive keyboard ballads seem like simple-minded mush; U2's powerful anthem "Sunday, Bloody Sunday", made Michael Jackson's "Thriller" seem both self-serving, and juvenile. The smooth, haunting voice of the lead singer for the Police, Sting, made American icon Bruce Springsteen sound to me as though he were gargling milk (it does a body good) as he sang.

The Eurythmics, Spandau Ballet, Genesis, Simple Minds, General Public, Adam Ant, Tears for Fears, Frankie Goes to Hollywood, Naked Eyes, I loved them all.

When our U.S. musicians crowed: 'WE are the World', I noticed the Euro-rockers wondered aloud, 'Do THEY know it's Christmas?'

As the fall semester ended in December of 1984, Jeff's musical offerings had truly proved to be eye opening for me.

But by far, my favorite musician of the time became William Michael Albert Broad, or rather, Billy Idol. *Rebel Yell* was the first cassette tape that I purchased while at college, and I played it almost every day during the school year of 1984-85, including those portions that contained the haunting. If someone had decided to rush, unannounced, into my room, they might have found me flailing about C2D1 in mock Billy Idol fashion, with a black indelible magic marker serving as my makeshift microphone.

I knew every word, every beat, practically every musical nuance of "Flesh for Fantasy", "Rebel Yell", and "Eyes Without a Face". The raw energy, the retro Elvis lip curl, the emotional delivery all had me enthralled. At a time when some of my friends were claiming that they wanted to be me (due to all of my lady friends), I wanted to be Billy Idol!

The song on the album that most affected me was "The Dead Next Door". It was plaintive and moving, and at the height of the terrifying events I would play the song in my room, hoping that the ghost might feel some element of remorse, or perhaps even some sense of understanding through it. The line: "One error, silent terror" captured how I viewed the time. The song served, to my teenage thinking, as a potential musical olive branch to my enemy.

I was also influenced by a wide variety of thought-provoking literature through the various courses that the college offered.

The resonating imagery and erstwhile glimpse into both the character and behavior of men (and nations) expressed in Joseph Conrad's classic *Heart of Darkness* impacted me as no other book before or since. One reason was that just as the character of 'Lord Darcy'(from *Pride and Prejudice*) became an apt descriptor for Jeff, the young Russian – or harlequin character – in Conrad's tale, seemed a close match for me at a time when I was still in the important process of defining myself as a person.

As I turned page after page, new concepts and philosophies were forcing my brain to a higher level of self-reflection. I drew in a gasp of surprise when I realized the Russian's favorite catchphrase was that Mr. Kurtz had 'enlarged' his mind!

Physically, the harlequin was possessed of a fair complexion, with a "beardless, boyish face, very fair, no features to speak of, nose peeling, little blue eyes, smiles and frowns chasing each other over that open countenance like sunshine and shadow over a wind-swept plain." Had Conrad written that description about *me* in 1985, it might have been just as apt.

He also wrote of the Russian's 'glamour of youth', and that was precisely the stage of life that I found myself at as the haunting drew near. I had been somewhat quiet and shy growing up, but the combination of steady advances from the college girls and admiring comments in the locker room from my male counterparts, had me increasingly proud of my physical appearance. When I was able to, I showcased it.

I was nineteen.

"In the woods too, a man casts off his years, as the snake his slough, and at what period soever of life, is always a child. In the woods, is perpetual youth."
— Ralph Waldo Emerson, *Nature and Selected Essays*

It was not unlike me to bound – naked and free – through snow drifts during a Western New York winter storm, with friends following behind clapping, hooting and nervously looking out for the college's Public Safety vehicles around every corner.

Corners are important.

"That's *Chris*," Jeff would offer while shaking his head back and forth in practiced amusement, hoping that my "Joie de vivre" (joy for life) would not end up actually taking it from me.

In warmer weather I would try to find my way to places such as Letchworth State Park (the Grand Canyon of the East) and to Fallbrook, which held the most remarkable waterfall, and was just a short walk from the south side of the Geneseo campus. Nature became my playground. And that long ago piper cub flight was transformed from a purely physical event into a more spiritual one.

My mind embraced thoughts and images of humanity's search for the heavens, for meaning, and for purpose.

Even the path of a baseball off the bat, the ball rising to the skies, always to fall short – but still able to be celebrated – now seemed to me to be a step on the road to understanding the inherent value of the experience of life, of simply being *alive*.

I pored through Edith Hamilton's classic *Mythology: Timeless Tales of Gods and Heroes* with the veracity of a wolf in winter time. I was enthralled by the stories of Daedalus and Icarus with their flying wings of wax and feathers; of Hermes, the fast-running messenger of the gods who would lead souls from life on Earth to death in Hades; and of Pan, son of Hermes, the god of the mountainside and the dark woods.

Though a devout Christian, and fully understanding my faith's Jewish foundation, as a student who was familiar with more than a few sections of the Quran, nowhere could I find tales or events as personally applicable as in this long dead Mediterranean religion ... this Greek Mythology. The monotheistic faiths had taught me everything that I knew about God; the writings of the ancient Greeks were teaching me more and more about humanity ... and me.

The ancient Greeks had a term: *Arcadian.* This referred to more than simply being from a physical location heavily adorned with farms and vineyards, and roaming shepherds. It was also an approach to understanding life, expressing a vision of man's harmony with nature.

As a distance runner my training would have me running through forests, up and down mountains, and through fields and meadows. I began to feel as though I was becoming a minor part of some valuable whole. In my mind I had become an 'Arcadian'.

Once to a wooded – or low foot-traffic location – I would typically cast off as much of my clothing as I could and sit myself down in some brush to relax, or sprint from tree to tree as though I were some character in the John Boorman movie, *The Emerald Forest*.

Aside from post-race synopses, I wasn't much of a chronicler, like Jeff was. But I did take the time to write in great detail about the experience of standing inside the cold waters of a rushing waterfall:

The waterfall was majestic and alluring. Stepping into the stream below it, I stood motionless for what seemed an eternity. The stream bed shimmered in the sun's light, illuminating an outcrop of black rock. Thick, healthy, green moss drank the droplets of water that sprayed its way. I had been taught that the human body was comprised of 90% water. If that is the indeed the case, then there is no material that we are more like than water!

Water: essential for life.

The fluid was so pure, so cold, so cleansing, that my only desire was to feel more of it. It rolled over my fully exposed body as though it were protecting me from some harshness. I could hear only the wet rush of life over my ears and the strong, rapid beating of my heart. I opened my eyes and saw an ever-changing image of shape and color. No longer was there a flecked arrangement of separate hues on a canvas, but rather one dynamic design.

"Water is the driving force in nature." — Leonardo da Vinci

"One Grand Design," I thought to myself through timed gasps for the warm air, "Everything, everyone is different, yet we are all a part of this one Grand Design called life." I no longer felt conspicuously different or apart from the norm. I was quite simply a human being discovering that I was one small, hopefully valuable, piece of the whole. It was exhilarating!

130

My idyllic love for body freedom kicked into high gear my second year at college. I was able to make a few extra dollars by posing for art projects as a figure model. The work requirements were easy enough: "Take off your clothes, and don't move." Although you'd probably be surprised at how itchy your skin can become when you aren't actually allowed to scratch it!

I made a whopping $69, an exact amount that would lead to a whole slew of terrible jokes from my friends. Most of that money was happily used purchasing salami and provolone subs at Aunt Cookie's up on Main Street.

Although I tried to downplay where I was going some nights, word of my modeling eventually spread to the girls' building and that would reward me with the 'super pickle' doll that everyone always asks me about; the one hung from the ceiling in room C2D1 above my bed, and that appears in the now famous ghost picture.

I hear they sell for a lot of money now.

It also led to a bizarre demand for locks of my hair. Jeff could only shake his head at the delirium that surrounded me. The curls ended up taped to dark-colored pieces of construction paper which were then triumphantly displayed on the girls' dorm room walls; something about that curtain and carpet thing again. College girls are weird.

I even harnessed the unthinkable courage to use my sketched bare form in a comic strip, the one that Jeff and I had been working on the night of the Warren presentation. And with the exception of the fact that we taped the caption on a bit crooked, it turned out pretty well. I sometimes wonder what we could have developed it into, if the haunting hadn't consumed most of our time and energy.

Eventually even Jeff, as proper-minded as a person could be, came to accept the value and joy I found in just being myself: a living part of the natural machine.

He began to use some of these excursions as creative photo opportunities, capturing my wonder for the natural state, the world, and the natural order of things, through his 35mm lens. Although Jeff did note that he would have been more interested in catching snaps of nubile forest nymphs than fleet-footed Pan!

For Jeff nudity seemed to be defined as the few elapsed seconds between leaving the shower stall and wrapping an impatient towel around his waist. And while Jeff adamantly refused to join me in eliminating any clothing, he had his own method of enjoying nature: catching it!

Whereas I flitted around as though some carefree, golden-hued, dragonfly moving from location to location with seeming abandon, Jeff had the skills of a silent, effective, and stalking, predator. Skills demonstrated to him by his father who used them to survive the horrible after effects of World War II in Germany.

In the spring of 1985 Jeff invited me to his family's home in Webster, NY just outside the city of Rochester, and less than one hour's drive from the college. Located on Drumm Road, it was actually an estate, crowned with a beautiful home and nestled amongst acres and acres of forestlands not very distant from the southern shore of Lake Ontario. It even had a name: Wolfern. It was named, I am told, after his dad's family's farmstead in the 'old country'.

Jeff himself resided in the basement and his room, which seemed large enough to me to ride horses in (or maybe small ponies), was chock-full of ancient leather bound tomes of knowledge, with an assortment of smooth rocks, driftwood and far too many hand blown glass bottles of varying color shape and size to count. I was taken by the small bubbles inside the glass walls of the bottles, remnants of an earlier world. The articles in Jeff's room caused me to wonder if he might have been an alchemist had he lived a few hundred years earlier. I could imagine him slaving away under dim candlelight in some ivy-walled castle in the attempt to turn lead to gold. What I could not imagine was what I would witness the following morning.

The fast-flowing stream was a good fifteen feet across in some areas, and at random intervals ran as deep as three feet. For all of my vaunted love of nature, I certainly wasn't about to risk getting pulled out into the frigid waters of the vast Great Lake at whose doorstep the mouth of the stream knocked. I remained safely on dry land – terra firma – as Jeff slightly cuffed the bottoms of his blue jeans (perhaps more for effect than purpose) and wade knee deep into the bitter flow.

"What are you doing," I asked with what had to be a look of sincere concern.

"I'm going to catch a fish."

"With what" I asked, seeing no fishing pole, net or bait.

He stopped for a moment, met my gaze and smiled: "With my hands."

Moments later he was stepping cautiously though the water, his hands raised just inches above the sparkling surface as though he was reading some type of invisible signal.

With a startling suddenness, he plunged his hands into the water, focused, and extracted a large fish that seemed as shocked as I was.

Jeff would, on many occasions, claim to be in awe of me. In awe of my courage, my social skills, my running success, the way that I could light up a room, or run naked through it. Truth be told, I would have considered trading in all those things to be able to do what he just did.

He was cool. Cooler than the French Bayonet sword he purchased when he was ten, cooler than his collection of silver Peace Dollars (even the rare 1927 one). Cooler than I ever could or would be.

I was proud that he allowed me to be his friend.

Lightning fast: It took Jeff less than two minutes to wade into a large stream on his property … … and catch an eight pound steelhead trout with his bare hands.

My streak of good fortune in Erie Hall continued, and without so much as stating a single position, and with no prior experience, I won a place on the dorm council by carrying almost all of the male vote and 70% of the female vote ... against a female opponent.

There were five of us on the ticket, and in a tip of the cap to adolescent ignorance and unrestricted free speech, we called ourselves The Fourth Reich Party. We weren't quite able to figure out what the first two 'Reichs' had done, but we figured the third one (Nazis) was so debauched that we would shine by comparison. Of course, it probably did not help that we were all blue-eyed and blond-haired. But it was all part of the tongue-in-cheek joke, we thought, as none of us believed we had a snowball's chance in hell of winning, anyway. We just didn't want those in the ruling party to run unopposed again.

We were all stunned when I won, maybe me the most.

My opponent, who was justifiably staggered by reports of her loss, demanded a recount on the spot. After the recount had been finalized (which again verified that I had won) several of the girls who had supported me were asked by their suitemates why they would 'break ranks' and vote for a guy. The most common response was a helpfully shallow one: "He's cute, and we like him!"

I wasn't sure if it might have had something to do with the locks of hair on those walls.

Jeff was so astounded, that he offered up a theory that I might be possessed of some type of 'super pheromone'. When I shot him a quizzical look, he explained to me that pheromones were a form of 'chemical cocktail' that is transmitted through the air in order to aid a male in attracting a female mate. I laughed, made reference to a certain cartoon skunk, and announced: "Le pew!"

Jeff didn't laugh; tough crowd.

Meanwhile, none of this 'pheromone talk' sat particularly well with my opponent who had, over the prior weeks, actually taken the time to develop a well thought out agenda in the clear expectation that she would win. It didn't take long for me to notice how distraught she was, and how much the position truly meant to her.

I offered her my resignation that evening down in the dorm lobby where the makeshift ballot box still sat. When she realized that I wasn't joking with her she thanked me and then scrambled rapidly down the hallway yelling to her friends: "Hey, I'm in! I'm in with you! He just resigned! Just now, he resigned!"

Her running form might have been terrible (really terrible) but her effort was certainly impressive.

My political career had lasted just under 90 minutes, but I was still able to celebrate the accomplishment of having won an election. For a few hours I had felt like Ronald Reagan with my 'landslide' victory, the next day when a female student in my communications class called me a Nazi, a bit less so.

But the truth was life was good in Erie Hall. It seemed as though I had everything I could possibly desire at Geneseo in the early winter of 1985: academic and athletic success; awesome friends; excellent health; and great happiness. And the icing on the cake for me was that I didn't have to smoke pot, drink alcohol, cheat on an exam, or lose my virginity to have it.

As the Warrens rolled their way out of town, my life seemed charmed (no offense to Billy Idol). The 'Golden Boy' was on a roll, people, and he didn't have the time for – or any interest in – the madness that a haunting might possibly bring with it.

Anyhow, while we were talking, Chris went
through the motions, he went through before —
fumbling with the candy "Hot Tomales" box — he had
been trying to open — when suddenly he stopped,
uttered something and averted his eyes, claiming

"Every great thinker keeps a journal, you know."— Trenton Lee Stewart, *The Mysterious Benedict Society*

12. After Effect

No one is answering!

I can hear movement behind the door that leads into C2D2, but for some reason no one is opening the door! I increase both the rate and the force of my fist pounding.

"Help, I'm in TROUBLE!"

The terror that drives my fear leaves my hands numb to a pain that would normally be coursing through them after I had banged so vehemently on the unmoving door. I don't understand why they won't open the door. Can't they hear my voice? It's me, Chris!

"OPEN THE DOOR!"

Only the Hawaiian-shirt-wearing dog with the sunglasses on the beer poster in the hallway seems willing to notice me in this state, and he is no help. Being forced from my own college dorm room was bad enough – having no safe place to go now seems worse.

"HELP ME, PLEASE! PLEASE!"

I bang some more, and I hear some nervous mumbling behind the door. I watch as the silver door knob moves slightly as though it is being unlocked from the inside. I stop my screaming and try to catch my breath.

As the knob begins to turn, I am hoping that I am actually asleep in my bed, simply trying to work through a vivid and nonsensical nightmare. I will awake safely in the morning with the sun's light trying to peek through the blinds. By the time I walk to the bathroom to shower and brush my teeth, I will have forgotten all but the most trivial aspects of this dark dream. That's what is happening right now, I am sure of it.

My hopeful delusion is short lived, and replaced by a bizarre reality as a very worried looking Ed opens the door to C2D2 and I realize that I am still out in the hallway with the specter of death possibly still hovering in the room behind me.

Ed's eyes halt for a moment, as he takes stock of who is at his door, and then cranes his neck to look behind me for signs of anyone else. I fear that the *thing* will be there, so I do not look back.

The alarm in his voice is sincere when he asks: "Are you all right, what the *blazes* is going on?"

"I need to come in, please. Something *horrible* just happened!"

Ed steps to the side so that I can enter the room, and asks in a concerned tone with both arms raised:

"What, Chris? *What* just happened?"

I look at him. He looks confused and exasperated. It dawns on me at that moment that I can't be exactly sure what had just happened, only what I had done: panicked.

Oh, no. I panicked.

It is common knowledge among those who follow horse racing that when a thoroughbred race horse breaks its stride; the race for them is over. Likewise, a successful athlete must never panic. They needed to trust in their conditioning, in their strategy, and in their ability to problem solve through even the worst situations. Panicking wasn't in my training. Even when the cramp slowed me at Marist College, or when the piper cub hit the turbulence, my mind immediately began to problem solve.

I didn't do that this time … I panicked. Whatever that thing was, my fear of it was greater than my ability to control it. You lose control of your environment, you lose the race. Apparently, I had just lost the race for my own sanity …

This understanding is devastating.

Race horses are often equipped with blinders when they race in order to keep them focused on the task at hand, and to keep distractions from 'spooking' them. Moving forward I would need to find my own set of blinders if I am to retain any sense of sanity.

…

When I was nine years old my uncle Patrick, now aware of my near obsession with Bobby Murcer and baseball, began the practice of giving me his baseball books and magazines after he had finished reading them. My favorite quickly became the 1974 *Complete Handbook of Baseball*. The undersized paperback was loaded with player profiles, picture and statistics. Within a few weeks I had the entire book near memorized. I could now reveal to any friend who might ask (none ever did) that Joe Morgan's baseball glove was dubbed "The pea model", that Dave Duncan looked like Prince Valiant, and that Ron Cey's nickname was 'The Penguin', for the waddle in his walk. I knew that Mike Lum was the only player to have pitch-hit for Hank Aaron, and that Joe Rudi was

Norwegian not Italian as was so often thought and that Yankees' pitchers Fritz Peterson (who had also been a semi-pro hockey player) and Mike Kekich had traded wives.

What I knew most, though, was that Bobby Murcer was an 'established star' and that he 'has hit .331, .292 and .304 over the last three seasons with 80 homers ...

For the next ten years, even up until the haunting, I read the book almost religiously, barely a day passed in which I would not try to improve my knowledge and memory. I accessed the book's National Past Time wisdom so often that I eventually had to preserve its structural integrity by plastering the spine and both covers with thick strips of black electrical tape. Altering it in such a way forever diminished any future resale value, but this meant nothing to me as I would sooner part with one of my testicles. I carefully practiced holding the book in its middle to help preserve the corners.

Corners are important.

The page I gazed at the most featured an action photo of Murcer, the tag line below it read: Bobby Murcer was one of few consistent Yankees in '73 folly.

The Yankees who had been in first place in early July (during the time that I had watched my first game of baseball with my uncle) had faltered badly, finishing below the .500 mark. But that only increased my admiration for Murcer who still managed to hit over .300 despite the duel burden of being the 'next Mickey Mantle' and restoring the Yankees to their dynastic ways. As my favorite player, his quest for success soon became my quest as well.

There was something about the picture. Maye it was the way in which his eyes focused on some unknown future as the ball made its way – somewhere – ahead of him. Or perhaps it was the respect with which he was placing his bat, his trusted ally, on the ground beside him as he ran. No callous bat flips, no pretentious grand standing.

I drew a personal connection to many of my childhood heroes, and when the malicious front office denizen Gabe Paul traded him away to the Giants, I cried, it felt as though I had been traded away with Murcer. Murcer had been the Yankees' Golden Boy.

I understood that.

I also understood the unseen pressures and expectations that went along with it, like the race at Marist College.

Bobby Murcer was one of few consistent Yankees in '73 folly.

Much as a votive candle shrine, a lucky rabbit's foot, a Star of David pendant, or prayer beads and urns of ashes, gazing upon page 168 would become my solace during the haunting. First Paul, then Jeff, then Beth and Judy and others would watch me as I hunched over my desk, or huddled under my bed sheets, for hours, with my most prized possession clutched within my anxious hands.

I have recreated it here in this book in order that you might want to turn to it, just as I did, as you move through the more frightening moments of the haunting.

In early 2015 I was able to purchase the original photograph, editor's markings on the back and all, used in the printing of the 1974 baseball book that became my young adult security blanket.

The book and the image within it would become my personal 'blinder' keeping my eyes focused on pleasant memories of the past (sunny Saturday mornings, playing ball with my friends on hot, cloudless summer afternoons, rows of baseball cards lined across my bedroom floor according to lifetime RBI totals) and away from the dark shadows and misty forms that swirled around me. It would help keep me from breaking my stride, from getting 'spooked'.

...

But I haven't figured that out yet. I'm still trying to catch my breath, and hopefully a degree of sanity as Jeff rushes in behind. I sit myself down on the closest bed. I feel dizzy and nauseated and cold. I glance rapidly about the room. My eyes are drawn to, and then focus upon a black and white image on the wall. It is of a young girl, both of her hands are placed on a static-filled TV screen and the caption reads: "They're here."

The *Poltergeist* advertisement on the wall in C2D2 was likely a coincidence, but had me wondering if the haunting had been inevitable.

I clench my hands together, and I wonder why the poster had never bothered me before. Now I am quite sure that it *should* have bothered me because ... something *was* here!

Jeff leans in towards me and puts a hand on my shoulder. His eyes, which are protected by a pair of wire-rimmed reading glasses, are actively seeking clues, searching for information.

"Chris, look at me," he states with an affect that suggests to me that he has experience with people going through emotional crisis. My eyes meet his and I can tell – in an instant – that the sheer terror in them has struck home with him. He has never seen someone this scared before. A feeling of guilt adds to my shivering terror. I don't want him and Ed to suffer because of me. I should be in my own room, taking care of this myself. But I can't go back there; I am too afraid of whatever that *thing* is in there, and too afraid of what its continued presence might do to my mind. I don't want to be broken. I don't want to panic again.

"Chris, you need to tell me what's wrong."

Jeff's choice to invest in my well-being first, to ask about *me* and not about … *it* … beckons me to take a risk. It is a very dangerous risk. I need to tell the truth. My brain gives the daring order:

"I panicked, Jeff! I can't believe I panicked! It was horrible! The head was tilted! It looked at me, Jeff, right at me! I panicked! I can't believe I panicked! It kept looking at me!"

"I don't understand, Chris. You're not making any sense. *What* looked at you?"

"The ghost, Jeff! The *ghost!*"

"The darker the night, the brighter the stars,
The deeper the grief, the closer is God!"
— Fyodor Dostoyevsky, *Crime and Punishment*

13. A Slow Reveal

My paternal grandfather, Vito Di Cesare Sr., had shared with me the story of when he and the other newly minted army recruits were heading out of the San Francisco Bay; the officers ordered all of them locked inside of their rooms. The newspaper headlines that morning screamed of a recent Japanese attack on a U.S. vessel, and the men in charge wanted to make sure that none of the fresh-faced soldiers had the opportunity to jump ship on their way to the steamy Japanese-held islands of Southeast Asia.

In the movies, whether it is a Western, Science Fiction, or Drama, the hero is typically portrayed as stoic, determined, and brave as he saves the day, rights a wrong, or simply wins the love of another. Therein was the major difference between cinema and reality: inevitability. In a scripted scenario, the hero always triumphs; the tension comes only from overcoming or surmounting ever growing manufactured difficulties as the film progresses.

Reality has no script. Rather, it is a series of connecting possibilities or likelihoods that must be safely navigated and learned from. Some outcomes can even be sketched as they are realized, such as the vertex of an axis of symmetry when plotting a quadratic equation. Most other likelihoods tend to be more elusive.

Revealing to Jeff the source of my panicked fright could have resulted in a wide variety of scenarios; most of them were likely to be negative. Had he looked at me and broken out laughing while questioning my sanity, I have no idea what would have become of me. But just as I had selected the baseball card pack with the Bobby Murcer card in it when I was nine, almost ten full years later, I had the uncanny luck or ability to select Jeff as the person with whom I could safely confide my terrifying experience. Not only was Jeff open to the concept of the paranormal, he actually had a passing interest in it. As a young boy he would watch shows such as *In Search Of* and would, on occasion, take a flashlight out into the dark fields behind his home and shine the light into the sky just to see if anyone ... or anything ... was out there. He had been waiting for an answer ever since.

Zoologist and author Desmond Morris (*The Naked Ape*) wrote that there is a tendency to be attracted to novelty, neophilia (love of the new) that is naturally contrasted with neophobia (fear of the new). With neophobia everything unfamiliar is potentially dangerous. As such it should either be approached with caution, or avoided outright. But, he questioned, if it was avoided then how shall we learn anything about it?

Now, being presented with testimony that an actual ghost might be in the room next door, Jeff felt compelled – perhaps even 'called' – to see this ghost himself. Years later, he would recall the moment vividly. "It wasn't [necessarily] that I believed it, it was that *he* [Chris] believed it."

My terror was so palpable, and so convincing, that Jeff sensed this was indeed a moment that he could not let pass by him.

Nor could he sit idly by as his friend suffered so.

I fed him the facts, through my fear, as best as I could. For some reason I ended up curled in a ball in the corner of the room at the foot of Jeff's bed. It was the same spot that, almost exactly one month later, I would leave wet footprints on after Jeff pulled me – exhausted and bleeding – out of the bathroom.

It was now nearing 10PM, and trying to recall what I had seen was burdensome. Even now, a half hour removed from the event, each time I considered what I had seen, it sent a chill of panic through my exhausted and continually trembling body. I was making 'best guesses' of my initial impression that had left me in a near state of shock. But Jeff found strong testimonial value in the immediacy of the discussion.

A physical description of the ghost was recorded on the second page of Jeff's "C2D1 Journal Notes":

"A 12 or 13 year old, brown-haired boy, with a yellow and blue striped shirt, navy blue sweat pants, who was hunched over, looking at me."

But none of these statements, as they are recorded, may have actually been true. Or all of them may still be. The difficulty in recording impressions is that there is a subjective process of refining and defining as it is done.

Here we are assembling the now infamous 'C2D1 Loft' on September 3rd, 1984. Paul's father is far left; my father sits atop the loft; I am holding the loft at its center; and Paul (who is partially obscured) is sliding the section of plywood that would support my mattress during the haunting forward.

The very act of recalling an event creates a chemical change in the brain that can alter it in some way. This is called memory distortion, it can happen within seconds of an event, and it can reshape your recollection.

This is why photographs and recordings are often so critical not just in terms of the paranormal, but for any memory someone wishes to preserve. And we hold on to those tokens (a vacation or wedding souvenir, an old gum wrapper or empty bottle of perfume) to keep a piece of that moment, or that person, with us.

But even that valuable act of preservation can serve to distort, as it overemphasizes that one particular facet of the event.

Nonetheless, here is what can be stated with certainty some thirty years later: The thing … the apparition … was male.

When I was working through that frightening life changing moment with Jeff in C2D2 (with Ed listening at the edge of his chair just a few feet away) my pronouns were decidedly masculine: 'he' and 'his'. Its brown hair had me searching, after the fact, for which – if any – of my friends from high school or college it most resembled.

At one point, I offered to Jeff as close a physical match as I could make. But apparently the comparison worried me to the point where I asked Jeff to strike it from his notes, which he did. The crossed-out section can still be seen with a comment scribbled next to it that reads: "(removed by request)."

Looking back, if I could change one thing about the choices we made back then, I would not have asked Jeff scratch out that line.

The rest of the description should also be broken down and examined – something that I have held off on doing for almost three decades.

The human eye, much as any receptor, can be used in varying ways with varying results. I learned as a child that if I squinted my eyes that it could increase the contrast of the image I was looking at, blocking out some of the colors and reducing the object to an almost black and white simplicity. Likewise, in a darkened area, the eye lids as well as the pupils will instinctively open wider to allow more light reception. Yet, even a person with 20/20 vision has more difficulty in observing detail on a moving object than they would one at rest.

When an object is in motion, as the apparition's head was, telling details such as wrinkles, freckles, scars, and other potentially defining characteristics are oftentimes 'blurred' away. Take away razor stubble, a developed Adam's apple, or skin creased from aging and you might well perceive an adult to be a child. And let's not forget, we all age and mature at different rates. Even in the flesh, almost all of my own college contemporaries believed I was only twelve or thirteen years old when in fact I was almost twenty years old as well.

In fact, during my own orientation at SUNY Geneseo, the tour guide mistakenly thought that one of my younger sisters was the incoming college student, not me. She even took the time to ask me what grade in high school I was currently in.

I replied "13th grade" and smiled.

Arriving at Erie Hall in September of 1984.

To further complicate matters, the apparition was somewhat transparent, another factor to consider as even more facial characteristics and details would then be obscured.

The description of the clothing also needs to be addressed. I had mentioned to Jeff that night that I had never seen a shirt – or pants – similar to the ones that the ghost had. So what Jeff helped me to do was whittle down the possibilities and select the closest 'contemporary' styles of clothing in order to establish a baseline understanding of the garments. The pants, in particular, looked odd to me. They approximated the dark navy color of blue jeans, but had the visual consistency of old-fashioned wool leggings, thus: sweat pants. The torso was covered by a blue garment, with flashes of yellow, which had buttons running down its front. The 1985 conclusion: some type of Rugby shirt.

Even the observation detailing the apparition bending or leaning forward needs to be considered with care as I had already noted that the head itself had moved forward away from the body. For a living human being this would presuppose that the person is bending forward or leaning over, but then this was *not* a living human being!

This critical review in no way discredits the journal notes in any fashion, as they accurately detail the discussions, observations, and conclusions made at the precise time the events occurred. As such, they are an invaluable, raw, and rare primary source tool that details the day-to-day horror that all of us were exposed to in those dark times. The fact that my name is spelled wrong on the first page of the notes (De Cesare) underscores that while today people tend to 'polish' facts and proofs to make them more 'credible' – and for the chance to appear on television for five minutes – back then we were concerned with one thing: surviving.

Rather, I am attempting to illustrate how the human mind is capable of shaping things, forming things, expressing things in ways that are the most comfortable or reasonable for us. The danger is that, in the final analysis, this might not lead you to an accurate explanation, only an accepted, possibly inaccurate viewpoint.

In the present-day environment where it is not uncommon for a novice researcher or paranormal group to claim that the reflection of a coat rack in a window is the ghost of Abraham Lincoln, or that a speck of floating gray dust in an old building is the spirit of Robert E. Lee, it can be noted that people sometimes see what they want to see, facts and other possibilities aside.

There is a term that I have heard J. Jeff Ungar use: *pareidolia*. This concerns itself with a tendency of the mind. It is the tendency that allows us to so quickly 'see' the shapes of dogs, whales, select body parts, and umbrellas in the clouds ... when none are clearly there. For me it all goes back to what my 9th grade English teacher at Valley Central High School, Mr. Mooney, suggested to the class: Let the facts shape your argument, don't try to shape the facts to it.

He then shared a quote – "All is jaundiced to a yellow eye" – that again underscored the danger of seeing things only the way in which you want to.

Regardless of any potential distinctions between Jeff's 1985 notes on the ghost's appearance, and my contemporary understanding, the fear that the apparition created in me had one undisputable effect: I did *not* want to go back into that room!

"We never stop investigating. We are never satisfied that we know enough to get by. Every question we answer leads on to another question. This has become the greatest survival trick of our (human) species." – Desmond Morris.

14. The Burden of Proof

The Robert Moses State Park on Long Island is one of the premier beach locations in New York State. The beaches are made up of warm, tan-colored sand and vendors selling Italian Ices and soft drinks crisscross in front of and behind the large gatherings of families and friends enjoying a brief weekend respite.

As a youth there were few things that I looked forward to more than a day at the beach with my family. The breeze at the beach was always warm and often accompanied by light granules of sand that landed on your skin. While the water always seemed too cold to actually be comfortable, wading into it was refreshing and I had no aversion to the briny taste of the Atlantic Ocean when a random waved knocked me off my feet only to deposit me on the shore a few seconds later.

Building sand castles was my favorite activity. Much like some Grail Knight at King Arthur's Round Table, I would work my palms and fingers tired and raw, scooping and building and repairing as wave upon wave of marauding water assaulted the castle's walls. Paying no heed to the irrelevant burning of the skin on my back, neck, nose, and shoulders – until my mother forcefully intervened with sun block – I could only rest once the tide had receded.

The ride across the bridge on the Robert Moses Causeway was memorably beautiful. The sunset was creating reds and oranges and pinks and purples on the western horizon and white and gray seagulls were flitting around in the warm salty air searching for sources of food left behind by the crowds of people now returning to the mainland.

My mother's family lived on Long Island. My grandparent's home, the one where my sister first counted to ten, was only a quick fifteen minute drive from the ocean when there was little traffic.

We were bumper-to-bumper now, the tail lights of the car ahead of us casting a soft rose hue across the front windshield of our car in the fading twilight. The radio, tuned to WBLI-FM, emitted the catchy melody of the Hughes Corporation's 'Rock the Boat" *which was enough to keep my sisters and I occupied as our sun-warmed bodies relaxed comfortably in the back seat.*

When our car finally rolled to a halt in front of the house my mother had grown up in, I was happy to see that we would not be alone. My mom was one of six children, and it looked to me that most of them – and their spouse if they had one – were there ready to greet us.

I was born with the gift, the gift of grandparents, and it seemed to me that they were good at making aunts and uncles.

One by one, my mother's siblings greeted us: Uncle Tom, Aunt Diane, and the blond-haired twins Sandy and Susie who were not much older than me.

My Aunt Lynn was the last to make it over because she had been by the kitchen table sharing something. When she saw me, she exclaimed:

"Christopher! I know that out of everyone you will be especially happy to see these!"

She gave me a welcoming kiss and then handed me a stack of photographs to look through.

It was Elvis! Elvis Presley, the King of Rock and Roll!

She had seen him perform at the Nassau Coliseum just days earlier and she knew that I loved big music. I would wake up almost every weekend morning and, before the rest of my family had begun to stir, quietly pop in the Pure Gold *cassette tape and sing along to "Kentucky Rain", "It's Impossible" and "Loving You".*

My aunt then offered, as long as my parents were OK with it, that she would bring me to see him. It was Christmas in July. What could I possibly want more?

I was 'too young', came the response. I might be able to go when I was twelve. So I counted. I counted down the days until 1977. Then I counted again when it was announced that Elvis would be coming back to New York in September. But I didn't get to finish counting.

Photograph of Elvis Presley in concert taken by my Aunt Lynn (Hubley) Natale.

On August 16th, Elvis was found lying face down, on the shag rug in his bathroom. The king was dead.

No need to dwell on things that you can't change; right?

...

Now Jeff wants me to look for a ghost, a ghost who is responsible for the only other interrupted count in my entire life. The first interrupted count, to see Elvis Presley, had a very painful ending ... I worry that this one might be even worse.

He crouches down in the hallway and gazes through the doorway that I had left wide open in my mad dash to his room earlier in the evening.

"I don't see anything out of the ordinary," he whispers, "Do you see anything now?"

I truly have no idea why I am even standing behind him as I nervously wring my hands together in front of me. If I were smart, I would simply retreat back to the safety of his room, and try to forget any of this ever happened.

No need to dwell on things that you can't change; right?

Hearing no reply, he glances back at me, "Do you see anything, Chris?"

"No."

I hadn't actually looked into the room yet, preferring instead the boring comfort brought on by examining the worn hallway floor tiles under my feet. It was Ed, who nodded at me to make the effort, and said: "Why don't you go in real quick to see?"

"OK. I'll go in," I whisper over my fear.

Jeff is pleased by this; his reconnoitering will be greatly aided by an advance forward into what has suddenly become a paranormal 'ground zero'. He lifts his 35mm camera up to his face, turns his head quickly to the side to loosen his neck, and then places the view finder to his eye.

[Flash!]

Elevating himself to his full standing height, Jeff glances up into the loft area once and then turns his gaze back to me.

"Where did you see it?"

I point to the general area between Paul's desk and stereo, but the vagueness does little to help Jeff pinpoint the exact location that he wants. So I step gingerly by him, and (with a careful eye on the closet door) I sit down in my desk chair. I run through the whole encounter, several times, as best as I can. My hope is that I am not speaking too fast to be understood, even though I wasn't sure I was capable of slowing my rate of speech if I were asked to do so.

Jeff jots some words down and turns to Ed, who is standing in the doorway, and announces, "The room isn't cold, and that's a good sign."

Ed nods.

"What does that mean?" I ask.

Jeff explains to me that spirits have been alleged to drain the energy from a location, and that many people who report having an encounter with a spirit claim that the room the ghost is in becomes uncommonly cold.

This certainly matches my experience, if it *was* a ghost that was actually plaguing me. I noticed the room temperature had been icy cold when the closet door had opened; also when I saw the … thing … the wicked thing … appear less than an hour ago, and when I was hiding in the shower stall and Paul came running in out of breath claiming he had heard a disembodied voice. In fairness, though, I had been undressed for two of those instances, which may have played a role in my perception of it being colder than usual.

The possibility that Jeff might be bringing some practical information regarding hauntings served to add an air of both structure and stability to the entire situation. Whether the information was accurate or not, I could not say, but I welcomed the conceptual input. The Greek philosopher Socrates was credited with having shared: "I am the *wisest man* alive, for I know one thing, and that is that I know nothing." So who was I to pass up an experience to learn?

Jeff asks why there are red candies scattered across the floor, which allows me to explain the horrific encounter in even greater detail. I pick up the now empty fire red candy box in order to scoop the candies up off of the bedroom floor. Whether or not I am suffering from a flashback – or the creature has temporarily returned to the room – I see it standing inside the stereo again as I move to collect the candies from the floor. I try to screen my eyes with a hand as I scream: "It's there again! I see it!"

Both Jeff and Ed strain their eyes to see what it is that I am referring to, but nothing is visible to them.

"Chris, I don't see anything," Jeff yells to me.

"What if I'm going crazy? Can we get out of here, Jeff?"

Jeff agrees that exiting the room is the best strategy, perhaps fearing for my mental health. Ed is already halfway to his room, visibly shaking his head in frustration. Jeff and I take one quick glance back at the room.

"Do you see it now?" Jeff asks.

"No. Thank God," is my reply.

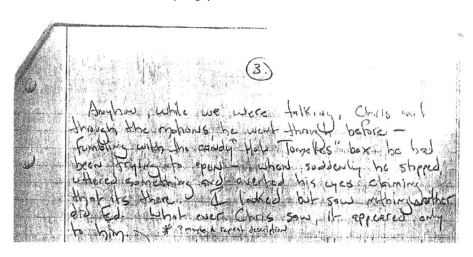

Jeff closes the door behind us and we proceed to his room. Ed is nervously brushing his hair as he looks into a well-placed wall mirror. I sit down at Jeff's desk, not enjoying the image of the girl with her hands on the non-working TV.

"What is that for?" I ask Jeff.

It turns out that it is an advertisement for a movie called *Poltergeist* that was released almost three years earlier. When I ask Jeff why he has it on his wall he replies that he thinks the image is very powerful.

I can't argue that.

Meanwhile, my mind is still churning, looking for any logical explanation for what I have been experiencing. I recollect that I had not seen the ghost, the first time, until I began eating the Hot Tamales, and I saw it again only when I began to pick them up off the floor thirty or forty minutes later. I ask Jeff if he thinks that the candy might be linked to the ghostly appearances. He feels that it is extremely unlikely.

My embarrassment over having asked the question makes me promise myself to screen what I say from now on … *before* I say it.

Adding to the pressure of the situation, it is obvious that Ed wants to turn in for the night, and having a trembling college student – who claims to have just seen a ghost – blabbering in the room is not going to help matters. I ask Jeff to accompany me back to C2D1, which he quickly agrees to do.

As we stand in the hallway, I ask Jeff if he will write down what has been happening, what I've been going through. If nothing else, it will provide a psychiatrist with a blue print to my illness from the moment that I first noticed it manifesting. To my relief, Jeff is more than happy to oblige, stating that recording the events is something he is very interested in doing. He was already hoping that I would give him permission to do so.

The C2D(1) journal is born.

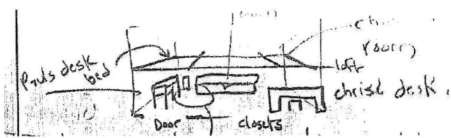

Sketch John Jeff Ungar made in his journal of the C2D1 room layout that night.

I do ask him not to tell Paul about what I am sharing with him, as I don't want to cause him any unnecessary angst; he was clearly already on edge. I am still hopeful that tomorrow morning will bring a much needed clarity to, and space from, events that should not be occurring.

Paul returns shortly after 11PM, looking much more relaxed. Opening the door into the suite, he questions why I am standing outside of our room, by myself, in the hallway. The obvious answer is that some freakishly scary undead creature might still be in there, but my answer to him is that I am simply 'getting some fresh air.'

A look of comical confusion crosses his face, it was good to see someone smile around here for a change, and he asks, "You are getting fresh air ... across from the *bathroom*? O-kaaaaay!"

Fifteen minutes later we are both lying atop the loft on our respective mattresses having brushed our teeth and changed into our sleeping clothes.

My eyes are exhausted. My arms are exhausted. My legs are exhausted.

As I lie in a futile attempt to stay awake, I am debating whether or not to tell Paul about what had transpired after he'd left the room.

Honest people should not keep such secrets from their friends, especially ones that might help them to know. But I am afraid he will think I am crazy. I already know that Ed thinks I am, and for all I know, Jeff might think so as well. Plus, I don't want Paul to leave.

Sleep seems to be a better choice.

"I know God won't give me anything I can't handle. I just wish he didn't trust me so much." – Mother Teresa

15. Haunted

For most of us, there are few things in the world more comforting, more healing, and more welcoming, than a good night's sleep. I lie in my bed with my feet slowly moving back and forth under my recently washed sheets. I am warm. The soft pillow that I have faithfully carried with me from my home gently supports my tired face. I hold the edge of the pillowcase in between my fingers, something my mother tells me I have done since I was an infant. Lying on my right side, intentionally facing Paul in order to make sure that I can see if any harm should befall him, I fall asleep.

Unlike most things in life, where we are aware of the details of what we are doing, it is hard to know – with certainty – the exact moment that we fall asleep. In fact, many people don't even know that they've fallen asleep until an annoying alarm clock or the intruding sunrise wakes them up.

At some point in the night – my distant recollection was that it was around 1AM – my body craves a shift in position. Stretching my arms up over my head, I yawn, take a quick glimpse over at my still roommate, and turn onto my left side, facing the cool blue wall. I move my feet a bit and then doze back off to sleep. Or rather, I try to.

A tiny thought, a recollection, perhaps about the size of a grain of sand, is bouncing around my brain. It is knocking into synapses trying to get the neurons moving, it is shouting: *Do not go to sleep!* But I am bordering on exhaustion, and just too comfortable to remove myself from an opportunity for some healing slumber. I do allow myself, however, the chance to run through my last few actions to see if there was any credible cause for this microscopic-sized primal alarm.

It should be a quick and simple drill. While still in my closed-eyed half-sleep, I reflect back on the last few things that I had seen: Paul sleeping; the off-white colored, roughly textured ceiling; the light blue wall ... and the ghost's face.

Something seems wrong. As I am still not fully awake, I decide to run through the sequence a second time: Paul sleeping; the off-white colored, roughly textured ceiling; the light blue wall ... and the ghost's face.

Got it!

It was obviously the ghost's face that shouldn't be there. Having solved the cause of my angst, it would be back to sleep for me.

...

Wait.

...

The ghost's face?

...

I open my eyes, and there ... *right* there ... mere inches from my own face ...

"Paul! Turn on the light! Turn on the light!"

I am already out of my bed and sitting on the blue carpeted middle (or shared) area of the loft when he flicks on the light by his head.

"What's the matter?" Paul asks as his eyes strain to adjust to the room's sudden change in illumination, "Why are you yelling?"

"I saw something by the wall!"

He scratches the back of his head; his hair is tousled from sleep. "What are you *talking* about?"

Looking over at the empty space by the wall, I have to wonder myself. Now that the room was well-lit, there was clearly nothing visible by the wall near my bed. I *had* been half asleep ... still.

"Can you keep the light on for a while, Paul?"

"Dude, it's right in my face. I won't be able to sleep. Why don't you turn on your desk lamp under the loft? Maybe that will help."

It is a good idea. Technically I could reach down under the loft by my ladder and turn the light on near my desk. I wouldn't even have to leave the comfort and/or safety of the loft. As I crawl over to the edge of the loft, gazing down into the large open space below, Paul switches off the light.

Complete darkness. Paul laughs. I scream.

The mad dash back to the shelter of my bed covers and mattress is made without delay. Paul has no clue as to what might be in this room right now, and I still don't know how to tell him, but I am mad that he is making me take unnecessary risks.

"Why did you do that? It's not funny!"

"Go to sleep."

I point a finger, which he cannot see in the returned darkness, towards him and warn that if 'something bad happens' I will be blaming him! He lobs a sarcastic comment back at me, something to the effect of me 'having no balls', and then I hear the deep breaths of sleep once again emanate from his side of the loft.

Wonderful.

Pulling the tan comforter up over my head, I curl up into a fetal position; I leave only a barely visible 'air hole' from which to breathe in fresh air. I am petrified. My heart is beating hard enough for me to hear it in my ears and to feel its pulse in my neck. The irony of a successful athlete, and 19-year-old college student, hiding under his covers is not lost on me. Sadly, I have no better idea. If I needed to 'wait out the night' in this fashion, then so be it.

The soft sounds of the song "Glamorous Life" (by Sheila E.) make their way through the closed windows of a car that is slowly passing the dorm. I wonder if it is the quiet girl who lives across the walkway that is in that car; I know it is her favorite song, and I push my head out of the bed coverings to look through the blinds. The street light is reflecting off of the slightly fogged windows, leaving me at a complete loss as to whether or not it is her in the car. I worry about her as she seems to be unusually quiet, as though she's still coping with some type of trauma that had defined her early years.

Pulling my fingers back from the blinds I notice a marked chill in the air. It is time to see if Jeff's theory about the change in temperature is correct. I direct my gaze over to the wall beside my bed, fully determined to see nothing out of the ordinary.

It is smiling.

...

"Chrisss."

...

"Chris, wake up."

...

"Chris!"

...

Waking with a startle, my mouth which apparently has been open while I was sleeping, is almost totally dry. I moisten it with my tongue as I look over to see Paul's barely visible silhouette sitting up on his mattress. My eyes do not want to stay open.

"Whaaat?" I ask with a slight rasp to my voice.

Paul is sitting perfectly, and unusually, still. I recognized this reaction. It is the reaction I had when I first saw the … thing. This can't be good.

"There is someone 'downstairs'," he says, referring to the area under the loft. There is no hint of emotion in his voice. He is doing a 'survival shuffle' with his emotions. I have been there.

"How do you know?" I whisper back.

"I heard someone moving my desk chair across the floor. I'm serious."

Gone now is the Paul who so cavalierly turned off his light leaving me in darkness. Gone now is the Paul who questioned my courage. I missed the old Paul.

Listening carefully, I too hear an unusual sound … a 'hissing' sound. Promising myself I will not look behind me at the wall again, I try to compose myself.

"Do you hear that, too?" Paul asks.

Even though he probably can't see me, I nod my head in affirmation. There remains a (very slight) chance that one of us forgot to lock the door prior to going to sleep. The source of the noise could be anything from a drunken student who has mistakenly passed out in the wrong room to a person trying to steal from us. Or … I don't want to consider the 'or'.

"Go check it out," Paul timidly commands.

When I shoot him an angry glance, one that he can probably feel through the darkness, he explains that the sounds are currently coming from my 'side' of the room. I do not argue with him. It was no worse of an excuse than I had given to Luke about not going to the toga party back in January, and was being made under a much more stressful circumstance.

As I begin to back down the loft's ladder, I have the horrific thought that whoever … or *what*ever is down below is going to grab me by my feet and pull me down to the ground. I am immediately angry at myself for even thinking it. If all of this was some type of 'mental creation' I did not want to add any fuel to the fire.

The 'hissing' sound was much louder below the loft, and Paul's nervous assertion that it was originating from my side of the room is actually correct: it is my tape recorder. A power surge must have turned it on. This problem is easy enough to solve, and I press down on the 'stop' button with my right index finger. A warm silence quickly engulfs the room. Walking over to the room's only door, I give a quick tug on the door handle. It is locked. I wonder if maybe Paul has been sleepwalking because it is evident that no one has entered the room.

"Leaving the Caves of Plato, State IV" by J Jeff Ungar, 1985

Confirming that Paul's chair is indeed pulled out from his desk is disconcerting. That feeling is amplified when I notice, after I had pushed the chair back to its customary location, that the door to my closet is open … just a bit. Open just enough for someone to be watching.

Bleh.

I climb back up the ladder with an air of accomplishment, but it is short lived. At the precise moment I place my head back down onto my pillow, the hissing sound returns. Paul hears it, too. But he refuses his turn to go down and address the situation.

"You need to go back down," he says, "you didn't fix it right last time."

I want to punch him. I even threaten to, but ever since my conversation with … I purposely don't 'think' her name …

"You should have said 'yes'."

I have a hard time saying 'no'.

Again, my tape recorder is powered 'on' and the tape inside it is spinning slowly around emitting the hissing noise. This time I will allow for no more occurrences: I unplug the device from the wall outlet, wrap the chord around its sturdy rectangular body, and then shove it into the bottom drawer of my desk.

I call up to Paul through the support beams of the loft that I had taken care of the noise and that I wanted to kick his butt for making me go downstairs twice. It wasn't fair and he knew it.

Trying to ignore the fact that my closet door is still open (I decide that I will close it in the morning) I turn to make yet another ascent up the thin wooden-rung steps that by now had the insteps of my feet aching.

My concentration, as I prepare to climb the ladder again, is broken by the hint of movement in front of me. Gazing through the ladder steps, I see a figure in silhouette standing in front of the window. Its head, which is extended part way up into the loft, is tilted to the side, resting on a neck that looks either damaged or snapped.

It is staring at me.

"Oh my god, Paul," I scream, "I was just standing where it was!"

As I begin my mad scramble up the ladder, the thought careening around in my head is once again the fear that the … thing … will grab me by my bare feet, its ice cold nails sinking into my warm flesh, pulling me down to the ground, helpless. I don't have time to be angry at myself for thinking this again; I am more focused on the fact that … the thing … the *wicked* thing … is standing exactly where I was when I had spoken to Paul up through the loft. How long has it been there? Was it standing beside me at that moment, with its mouth and eyes and face mere inches from mine? I want to hide like a child; I need to find a safer place.

Wait.

Stop.

I am not a child, I am an adult.

Steeling myself as best I can, I nervously step back down to the floor. There is a slight tremble in my legs. The thing is still there. I am not sure if I am happy – or even more afraid – by the fact that it is barely moving. Only its head has moved, slightly, perhaps to better follow me when I move towards the stairs. A portion of my brain is still not sure that I am actually seeing this; maybe it is some type of trick of light, a reflection being cast – somehow – across the room.

I am taking no chances.

The only semblance of a weapon I can locate is my hard plastic hair brush; and after snatching it off of the side of my desk, I throw it – just as I would a baseball – at the foul intruder.

For a split second I am encouraged by the brush's trajectory: the solar plexus. Sadly, my joy is short-lived as it passes *through* the … thing … and then caroms in billiard ball fashion off of the back wall, the side of my dresser, and then finally hits the metal base of my standing lamp with a loud 'clank'!

Then there is silence. Until I yell: "Shit!"

My muscles strain, harder than they have ever in any race in my life, to get me safely back into the loft. I am already halfway under my protective bed covers by the time Paul has the chance to ask me what is happening.

"Don't talk to me!" I yell from under my covers. The fact that he has steadfastly refused to go down, and I had to, is not making me any happier right now.

As my mind tries to wrestle with the utter insanity that is swirling all around us, Paul cries out:

"Someone is looking at me!"

I say nothing. I do nothing. I hide in the darkness like a child who knows that the person who molests them at night has just entered the room.

"I can see someone at the foot of the loft!"

Suddenly, I recognize this as a critically important moment.

This is my chance to corroborate, or refute, the similarity of our shared experience: to see if I am going mad, or if the world around me is.

I ask Paul from my self-imposed prison what the person looks like. I am very careful not to use any gender-specific pronouns or detailed characteristics. I decide to use the term 'they'.

"What do *they* look like?"

Up to this point I have not shared with Paul what I have been seeing. He has no knowledge of my earlier encounters other than me repeating that I was seeing *something*.

I wait for his response.

Opening up the breathing hole in my comforter, I can make out Paul's form, as he leans slowly forward. Both of his arms are behind him, elbows locked, palms flat on the mattress.

I watch as his mouth opens in horror, and he yells:

"It looks like his neck is broken!"

I consider: His. Neck. Broken.

I am very frightened. Paul looks at me, and I can see a white mist swirling around him.

He asks me: "Oh my God! Are we going to *die?*"

I am guessing the answer is 'yes.'

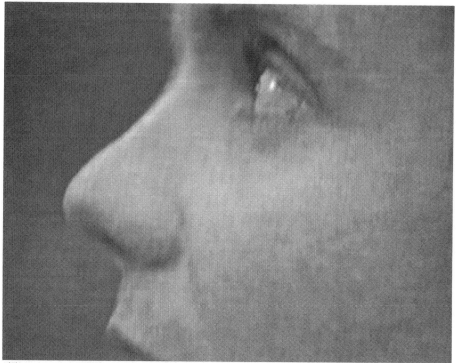

"The hardest thing to explain is the glaringly evident which everybody had decided not to see." – Ayn Rand, *The Fountainhead*

16. Where Angels Fear To Tread

The thin layer of frost on the ground is making the sunlit morning seem brighter than usual. I rub my eyes with the back of my two closed hands, removing any particulates that might have formed in them overnight. Not that there was much of a chance for that to happen. It is 9:16. Paul has just made his way to the bathroom to splash some water on his face. My alarm, which was set for 8:10, did not go off – so we will be missing our morning classes.

I wish that I was someone else, somewhere else, and anywhere else. I stare at the sundrenched blue pillow on my mattress, the one with the image of Jesus on it. I wonder where God is right now. Is He in some great cathedral in Rome? Is He in the eyes of a young couple falling in love? Perhaps He is in the heart of a new born child breathing her first breath? He certainly wasn't in our dorm room last night.

Something was.

I run both hands through my tousled head of hair and then try to lightly massage the tenseness out of my young neck. Closing my eyes, I recall the horror that plagued us once darkness fell:

"Oh my God, are we going to die?" Paul had asked. I didn't answer him as I was still trying to understand the significance of Paul seeing the same form I had, independently. This was no case of mass hysteria, nor was it some grotesque version of suggestion. An external factor was creating this fear, this terror, and this dread.

Moments later, Paul had yelled out, "It's gone! I don't see it anymore!" I did. The wispy, human-shaped black shadow – with the tilted head – had found its way over to the area of my closet. In the darkness of night, it was still a shadow. I moved my hands back and forth in the air in front of me. The slivers of light cast from the moon were sliding through the cracks in the blinds, and I was able to create shadows of my own. But the shadows that I made slanted to the left as the moon was in the eastern sky. The human shadow had no 'slant', nor was it of the same uniformity.

There was a dead thing in the room.

Nervously, and perhaps at great risk to myself, I had reached my right arm down into the dark, narrow space between the edge of the loft and the wall in order to pull my blue 'Jesus pillow' up off the couch below. That task safely completed, I pulled my Bible closer to me.

Paul and I then sat still in our beds for a period of roughly thirty minutes, neither of us able to decide what to do, as we tracked the swirling mist that floated throughout the room. All the while, we would catch intermittent glimpses of the dark shape that could be seen swaying slowly and in different sections of the room. I was too emotionally distraught and physically drained to contemplate what was happening. Having the comfort of both my Bible and pillow near me, I was going to try to get some sleep.

Paul nodded and indicated that he would try the same. It was nearing four o'clock in the morning.

The force that tore the pillows out from under my head seemed both impossibly strong and ... impossible. My head flopped down to the mattress top and the pillows were drawn away from me towards the wall. The abrupt motion sent a quick flash of pain through my neck muscles. I gave a preliminary pull on the pillows only to discover that they were suspended approximately a foot in the frigid air, unmoved by my attempt.

Those were my *pillows. I wanted them back!*

It wasn't difficult to grasp them – tightly – both fists clenched onto them. Nor was it too much of an effort to wrap my feet around the base of the mattress. Pulling my body together (which was much like executing a 'military crunch') in order to take back my pillows turned out to be more difficult. I had strained and strained, gritting my teeth as the force being exerted by whatever that wicked thing was, bent the bottom of my mattress up. My feet were slipping. I needed help.

"Paul, I need your help! You need to see this!"

His reply, from behind his bedding was a simple: "No."

But it couldn't end that way, I wouldn't let it. He had to know, everyone *had to know the extent of the physical manifestations. I knew that it would take more than just the word of one lone student.*

"Paul! If you value our friendship at all, you will look right now!"

Turning my head for a moment, I see the look on Paul's face. It is a look that says: 'No one should ever have to see this.' His eyes are opened wide, and I fear for his sanity, as I do my own.

"Let go of my pillows, damn it! They're mine! In the name of Jesus Christ I command you to go back where you came from!"

I used the phraseology that the Warrens had recommended.

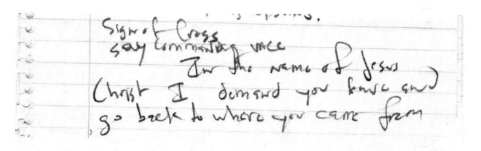

The sound of Paul sliding open the bathroom door pulls me from my uneasy reflection. I stretch out my legs and hop down the ladder rungs.

"Are you all right?" I ask.

He doesn't respond at first, then points and says, "Look. My chair was pulled out again."

There is no doubt in my mind that I pushed his chair back to his desk the night prior, although I fail to understand any meaning or purpose behind such a seemingly arbitrary action having happened a second time.

"There was a gold orb floating over your head last night while you were sleeping," Paul adds with the nonchalance one might use while indicating that the morning's toast was ready.

"Oh, really? That's ... uh ... pretty *strange*. Why didn't you wake me?"

"You had just fallen asleep."

My thoughts drift back to a discussion I recently had with a student named Dean who was in one of my communications classes. After I had given a required oral presentation that had gone very well, he jogged up to me and told me that the reason I was such a great speaker was that I apparently had a "golden yellow aura."

Right. Sure. That must be it. It couldn't have been all my hard work and preparation.

Therein lay one of the core challenges on the events that washed violently around us. Where is the leverage, the balance, the delineation between objectivity and subjectivity? How far would I need to search in order to know if my interpretations of the events were accurate? Was it feasibly possible that I had some type of gold 'aura'? Sure. Was I able to prove it existed? No. So then, was I to put stock in Dean's analysis when it was so easy to dismiss? To my thinking, the chance that the color of my supposed 'aura' had any impact on the effectiveness of my speech was slim.

But, what if I could prove that auras existed, and that their color (or shape or size) somehow did impact the effectiveness of our abilities? As phenomenal a discovery as that might be, it might imply that we had far less control over our successes, our choices and our lives than we knew. Moreover, it begged the question as to whether or not auras – if they existed – were borne of genetics, environmental causes or some divine order.

Jeff, Beth, Craig, me and a few others had, in fact, experimented with auras the night after I had shared with them what Dean had suggested. We faithfully followed the directions read from a book on parapsychology that Jeff had obtained from Milne Library, and took turns reading our auras. The method called for gazing through a clear bottle with colorless liquid (we soaked the label off of a large bottle of white wine) at a person who was lit from above, and had a black or dark background (three sheets of back oak tag paper taped together) behind them to create a strong contrast.

Several people claimed that they saw my aura, and noted that it was the most gold and largest of those that they could see.

I myself, felt pretty confident that I could see energy patterns around their heads too. But was that what we were really seeing? Objectively, I had the blondest and fullest head of hair of those present, and it seemed just as likely that they were seeing some aspect echoed from that.

Or, maybe we were seeing auras.

The continual onslaught of questions that puzzled my brain was exhausting, since the specter of death had arrived, and they typically created even more questions when I took the time to consider them.

Just a week earlier, I had read the *TIME* magazine article, 'Discord in the Church', which examined the tenuous balance between Pope John

Paul II's conservative ideology, and those Catholics who were pushing for reform in such areas as birth control, the role of women in the church and abortion.

The pope, much like Reagan, had also achieved mythic status in the eyes of many, as he too survived an assassination attempt, going so far as to meet face-to-face with the shooter and forgiving him. To my thinking, it was through the sheer power of his earned popularity that these rifts in the Catholic Church did not fester more than they already were. But what was he to do? He was charged with leading the millions of faithful people who turned to him for spiritual guidance. It must be humbling. It must also be terrifying.

I reasoned that the pope likely had a strong belief in the presence of a God, and that he believed in the value of the words written in the *Bible*, which I too considered to be the greatest piece of literature we had. There was no concern there. But what of the millions who hung on his every Latin phrase, who waited for hours on foot to wave at this striking figure clad in bright white, who was said to be a conduit to the will of the heavens? They were fair questions, and I had only recently concluded that it was a construct, although potentially flawed, built on the premise of hope, love and salvation. As an athlete I knew that effective teamwork was the essential component of victory and that individual sacrifice was necessary in order to achieve it. To see these people of all races, genders and ages push together towards a bright light, a noble concept; perhaps God was inspiring us through him.

Yet, the ghost had shaken me awake. It had made me angrily, and against my will, accept that life might not be quite so simple or quite as easy as I had wanted it to be. I didn't enjoy what I now had to consider: Can we really ever prove that we are 'right' about anything? Should we force ourselves to try?

Should I accept Dean's unprovable explanation and consider the implications behind it, or would it be better to simply discard it, and hide safely and comfortably behind what I thought I could prove?

Turning away from my thoughts, I glance over at my desk … oh no. Oh no.

My eyes begin to well with tears.

"What's the matter?" Paul asks with an unmasked sincerity.

The picture frame on my desk – the one with the photo of my young Godchild Kara in it – has been pulled apart. Pieces of it, and what it had held, are scattered across my desk top.

"The damned thing is taking my stuff apart!"

"At least you got your pillows back," Paul offers; and he is right.

But I now have a more frightening problem to deal with: the ghost found what I had hidden inside the frame ... the picture of Paula, who was killed hitchhiking home.

It knows. It *knows*.

"You should have said 'yes'."

"It is better, I think, to grab at the stars than to sit flustered because you know you cannot reach them." – R.A. Salvatore, *Sojourn*

17. Reaching Out

February 14th, 1985 - Valentine's Day: All throughout the campus balloons, decorative hearts, and curled paper streamers of deep red adorn the walls, doorways, windows, and tables. The song, "I Want to Know What Love Is" from Foreigner – appropriately – is echoing out of the many dorm rooms as the girls fret over their makeup, and the guys search in vain for a pair of nice shoes to wear to a dance.

One rare exception is room C2D1.

The day prior, three of the ladies from the B-Building (Beth Kinsman, Linda F., and Judy Y.) had generously offered their assistance and helped us decorate the room in style. The main feature was the dozen balloons of red and white. Less than two hours after the girls had left, however, all of the balloons, every single one, popped. One at a time they popped, almost as though an unseen person was moving from balloon to balloon, pausing just long enough to gauge our reactions. Paul had yelled, "Stop it!" to whatever it was and then turned to me and shouted: "Something is breaking the balloons!"

He didn't have to tell me. I was watching, fascinated, by the occurrence. This wasn't happening in the darkness, this didn't involve barely discernible shadows or half-asleep impressions. This was empirical ... provable. Balloons could be weighed and measured, their remnants examined and discussed.

I looked over at Paul, who was sitting at his desk as I was at mine, and wondered aloud, "Why do you think this is happening?"

He leaped from his chair and ran down the hall, returning a few moments later with Brian from C2D3. Paul pointed out all of the now burst balloon fragments. Some were lying flat on the floor and some were hanging from pieces of tape or string. I could see that Brian was weighing whether or not Paul – with my help – was trying to get some type of gag over on him, playing him like a fool, or if we were actually serious.

Brian rubbed the back of his head and asked, "Do you know what's really scary?"

"What?" Paul and I asked simultaneously, wondering if perhaps the dread phenomenon was spreading.

"This!"

Brian dropped his pants.

Paul quickly punched him in the arm and then chased him out of the room, angrily cursing at him as they both ran down the hallway.

I stood up, closed the door, and picked up a deflated rubber balloon fragment. There was nothing unusual about it, with the exception of it being ice cold. 'Too cold' for having been in a room that was at a comfortable temperature, I considered.

Jeff had placed some light pressure on me earlier in the day to provide him with a name for the 'thing'. He preferred not to have to continuously use words like 'ghost' or 'apparition' in public ... or in his journal. He was hoping for something more precise ... more personally descriptive.

Holding a portion of the balloon in my hand, a name had found itself into my thoughts: 'Tommy.'

A slight smirk had crossed my slender face; that was the name of the blue-feathered parakeet my family had when I was young. Whatever, it seemed a safe enough name to use in public, one that wouldn't draw unwanted attention if it was used at a dining hall table or inside a classroom. After I had placed the balloon piece on my desktop, I approached the closet. It was just a closet, I reasoned.

Besides, I had run longer and faster – and through more pain – than most people could even contemplate. I was made of hardier stuff than most.

I decided to walk over and stand directly in front of the closet. The door was still opened a few inches, as I had not gone near it after I saw the shadow there the night before last.

Doing a tough guy impression, I called aloud: "Tommy, come out and play."

A low-pitched gurgling sound projected itself outward from the dark interior of the closet. My jaw dropped. For a moment I stood frozen in place as the door moved gently back and forth. My stomach wanted to vomit. I sprinted into room C2D2 to nervously share my questionable actions with Jeff, who shook his head in a rather concerned manner.

Now, at approximately 7:00PM on Valentine's Day (1985), Jeff enters my room. Paul has accompanied some friends uptown for a few hours, and – as Jeff will be leaving the following morning for a week-long family trip to Florida – he feels that this might be the ideal moment to try and collect some concrete evidence of the ghost's existence.

I have no objections. I haven't had a meaningful Valentine's Day since the 4th grade when Wendy Morin gave me a yellow candy heart with pink lettering that read: "Be mine."

I cast aside the most recent edition of the college newspaper that features John Cafferty and the Beaver Brown Band on its cover. I had been reading an unnerving article about a 19-year-old college student named Mary Hendler who was struck by a vehicle driven by 55-year-old Ed Engelbert of Retsof who was charged with failure to yield right of way to a pedestrian in a crosswalk. Hendler had been rushed to Warsaw Hospital with a broken arm and lacerations to her head.

What a mad world.

It occurred to me at that moment that the balance between life and death was a thing so frail that the most trivial mistake could cast the dice. It demanded a constant vigil. Otherwise, if one were taken from this physical life without warning or expectation, one might end up similar to the being haunting my room.

Having given some thought to my recent actions, Jeff's plan is for me to 'lure' the ghost out into the center of the room. He will then try to capture a photographic image of it … proof that it is real. While preparing his camera and jotting down some quick temperature readings, Jeff asks me if I have been able to determine some type of name for the ghost yet. I tell him: "Tommy."

He immediately stops what he is doing, casts me an examining glance, and asks me if Paul told me to say that. I shrug my shoulders.

"No. Why?"

"I just spoke with Paul a few hours ago, and when I asked him what he would call the ghost if he were to give it a name, he said: 'Tommy.'"

"Tommy is a common name," I tell Jeff as I try not to consider the true implications of what this might mean "I have an uncle that everyone calls 'Tommy'."

Jeff considers my statement, says nothing in reaction to it, and then carefully instructs me to push my arms out in front of my body. Apparently I am doing it 'wrong', and he physically adjusts: the height of my arms, the distance of my hands from my body, and the angle at which my hands are held.

I ask him how he knows to do this, unable to hide a slight smile of amusement.

"I saw it on a television show," he responds matter-of-factly.

As I prepare my attempt at 'calling a ghost', Ed sticks his head into the room, looking more than a bit perplexed by what he sees. To my continued dismay, Jeff asks Ed if he will take a few pictures to capture 'the moment'. It is obvious by the manner in which he reacts that Ed remains confused as to what exactly is going on, perhaps even *why* anything is going on, but he politely agrees to do so.

I attempt to stand totally motionless as Ed takes a few snapshots, all the while unable to rid myself of the notion that anyone who sees these images will think of me as a complete fool. It is not lost on me how I am now applying the very same 'pack mentality' that had bothered me so much at the baseball stadium almost a decade earlier: Society expects me to mock this endeavor. Even though I understand that this might be a valuable, potentially ground-breaking, even *life-saving*, course of action, I allow myself to mock it – through a slight smile – in order to not be judged too harshly by unseen people that I will never know.

The insincerity of my expression in this photograph 'haunted' me from the moment it was shot. I would pray for the opportunity to redeem myself.

In the picture I am a coward. As Ed departs the room, I silently counsel myself, hoping that someday I will be given a chance for redemption.

C2D1 is once more secured, and without the perceived threat of societal judgment, I rededicate myself to the task at hand. Jeff instructs me to "call" the ghost.

"Jeff, how do I do that?"

He offers that, while my arms remain outstretched, I should use the ghost's name this time – in a friendly tone – and formally invite him into the room.

Yes, this is actually *happening* – a part of my brain mocks the moment. *Welcome to yet* another *in a brutal series of dreadfully poor choices.*

I take one last glance around my room, trying to note every object and detail, wondering if this is when people, looking back, will say that I had lost my mind.

I begin.

"Hello, Tommy. It's me, Chris ... My friend wants to see you, and so he has asked me to invite you here."

Jeff is looking around in a fashion that suggests he is worried that he might miss the 'magic' moment. His fingers are poised, set exactly as they need to be, in order to take a photograph with as little movement, or time, expended as possible. He looks how I imagine a *National Geographic* photographer might look. Of course, I am the one standing on the savannah, calling the lion out of its den!

I can discern a grayish mist inside the darkened closet, and my exposed skin is now very aware of the precipitous temperature drop. Jeff is, too.

"If the thermometer is accurate, the room temperature has dropped from 66°F to 61°F in less than eight minutes. That shouldn't be possible in a closed room."

Focusing my sight into the closet, I watch as the mist seems to be shifting and growing in what appears to be a vertical fashion. It is happening. The ... *thing* ... is listening ... is understanding ... is complying. I wonder if, in Mary Shelley's mind, Dr. Frankenstein felt the way I do right now, when his monster's heart beat its first beat: dizzied excitement mixed with deep-seated fear.

The face is now visible: the pale unblinking eyes, the hint of what should be a nose, the misshapen mouth that is once again beginning to open.

Make it stop! Make it stop!

My throat tightens and my muscles constrict. I try to tell Jeff that the ghost is here, but I cannot utter as much as a single sound. The horror is overwhelming. *I've made a terrible mistake.*

I try a second time to speak. Nothing.

I need to problem solve. I recall a particular technique that some runners use to reduce air trapped near the rib cage in order to reduce cramping. The technique involves slightly compressing the solar plexus. Using my back and stomach muscles, I am able to slightly reduce the length of my spine. This in turn puts added pressure on my lungs.

The third time is a charm, and I am able to emit a slight, raspy, soft breath: "Hhhhhhhhhh ... "

Out of the corner of my eye, I can see Jeff scrambling in front of me and to the right. His back is now to the door. I am frozen with fear, my navy sweatshirt being blown back at its sleeves and into my torso ... a truly tangible indication of the spirit's presence.

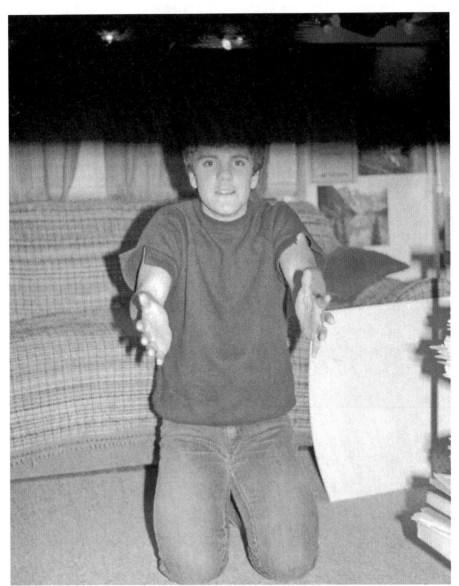

The image taken by John Jeff Ungar on Valentine's Day, 1985, that may forever be associated with identifying me as the 'The Ghost Boy of Geneseo'.

[Flash!]

"Got it," Jeff announces.

This time my faint smile is different: it is a cautious triumph. I know that Jeff might have just captured what my own testimony would have difficulty proving ... there will now be 1,000 objective 'words' in the image.

I do not know it at the time, but this photograph will someday grace the cover of a book; it will become the 8x10 picture that I will sign for fans at conventions; it will be how the paranormal field will likely remember me ... as 'The Ghost Boy of Geneseo'.

My celebratory mood is short lived. The flash or perhaps it is Jeff's quick movement across the room just prior to it, sets the wicked thing into motion and it is coming straight towards me!

...

It is my first ever baseball game and I am too afraid to bat. My father, who is the Colden Park Little League coach, asks me what is making me afraid.

"The ball is going to hit me in the head," I tell him, nervously squeezing my seven-year-old hands together until they are sweating.

Putting his hands on my two shoulders, and looking me directly in the eyes, he says in a reassuring tone: "The ball is not going to hit you in the head, Chris. I've coached baseball many times, and I've never seen anybody get hit in the head. You're making yourself scared. You just need to relax."

He crouches down next to me as we watch the batter in front of me approach the plate. His name is Mike; he is two years older than me and is the team's top hitter. The third pitch is across the plate, and he lashes out with his bat and connects with it. The ball lifts into the air and Mike bolts out of the batter's box towards first. The left fielder and centerfielder converge to where the ball is headed, but neither one can make it to the spot in time. The ball falls in for a double.

"All right, Chris, pick a bat and give it a try."

There are several bats to choose from, so I lift each one to see which best fits my hands. The one with the royal blue stripe seems the best. The number '27' is on its end. I give it a few uneven swings and cautiously walk into the batter's box.

"Remember, only swing at the good ones," my dad counsels.

"C'mon, Chris" Mike yells with a look of encouragement on his face.

The pitcher goes into his windup, and releases the ball.

CRACK!

The ball hits me in the head.

...

There was nothing I could do back then, and there is nothing that I can do right now.

As the creature approaches me, its physical details mercifully begin to blur into a whitish-gray energy – sparing me seeing its eyes, mouth, and teeth as they approach my face. As the thing passes through me, an uncanny awareness comes over me, and it feels to me as though I can sense every single cell in my body freezing, like ice, and then unfreezing just as rapidly. This forced encounter leaves me angry, afraid, and drained. I immediately fall forward onto the floor of C2D1. I want out.

Jeff is yelling to me: "Chris, where is it? I can't see where it went!"

He is darting back and forth around the room, his camera at the ready. I use the side of Paul's dresser to help pull myself off the carpet. It feels as though someone has just punched me in the chest.

"I don't care where it is," I complain, "I'm getting out of here!"

"Chris!"

Jeff has not given up on his mission, "I don't see it! If you see it, tell me where it is!"

I collect myself and begin to scrutinize the room. I look for any mists, shadows, or odd distortions of shape. There is nothing by the closet door, or Paul's stereo. It is not crouching by my desk or near the window. As I open my mouth to share the disappointing news with Jeff, I see *him*, suspended near the ceiling above my bed. Tommy, with his dead-looking eyes, is looking right at me!

"Jeff, over there" I scream, pointing with outstretched arm to the area above my pillows. I really hate that he is by my pillows.

Holding his camera in front of him, Jeff runs over to me to better line up the shot, but he apparently sees nothing. I am confused as I can see the ghost as plainly as the poster on the wall near him.

Jeff seems frustrated, "Where, Chris? I don't see anything!"

My mind is boggled as I can discern 'Tommy' as clearly as if he were a living person.

"Right *there*, Jeff – the thing staring at you: *that's* the ghost!"

I continue to point at it in order to direct Jeff's line of sight, but in spite of his honest efforts, he simply cannot see the ghost.

Then an idea strikes him and he says: "Chris, take my camera. If you can see him, then you take the picture!"

I am hesitant as I have only used a 35mm camera once before (at the toga party) and I don't want to be the one blamed for letting 'the big one get away' if I screw this up.

With an encouraging nod from Jeff, I place the view finder to my eye, line up the ghost in its center, and press the button.

[Flash!]

I hand Jeff his camera and run out of the room.

"Reality is that which, when you stop believing in it, doesn't go away." – Philip K. Dick, *I Hope I Shall Arrive Soon*

18. The Evidence, Please

By the time Jeff had returned from his Florida trip in late February, my friendship with Paul was beginning to fray. Tommy's daily activity had taken a toll on both of us, and Paul – who still desired to keep the haunting a private matter – became upset with me when he found out that I had spoken of it to some of the girls in the B-Building. In the absence of Jeff as my confidant, and considering Paul's reticence to discuss matters, I turned to my lady friends.

Everyone copes with crisis differently, and Paul and I were certainly in the midst of a crisis of epic proportion!

On the night of February 16th, we were again terrorized. I had fallen asleep relatively early that night, but was plagued by a frightening dream that involved being trapped by a spike that pierced my right foot as I attempted to escape from an enormous glowing sphere that resembled a ball of twine. I awoke with a terrible 'Charley horse' (an intense muscle spasm) in my right calf that had caused my entire foot to stretch and then cramp. The pain was extreme.

My moans of discomfort woke up Paul, who was very relieved to discover that it wasn't another Tommy episode. I laughed aloud –

almost uncontrollably – when it had dawned on me that things had gotten so bad that one of us being in immobilizing physical pain was now considered a 'positive' situation. Laughter tends to be contagious, and soon Paul was chuckling as well.

The laughter slowly subsided, and I turned onto my left side.

Tommy's ghostly face, which was now just inches from my own – and with an impossibly broad smile torn across it – greeted me. The sight was so frightening that, had I not taken care of matters just prior, I would surely have defecated in the loft. I screamed, and blindly leaped from the five foot loft; too much adrenalin was flowing through my body to feel the pain of smashing my knees, shoulders, and elbows on the floor.

I found a quiet spot in a nearby lounge and sat myself on a well-cushioned chair, pulling my legs up to my torso ... just the way that my childhood friend Joe S. had the day he told me that his mother had been killed by the drunk driver back in 1977 when we were both twelve.

Her name was Grace. I had a grandmother named Grace. His mom was working as an overnight nurse at a hospital across the river. I remember she had a towering beehive mound of platinum-bleached hair atop her head and usually wore a smile whenever I happened to see her. I thought that she was glamourous and would sit on my front lawn in the hopes that she would smile and wave at me. She left behind three boys, my friend Joe being the youngest.

It was my mother who had sat me down and told me the bad news. My first thought was that I was thankful that my Grace was alive, and sad that Joe's Grace was dead.

A few weeks after his mother had passed I saw Joe while I was in my front yard hitting a plastic ball with an oversized plastic bat. We sat down under the red maple tree in front of my house. I'm not sure why, but I was relieved that he looked the same as I had remembered.

With some hesitation, he asked if he could tell me something. I nodded in silence, eyes opened wide. Joe then verified, after pulling his long, skinny legs up against his torso, that his mother was killed by a drunk driver. What confused him he said was that while his mother was killed, the drunk driver – who had caused the accident by veering into her lane – was not. Apparently he wasn't even badly injured.

We both made a promise on that day that if we ever saw a drunk driver coming at us, we would relax all of our muscles so that we would live, just as the man who killed his mother had likely done. Our reasoning was that stiff things, such as peanut brittle or a tree branch, snapped. Loose and flexible things, like rubber bands, stretched. Arranging our bodies in various positions we attempted to approximate virtually every accident scenario that we could envision. It was a worthwhile distraction from his terrible loss, but eventually the sadness washed over his face and I could see his brown eyes darken. His large lower lip trembled for a moment, and then he stated with as much force as he could muster: "I know one thing for sure; I'm never going to drink and drive."

"Me neither," I vowed.

He was very afraid that day, afraid of what might someday become of him (he would die in an alcohol-related car crash when twenty-one) … I understood that feeling now.

Before he had left, Jeff had noted in his journal:

"As I'm writing this, Chris and I are in my room. He is extremely reluctant to be alone in his room, especially at night, the witching hour, 'when fancy stalks outside reason and malignant possibilities stand rock firm as facts'" (Thomas Hardy, Tess).

My admiration for Jeff, and his bravery in the face of the unknown, was ever increasing. He would be back in eight days.

The rhythmic electrical hum of the nearby vending machine was at once relaxing, and annoying. After collecting myself for a few minutes, and putting my thoughts of the death of Joe's mom to rest, I uncurled my legs and walked back to the room. The door was still open as I had left it, and Paul was sitting up on top of his mattress with his light on.

"You OK?" he asked with a tired voice.

"I saw the ghost," I informed him as I climb back up into the loft, "it was right next to my face, smiling a grotesque smile at me."

"I know," he said, "that's why I put the light on. It was looking at me too, from where my desk chair is. Its head had that weird sideways tilt again. I can't take much more of this, you know."

The way in which he had added "you know" at the end of his statement suggested to me that he was trying to get me to understand something that he was not actually saying. I wasn't sure exactly what.

"We have to do something or we might die in here," Paul continued in morose fashion. I felt my innards tighten. It was a possibility that I did not want to have to consider. Maybe he was right. All I could do was reply, "I know."

He shifted his legs a bit and added: "Looking at that thing, it might be a very painful death. They may not even find our bodies." Paul's eyes were a study in seriousness.

"Please, stop," I requested, "saying all of this is only going to make us more afraid, and … (I whispered) … you might give 'it' some bad ideas."

Paul nodded his agreement and, after looking around the room, said, "We need to do something. We need someone to help us get rid of the thing."

The thought was not new to me, but hearing someone else echo it brought me a degree of comfort. On several occasions I had considered simply packing my bags and heading home, leaving both Geneseo, and the creature, behind forever.

What had stopped me – each time – was the never ending shame that such an action would carry with it. My father was the first Di Cesare to attend college; I did not want the ignominy of being the first Di Cesare to drop out.

"What do you want to do?" I asked Paul, almost afraid to hear his answer.

"Let's get a priest."

. . .

February 25th, 1985, Jeff has returned from his trip. He looks tanned and relaxed, and he is speaking of warm weather, theme parks, and the assortment of foods that he sampled.

He has apparently brought the warm Florida weather with him, as the temperatures this weekend reach up into the mid-fifties, after having been below freezing for most of the month.

Gathered in a sun-drenched C2D2 – as Sunday's rain clouds clear away – Paul, Beth, and I recall the events that Jeff missed while away. We talk of the early morning walk into the village and how we had resolved to go to St. Mary's Catholic Church with our request for aid. We take turns relaying to him how the priest would not see us, but that a woman who was working there had provided us with a slip of paper, and a name.

Jeff asks to inspect the pencil written message on the rectangular cut scrap of gold stationary.

On it was the name of the priest (who, we were advised, had mentioned a story about ghosts at some point in the past) as well as his office number at the college's Interfaith Center.

"Are you going to speak with him" Jeff queries, peering at us from over the top of his wire-frame glasses.

Both Paul and I shrug.

"Maybe," I say.

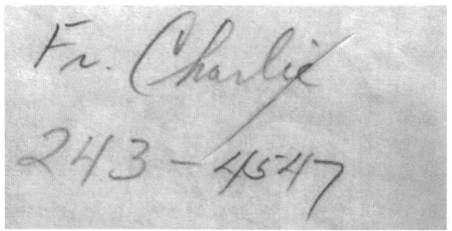

Above: the stationary with Father Charlie Manning's phone number across it.

Beth relays an incident that had occurred on February 18th when she and I were studying in C2D1: a pencil fell from the ceiling near the closets and rolled around on the floor for an odd length of time. And she tells of how we had decided to move our studying out in the C2 common area after that.

Paul says nothing when Beth speaks. The tension is palpable, but it does not dissuade Beth from maintaining her new-found place in this circle of friends.

I share a particularly unnerving experience from February 22nd that began with me sitting at my desk, wearing only a pair of nylon running shorts, while working on a school assignment. I had not done my laundry for a while, due primarily to my fear of unintentionally interacting with the ghost, which I felt might occur if I attempted to retrieve my basket of unwashed clothing. The abrupt waving motion of the light brown curtains was the first clue that Tommy was making an appearance.

I reached for my baseball book and opened to the Murcer page: emotional control must be maintained.

What was particularly unusual about this situation was that it was daytime. Except for the initial encounter, the one with Paul's headphones and the voice calling my name, the ghost always appeared in the evening hours, when darkness was surrounding us.

Being that it was daylight, and comforted both by the sounds of students bustling about and my baseball book, I chose simply to ignore him.

Yet, as I continued to stare at my book, that familiarly unnatural coldness began to move in towards me, its faint caress washing over my unguarded skin.

"Disbelieve," I told myself, "it is daytime."

The night time might belong to the creature, but the day was mine; mine to go to classes in and to run in and to talk with my friends in; and mine to eat in and to function with some semblance of comfort. It was important to me that I felt safe, and in control of my environment, for at least minor, set portions of each day.

"Leave me alone," I had stated, my eyes not leaving my desk area, my head not turning to acknowledge its presence.

Sarcasm ran across my mind when I realized that the book I held in my hands just minutes before was entitled, *Man and His Fictions*.

Oh, how I wished it were that simple.

I noticed that it had drawn closer to me; I could now make out the outline of its head and upper torso in my peripheral vision, not unlike the night that it first appeared, by Paul's stereo.

"Not now!" I yelled aloud, still determined to ignore Tommy's intrusion into *my* day.

The icy cold breath on my right ear moved me into an upright, more rigid, posture. My rate of breathing had increased, while the depth of my breaths decreased. Perhaps instinctively, I drew my legs together, tightened my muscles, and pulled my head forward away from the ever-nearing frigid breath.

I waited.

I waited ... for the sickly whisper of my name ... up close.

It did not come.

Instead, what felt like frozen finger tips – thin, hard bones of dread – touched the skin on my neck!

Screaming, I fell onto the floor at the foot of the couch. I curled into the fetal position like a shelled shrimp on a plate of Chinese lo mien ... only much larger and much colder.

I understood in that cruel moment that it didn't matter how fast a person could run, or how smart they were, or how strong their body was ... if a person could not control their environment, or worse, *understand* it ... they simply could not survive in it. How many capable warriors over the centuries have fallen due to circumstances beyond their control?

The scene had felt like it was taken right out of the epic Gericault painting, *The Raft of Medusa*. And I was the young man lying prostrate on the front of the raft potentially unable to survive it.

The sharing of my recollection of the events from three days ago leaves the room in a sustained silence. It has my friends, just as it has me, deeply worried.

I can see it in their eyes.

When the silence becomes unbearable, Jeff reaches for a green and white, thin, cardboard, photo envelope, packed with 4"x6" images.

The full "C2D1 Ghost Image" (sometimes called the "Skeletal Apparition") taken on Valentine's Day 1985. This photograph turned a Western New York 'urban legend' into part of the global lexicon when it appeared on the internet in the 1990s thanks in large part to Dale Kaczmarek of the Ghost Research Society.

I know what they are.

They are the pictures that were taken on Valentine's Day. They are the proof Jeff had sought: proof of the haunting, and proof that a dead thing was following me around and whispering in my ear.

This is proof that I did not want.

Paul and Beth fumble their way through the double stacks of photos, most of which are unremarkable. Both of them pause, almost at the same time, on one particular photo.

It was the photo that I had taken.

"No way," Beth murmurs under her breath, "this can't be real."

. . .

But it was.

...

Jeff had shown it to me, just an hour earlier, and it had sent chills through me. Like the rest of the photos in the roll it captured the varied contents of room C2D1: the old television set; a PUMA shoes poster of marathoner Bill Rodgers; my mattress and pillow; a section of a poster of the New York City skyline; and the American Greetings 'Super Pickle' stuffed doll hanging watchfully from the ceiling.

There were two distinct differences with this photo however, this was the picture that I had taken, and in it, in the spot I had pointed to that night, in the area where I had seen Tommy looking at me, the place where I pointed the camera ... was his skeleton.

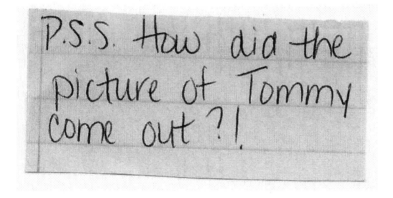

"God will not look you over for medals, degrees or diplomas but for scars." –
Elbert Hubbard

19. A 'Spirited' Analysis

The photograph weighed heavily upon me, like the world atop the shoulders of Atlas. Until its existence, all of this – no matter how many people became involved – could have been written off as some type of mass hysteria.

Not anymore.

Jeff retrieved an anatomy book from the Milne Library and was able to match bone after bone from the skeletal image in the photograph that I had taken with the illustrative chart in the thick medical guide. The photo was detailed enough for Jeff to determine that the figure in it was actually facing the wall!

His conclusion: Tommy did not want to be photographed.

This matched my impression, recalling that the ghost had bolted across the room, away from the flash of the camera, the night that it had passed through me.

So then, if the ghost did not want to be photographed, and I did not want to photograph it, then what right did the photo itself have to exist? What right did we have to show it to anyone?

I wondered if it should be destroyed.

With this proof came huge choices, and a potentially huge responsibility. Everything would depend now on how I would react to a proof that I just did not want.

A man who hires a detective to follow his wife on the suspicion that she is unfaithful ultimately wants proof that his worry is unfounded. He is, in a sense, paying the private eye in the hopes that he finds nothing untoward. If the detective returned a week later with an envelope full of pictures, I would guess that there would be some type of initial hesitation in the man before he decided to open it. For while his money was invested wisely, does he truly want to see what the pictures show?

In that scenario 'failure' brings a sweet relief, and 'success' provides a heart-breaking betrayal. Such it was for me and the photograph of the ghost.

Our 'success' had brought me only more suffering, more dread: something from beyond the grave was watching me.

...

With Jeff sitting at his desk, Paul sitting at Ed's desk, and Beth and I sitting on Jeff's bed we begin to discuss our options.

Paul recommends that we all try to spend as much time away from C2D1, or even Erie Hall, as possible. We decide that this plan will work for both Paul and Jeff, whose families live 40 minutes away, but not for me. I don't have the time – or the resources – to travel five hours each and every Saturday and Sunday. In addition, there is my running to consider. Coach Kentner called and expressed his concern that I have been missing too many practices if I want to stay on the team, and our meets are primarily on the weekends.

Beth mentions that Paul and I could ask the Residence Director for a change of rooms. I put a halt on that one as explaining to the person in charge that there was a ghost in the room would likely either have them thinking we are on drugs, or it might spread news of the ghost all across the campus, something that neither Paul nor I want. Besides, I feel that it would be immoral to simply stick some unsuspecting people in there during an active haunting while we turn tail and flee. Jeff agrees.

Paul offers that he and I ask our parents to allow us to change colleges. That is certainly worth considering, but it is more of a long-term plan, and we are seeking immediate remedies.

Beth mentions that she had taken a psychology class and that her professor, a man named Dr. Lawrence Casler, taught an entire class on parapsychology. She offers to get his contact information for us in case we want to reach out to him. This possibility immediately rouses Jeff's interest.

Then she turns to me, puts a hand on my thigh, and asks what I prefer to do. I hold up the golden ticket with Fr. Charlie's phone number on it. The church worker had indicated that he had mentioned ghosts in past conversations, and I see no reason why we shouldn't follow the lead that her generosity had provided.

Paul shrugs his shoulders as though to say 'why not?'

It is agreed. Paul and I will pay a visit to Fr. Charles Manning the following morning. As a back-up, both Jeff and Beth volunteer to call Dr. Casler to set up an appointment with him.

At 9AM on Monday morning, March 4th, Paul and I head up to the campus Interfaith Center. We take with us Jeff's journal notes, reasoning that it will be easier, and much less stressful, to have the priest read Jeff's notes, rather than us speaking back and forth – possibly leaving out relevant information – or getting our timelines mixed up. Credibility is the key; and for that, Jeff's organized notes are decidedly the best option.

Reaching the modern looking structure, I remind Paul that we promised Jeff that we will not allow Fr. Charlie to keep the notes. We joke about the likelihood that Jeff is watching us out of his C2D2 window ruing his decision to let us borrow them.

The priest who greets us at the door is younger, taller, and friendlier looking than I anticipated. To me he looks more like a collegiate football player than a distinguished 'man of the cloth'. I am hoping that this young man, who is certainly under thirty years in age, is a local seminary student who is there to assist.

He introduces himself as "Father Charlie."

My heart sinks a bit. If a dedicated, physically fit, accomplished athlete such as myself is being outmatched by the thing in that college dorm room, then what hope would this well-intentioned, slightly out-of-shape, casually-dressed young man have?

He would be cannon fodder.

If this were an episode of *Star Trek*, I mused; we would throw a red shirt on him, beam him down to the planet's surface, and watch him die at the hands of the Gorn.

Paul and I make eye contact.

Neither of us wanted to go in.

We go in.

After refusing coffee and other breakfast amenities, we get down to business. Handing him Jeff's journal notes, Paul and I sit back in two wooden chairs. Ten minutes turns to twenty, and twenty to thirty as the man of God carefully studies the fancifully-written words.

Only when he reaches the last sentence of the notebook does he glance up at us.

"I believe you, I want to help" he says with a look of steely resolve etched across his face.

I have misjudged him, and I am hoping now that he has not misjudged us.

He is clearly serious about his craft, and understands the importance of studying a situation before acting on it. His desire to help those in need, those who he barely knows, is ingratiating and it bathes me with some much-needed humility.

We will be in good hands with the young Fr. Charlie. I am glad that he has chosen to help us.

...

Two days later, March 6th, one day before a full moon, Fr. Charlie stands in the doorframe of C2D1. It is 8PM and the snow that fell earlier in the day remains on the ground as the temperature never climbed above freezing. But I am not concerned with events on the outside, I am solely focused on what is about to transpire inside.

"Is this the room?" he asks, now looking impressive in a large black overcoat – his priest's collar visible on his neck. He holds a large, dark briefcase in his left hand.

"Yes," I reply, "this is *the* room."

...

The tree, in the woods behind my house, had been knocked down by a violent winter storm. It lay on its side, bereft of leaves and life. I pondered how long it had stood guard over the forest before the end came. Like the great ship Titanic, there was nothing too large or too prestigious for Mother Nature to send to the grave. Months passed, and by summer I had used an assortment of silverware, mostly butter knives, to carve a makeshift control panel into the side of the tree. In my seven-year-old mind she had become my version of the USS Enterprise. Moving old logs and large stones from a long ago neglected farming wall, I had constructed my own Bridge, Captain's chair and all.

Weeks of solo adventuring had left me a bit bored and so I made a command decision: I invited two of my friends to join me. I now had a first officer and a doctor to assist me as I steered my imaginary space cruiser through the Solar System.

We drew 'rank' insignias and taped them to our t-shirts and 'planet-hopped' until the sun was setting and my mother said that dinner was ready.

Two days later I returned to find that my hard work had been vandalized: the chairs were turned over, the carved out controls had been destroyed, and the tree was lined with offensive words made with a can of white spray paint.

One of my 'officers' had talked.

Walking back home, across the old wood footbridge that connected the back of my family's property to the woods, I decided that some things in life were just too special, too sacred, to be shared with just anyone. Some experiences, some moments, some truths had to be earned.

...

Now, as Fr. Charlie politely explains to Jeff that he cannot be present for what is about to occur, I understand. As Paul opted not to be present, in the priest's mind this was now a matter between me, God, and the restless spirit. If I had not experienced the wrecked 'spaceship' incident, I would argue for Jeff's inclusion.

Jeff hands me one of his spiral notepads and a finely sharpened no. 2 pencil, and asks me to record as much of what the priest says as possible. I ask him why. He looks at me with a considered intensity, attempting to ensure that I understand, and says: "We may need to know how to do this in the future. If a priest is not available, it might be up to us."

I find it a compelling argument, and I carry the chronicling instruments to my desk as Fr. Charlie opens his briefcase to prepare for his ceremony.

Resting carefully inside it, beside his soft cover *Bible*, are three white candles, and what looks to be a container of Holy Water.

...

Approximately twenty minutes later the ceremony is apparently over.

I am not sure how I know, except for the fact that the Priest's voice falls silent for a period of time. Nor am I sure that the ghost has been expelled from the room but there is a great sense of calm echoing off of the four connected walls. It feels like I am sitting in a shelter now; a spiritual bunker of sorts. A sense of warmth, long since absent, has returned to the room with the colorful Christmas lights and posters. Still, I remain convinced that I can no longer put full stock or trust in my senses.

I ask Fr. Charlie, point blank, if the ghost can "get back into the room."

"Only if you invite him back," he answers without hesitation.

"*That's* not going to happen!" I assure him.

As the cleric puts away his belongings, I can state with an honest heart that there is no possible scenario in which I can imagine myself doing so.

"Call me if you need anything else," he says as he begins to walk out the door.

Fr. Charlie's Blessing of C2D1, as shown in the award-winning independent film *Please, talk with me ...* **(2012). Lead actor Kyle Shea did a stunning job portraying a nineteen-year-old me. While actor David Lanson gave the role of the priest the gravitas it required.**

"I will," I lie.

Just as I have no intention of inviting the 'dread Thomas' back into my newfound sanctuary, I also have no intention of bothering the priest a second time. It seems to me that to have to call him back would be akin to admitting a certain amount of failure the first time. It would be a failure that might point to my own lack of faith, or lack of follow through.

A history teacher might spend weeks preparing a lesson on the importance of the Nile River on ancient Egyptian civilization. The lesson might include maps and hieroglyphic samples as well as detailed contemporary analysis. Yet as organized, informative and effective the conceived lesson plan may be, there is simply no guarantee that every student would be inspired by it or fully comprehend it. Some students may still not answer the test questions correctly, and through no fault of the instructor. I do not want to be that student. Nor do I want Father Charlie's efforts to be wasted ones. Trust in him and a belief in the likely success of his blessing are not items that I choose to question. I am too overwhelmed with gratitude to even dare.

Jeff, while still somewhat disgruntled over having been excluded from the ritual, is quite pleased when I turn over my notes to him. I sit and talk with him in C2D2 for a while, no longer afraid of what might be lurking on the other side of the wall.

He quizzes me on the details of the ceremony. I provide him with what I can, although I do feel some pangs of guilt in doing so. 'A gentlemen never tells' is an adage that I was brought up on, and much the same, there was a sacred aspect to the evening that made it seem intensely personal and private to me. Father Charlie could have easily chosen not to have gotten involved, not to invest himself so fully in the events. An appreciative part of me knew that he was there not just to get rid of the ghost, but to help me as well.

Me.

Chris.

I look down at the crunched up poster in my garbage bin. It had cost me $20 at a time when I had not much more than that and the bronze-skinned, red bikini-clad, woman with the martini glass in her hand was certainly a pleasant distraction in my college room, but losing her was an acceptable loss if it means that the ghost might be gone.

That night I sleep alone in the room, and for the first time in twenty-seven days, I am not afraid.

"Not all those who wander are lost." – J.R.R. Tolkien, *The Fellowship of the Ring.*

20. The Post-Mortem

Last night, and for the last three nights, I have seen no sign of the ghost. He has not come into the room. I brush my teeth and throw on my running gear. The radio deejay announces that it is a balmy 51°F, and I am not going to pass up the rare opportunity to wear shorts in March.

I am running at a brisk 6:00/mile clip along the dirt roads that separate the local farming fields. The azure sky is lined with wispy clouds of white who are being hurried along by an unseen wind current.

It is so peaceful out here, almost meditative.

Almost a month has passed since I was last able to stretch out my runner's legs like this. But things are different now. The priest, Father Charlie Manning, had done his blessing, and the thing … that horrid thing … is gone.

In the three and one-half days since he raised up his cross, whispered his sacred prayers, and cleansed my college dorm room my life has returned to a healthy normalcy.

The ceasing of the harrowing events allows me an opportunity to consider what it is that Paul, I, and the others have just lived through. If I didn't believe in hauntings before, I certainly do now. Still, a number of significant questions remain for me, the most pressing of which is: why?

Why has all of this occurred?

According to Jeff, his prevailing theory is that the ghost just followed me home one day, much like a stray dog, on one of my many long runs; just like my run today.

Likewise, there is the possibility that attending the Warren lecture predisposed – or 'opened' – my mind to events that might have otherwise been overlooked. While I did listen attentively at the presentation, Lorraine's statement – that she did not want to 'know her future' – suggests that she felt some sort of 'gift' was a part of me already. In fact, at one point, Jeff speculated that my "noticeably undersized skull" might be pressing up against areas of the brain that might be contributing to my 'sensitivity'. My humorous retort at the time had been that my skull only *looked* small to Jeff, as he himself had a rather prominent dome ... like the rampaging Hulk's mortal enemy, the Leader. I enjoyed that analogy made Jeff the villain and me the hero; Jeff less so.

I can't help but smile at that now as I pass an old rusting farm structure to the side of the road.

Apparently, conventional wisdom has it that some young college student must have taken his own life years ago in what is now my room. The tilted head was perhaps indicative of a snapped neck on the apparition. I was told that colleges 'were known for' covering up events that might generate bad press. Of course, if colleges did cover such things up, then how would anyone know that they did this in the first place?

There are other persistent questions as well. Questions that go well beyond my own experiences, the first of which being: What *are* ghosts?

It still seems rather strange to me that we can view star systems millions of miles away, and view microorganisms in a petri dish, but we cannot see spirits, human souls, that are said to watch over us, guide us, and when things go wrong ... haunt us.

Even though it seems that everyone has a ghost story to tell, they are just ... stories. Quick – often nonsensical – tales of deranged asylum patients who walk the hallways opening and closing doors, or women in white who appear to drivers on lonely roadways, tales that are designed to send children scurrying away from the campfire and into bed so that the 'adults' finally had a chance to party themselves.

"I believe in everything until it's disproved. So I believe in fairies, the myths, dragons. It all exists, even if it's in your mind. Who's to say that dreams and nightmares aren't as real as the here and now?" — John Lennon

The only saving grace that I can afford myself in this mental exercise is that science can't prove what love is either. After all, even though we all profess to have felt it at one point in time, no one has been able to come up with a formula or machine to provide proof of it. What proves love? Is it placing a ring on someone's finger? Buying someone an expensive gift? Sharing oneself through sexual intercourse?

It seems to me, as I see the crossroad up ahead that if you felt loved, that you probably, in some way, were. Likewise, if you felt haunted … you might very well be.

I *know* I was.

I am approximately 3.5 miles out, and I turn left onto Rt. 20A and head back east. Over a railed bridge, and up some rolling hills, is the college.

…

Compared to the outdoors, the air inside the dorm is noticeably stale. As I climb my way up the stairs to the second floor, the melody of Julian Lennon's song, *Too Late for Goodbyes*, coming from behind someone's closed door, I am relieved. The feel of stale air is much better than the sense of dread that had emanated from here less than 72 hours ago.

Order had been restored, and almost no one ... not my family ... not the members of the track team ... not my friends back home ... would ever have to know that it had been temporarily lost.

"Paranoid? Probably. But just because you're paranoid doesn't mean there isn't an invisible demon about to eat your face." – Jim Butcher, Storm Front

21. Fear, Part II

"Chris, can you *hear* me? You're bleeding, what happened?"

A towel is wrapped, very tightly, around my waist. I mumble out: 'Thankssss.'

"No problem. Are you OK to walk? Here, just lean on me."

I follow the words to Jeff's face, and I can see that he has worry etched deeply across it.

Jeff navigates me across the hallway into the safety of his room. Ed is standing as we enter.

He looks concerned. I am shivering uncontrollably now from the cold, or the fear, or the exhaustion.

"And" Ed queries, raising both of his eyebrows in expectation.

"He was attacked, in the bathroom."

I stop looking at Ed when I hear him issue a pained and confused response: a long drawn out "Whaaat?" But I have nothing to say. And as Jeff carefully sits me down at the foot of his bed, my cold and wet feet leaving imprints on his floor, Ed apparently catches his first glimpse of the cuts.

"Oh my God …. Oh my God!"

There is a pause.

"This is *real,* isn't it?"

The view from C2D2: where I was taken to recover the day of the shower attack.

I reply in an undisguised and aggravated tone: "Do I get my Purple Heart now?"

Neither the pain from the back wounds nor the shock of the attack has lessened. And Ed's incredulous tone, as understandable as it might be, bothers me. He knows that something bad has been going on for over a month now, since the night I came banging on his door in an emotional frenzy. The understanding that it takes my blood being spilled for Ed to put any real stock in the situation does not sit well with me; at least, not while I am still actually bleeding.

There is a quick movement to my right, and as I am still exhausted, I do not turn my head to see what causes it.

Her voice gives it away.

"Is he OK?" Beth asks nervously, somewhat out of breath from what must have been a hurried trip to Jeff and Ed's room from wherever she had been.

"Chris was attacked," Jeff repeats.

I hear Beth emit a gasp of horror as she gets her first sight of the three bleeding scratches on my back. The blood-tinged towel doesn't do anything to improve the grim aesthetic.

With no advance notice, Jeff begins using significant force to try and push my hands up into my back. I wince in pain as my shoulders and elbows feel as though they might snap out of their sockets.

"Go easy, Jeffy," Ed cautions, "you don't want to make the poor guy suffer any more than he already is!"

"See," Jeff announces to anyone and all present, "he couldn't have done this himself. There is no way. Something *did* this to him."

"No duh!" I snap back indignantly in '80s lingo, "Can you please let go of my arms?"

"He needs to go to a hospital!" Beth counsels, her tone is severe.

"I am not going to a hospital," I yell, "they'll think I'm crazy. Then they'll medicate me and put me in a strait jacket! No way! If you try to make me go, I'll fight!"

"Well we have to do something," Ed advises, "He's just going to keep on bleeding otherwise."

Beth offers to run back to her room and get some cotton swabs and some bandages. I have some hydrogen peroxide in a first aid kit that my father had put together for me, one room over.

For the next 43 minutes – 47 if you count the time it took to decide who will do what – the painful process of pouring peroxide on cotton ball, pressing cotton ball on wound, and covering wound with bandage, repeats itself over and over and over again.

In spite of all of the pain, for me it is still preferable to being tranquilized by some drug in a psychiatric ward, completely unable to react if Tommy comes back.

Because I know now … that he will.

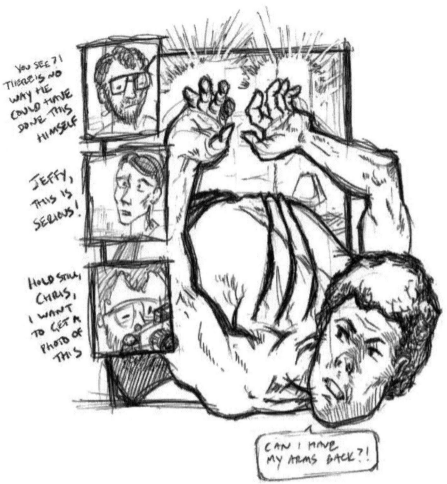

Above: A 'recreation sketch' of the tense moments that took place in room C2D2 following the March 10th attack by artist Kerry Lyon (2013).

It is nearing 4:30 and the skies outside of Erie Hall are growing darker. Jeff follows my gaze out the window.

"If we are going to get some pictures, we should do it now," Jeff informs the group, seeking tacit approval to do so, "before the natural light fades."

"No pictures!" I shout.

Jeff opens his mouth slightly, as if to begin explaining the medical, scientific, and journalistic benefits of taking the photos, but then he stops himself. He sees that I am suffering badly, and his expression suggests that he doesn't want to add to that.

"Thank you for not taking any pictures," I say to him.

"I just thought it would be helpful to have a record of this," he offers softly, "but I can understand why you wouldn't want that."

I'm still not sure about ghosts or love, but that's certainly how you prove friendship.

"The woods of Arcady are dead,
And over is their antique joy,
Of old the world on dreaming fed;
Gray Truth is now her painted toy."
-   William Butler Yeats, *Crossways*

22. Spinning Out of Control

Afraid that there might be more attacks, I retreat back to the safety of my room. C2D1, the place where for several weeks I had been too frightened to sit alone, now – thanks to the priest's blessing – is the one place that I feel safe.

How the blessing works in keeping Tommy out, I have absolutely no clue. Then again, I don't understand the concept of an infinite universe either; *something* had to have come before it. Nothing can come from nothing ... right?

Rather than second guessing the 'why' and the 'how' of the moment, I am just thankful that I have a place to go where I have some time to heal my wounds.

Making sure to lock the door behind me, I wad the bloody towel up into a basketball shape, drop it into a black plastic garbage bag, and toss it on the floor right next to my trash can. My mom had sent me back to college with three towels, so that 'losing' one shouldn't be a major issue.

Things happen.

I just need to make sure that I throw the bag in the dorm dumpster before Paul gets back. That is, *if* he comes back. I hadn't seen him since the day before the priest was here. He probably has no way of even knowing that the room is finally safe to be in.

I walk over to the plain, square mirror that hangs on the wall near my dresser. My eyes look the same. They are a light blue, passed on from my grandmother Hubley through my mother, just like my pug nose. Yes, my eyes look the same.

It is still me.

One of my high school teachers once told me that the human body is constantly changing with cells dying and cells being created. Eventually, he said, almost every cell in your body is replaced by another so that, in effect, after several years you are a completely different physical person. While I never completely bought into the application of that particular concept, I was impressed by an exercise we did in art class. We took a photograph of ourselves and divided our face down the center. We then reconstructed our faces by combining 'same halves' which accentuated how different each half of our face truly was. This, I suppose, harkened back to many models and actresses who referred to their 'good side' and their 'bad side'.

It suggested that we human beings had competing parts, perhaps a duality of sorts, of the same whole. An effective life, one could argue, might be a balancing of these two competing halves of the self: the preparedness, discernment, and strength against pacifism, forgiveness and kindness.

Perhaps it could be boiled down to the conscious and subconscious; or maybe it wasn't all that simple.

The ancient Essenes (or 'Essaios' meaning 'holy ones') an ascetic Jewish religious sect that some scholars suggest generated not only the intriguing Dead Sea Scrolls, but possibly produced both John the Baptist and Jesus as well, believed that we were all 'parts' good and 'parts' bad, up to a total of seven, equal to the number of days in a week.

In any event, I am relieved that I still look like I am 'supposed to', and for the first time in weeks, I let my shoulders relax.

A magic marker poster I made for art class that addressed the theme of the duality of the self. I also added a cool 'man descending from the stars' minor theme.

The 'Negative Zone', the old brown couch under the loft, that many of the residents of Erie Hall claim is the most comfortable place to sit in the dorm, looks welcoming. I drop myself onto it. Its textured cloth fabric, coming into contact with the backs of my legs and my bare bottom for the first time, feels a bit odd. Not alarming, just odd. I am careful not to place my injured back up against anything. I don't want to pull any of the loosely attached bandages off or get any of my blood on the couch, so I lean forward to a position similar to that of the famous sculpture, *The Thinker at the Gates of Hell,* by Auguste Rodin.

The quiet of the moment is soothing. The room feels much warmer since it was blessed. I dig my toes into the warmth of the couch cushions and I am thankful that they are no longer in the excruciating pain that they had been in, pushed painfully back, when I was lying on the cold, wet bathroom floor.

I smile slightly at the realization that I had not passed out from the pain … or the ordeal itself. No amount of money would ever be enough to entice me back into a situation like that: shivering, bleeding, and in pain … lying prone on the cold, wet, dirty bathroom floor …

Oh, God no!

I was lying in that *germ-infested* water for a long time! My hands, my legs, my …

I feel the muscles in my stomach convulse. Shooting frantic glances around the room, I realize that there is no water in here, but I have to clean myself!

Panic sets in.

I'm probably infected now and I can't tell anyone. I can't go to the infirmary, they'll see the scratches on my back and they'll ask about them. My mind is spinning out of control. I need to vomit. The bacteria is probably still on my knees and shoulders and worse ... my ears are ringing in my head.

...

I wake up, it is remarkably silent.

Sprawled face down on the brown cloth couch, my right leg hanging off onto the floor, I survey my surroundings. My black running watch, sitting on my desk, reads 2:09 am. I take that as a positive omen as my running hero Bill Rodgers had run times of 2:09:55 and 2:09:27 when he set his two American records in the marathon (1975 and 1979 at Boston).

I am looking for anything positive for my mind to grasp onto. My eyes are magnifying the entire room. I am able to see the fine granules of wood and old scratches in my desk chair as though my face were pressed up against it, even though it is several feet away. I understand now that while I slept, I dreamed of the green glowing sphere, like when I thirteen:

Gray ... total gray covers the sky, it is a numbing wall that can never be pierced and it blankets the earth with a stagnant coat. Next there are the wilted trees, branches barren and dying. I find myself alone, wearing only a thin, black bracelet that seems to weigh me down. I stand on a carefully-sculpted sidewalk that runs through suburbia and on through to a possible escape, a hope in the midst of the drab shuffle, a joyless paradise. A soul-dampening chill runs through me, the hand of the grave reaching out for me as though to drain away all the dreams of my youth.

Identically shaped box houses line the length of the street in a feigned perfection. Telephone poles, only eight feet in height, run alongside, stark crosses frame my vision, the wires only head-level off the ground.

On the other sidewalk I see the men walking in the opposite direction. They appear in suits of drab colors: black, browns, beiges; hats, watches and overcoats completing their outfits. Mandate of the American dream in person, from the perfectly groomed haircuts, to the square cut of their chins, to the immaculate gleam of their shoe polish. But without exception they all wear expressions of the greatest complacency. Everything is all right here. We know who we are and what we want. There is nothing new under the sun. All is as it should be. No hint of originality gleams in their eyes.

This is what you have to look forward to.

"... it was written I should be loyal to the nightmare of my choice."
— Joseph Conrad, *Heart of Darkness*

I walk forward and the men drop away behind me, having taken no notice of the 'child' in their midst. Ahead I notice a hillside set off to the left of the street, on the slope of which is an ominous cavern. The cavern has no place in this suburban vision, but nonetheless I approach as one who has found what was there for anyone else to see, had they only eyes with which to see. In front of the cave is gravel that shifts beneath my bare feet.

Inside is only darkness.

Daggers ran up my spine as I recognized the scene.

Oh God, here again.

The feeling is accompanied by a compulsion to move forward. The cycle must be completed. I step inside. Crossing the threshold is like stepping into the night sky, the cavern walls open up like the perimeters of the galaxy.

My attention is arrested by a sight at the heart of the cave, like the center of creation itself. A metallic globe glistens with a whitish-green glow. On the surface is a series of lines that show each time the light shifts, as though the gods have left their knitting yarn.

For a moment, I feel a transcendent gladness at the sight, like a lost traveler finding my home. This is always followed by. . .

The answer!

From within comes the awful truth, not yarn but needles radiated from the globe, silver needles whose touch cannot be avoided. Just to gaze upon so many pins hurts my eyes with a stabbing pain that pierces deep into my skull. The globe had sat dormant awaiting my arrival, anticipating this very moment, not striking until I know what it is -- my death.

I take a step back, then another, hoping for some escape from the inescapable. With each step the globe rolls towards me, and as it closes in I pivot back towards the gray world. The first stab pierces my left foot, spearing me into the world of the green rays.

There is no escaping myself.

One nail continues to hold me in place, as a wave of sweet, stabbing energy flows up to my torso, leaving the sensation of pins and needles numbing my senses. With the wave comes a paralyzing power that seems to resonate within the fabric of my soul. Then it hits the eyes, jolting me awake in breathless panic: home ... again.

Now that I am awake for the day, I wonder how my magnified sight might have been possible. Just as I had initially thought that my tape recorder had been turned on – twice – by a power surge, I wonder too if maybe some 'super impulse' from my brain (as a result of the intensity of the dream) had somehow overloaded my eyes with energy ... and an increased sight capacity.

I sound a bit like Jeff now. I chuckle.

Then again, I had been wrong about the tape recorder.

I look in my desk drawer to make sure that the tape recorder is still in there.

It is.

I think back to when I was thirteen. I had the same dream with the same preternatural result:

I woke up in my bed with cramps in both legs and energy literally shooting through my entire body. My fingers, my toes — all of my extremities — were humming with some vibrating 'pins and needles' that made them completely numb to the touch.

At first all I could see were swirls of color, with occasional flashes of white or gold, and then I swore I could even see the currents of energy flowing in straight lines through the walls until they reached a corner and were redirected to an outlet or a light switch.

Corners are important.

Not sure that it was actually happening, I called out to my sister Nicole, who walked sleepily across the hallway and into the doorway of my bedroom.

"Nicole," I stammered, happy to see her as she was the proof I needed that I was not still dreaming, "I can see everything like there is a magnifying glass over my eyes! Watch this!"

I instructed her to stand next to the Bobby Murcer poster that was securely taped to my bedroom door. It is the one put out by Sports Illustrated *in 1975 with Hall of Fame catcher Johnny Bench standing behind him as they both watch the trajectory of a ball that Murcer had just hit.*

I closed my eyes tightly.

"Now check and see if there is any writing, or any tiny words on the bottom somewhere."

"I see a bunch of tiny words on the bottom," she replied.

I opened my eyes. She was crouched down with her face inches from the poster trying to make out what the words said.

"Watch this, Nicole," I announced, and I proceeded to read each word as it appeared on the poster's bottom edge from a distance of over ten feet away. She was absolutely dumbfounded as to how I was doing this.

So was I.

I no longer had that poster.

One of my cousins, while throwing some sort of toddler temper tantrum, had torn it into pieces during a visit to my home a few years later. I was *so* angry with her at the time. It was the one relic of my past that I felt I had some type of – I don't know – maybe 'mystical' connection to.

But she was so young; I made the choice to forget the poster, its destruction and the incident that went along with both of them … until now.

I am not liking where some of the arrows are starting to point: at me.

My dresser drawers make commonplace sliding sounds as I open them to retrieve some clean clothing: underwear, a pair of white ankle socks, dark blue running shorts, and a light blue t-shirt with the words "Diet Pepsi 10,000 Meters Series" featured across the chest.

I find that I cannot put the t-shirt on over the bandages without the risk of pulling them off. So instead I walk over to my closet, and opening the door, I pull a large, blue winter sweatshirt off of its hanger. I hadn't worn it before as I normally don't care for baggy, loose-fitting clothes, but this seems a good solution to my current problem.

"But his soul was mad. Being alone in the wilderness, it had looked within itself and, by heavens I tell you, it had gone mad." – Joseph Conrad, *Heart of Darkness*

23. "The Horror! The Horror!"

The airwaves are filled with talk of the Kremlin choosing Mikhail S. Gorbachev as the new leader of the Soviet Union and of the Boston Celtic's Larry Bird scoring 60 points in a game.

"It should have been 63," yells a student who is telling anyone who will listen to him, that he played basketball himself back home in Bowmansville.

The dorm is unusually busy for being this late on a Tuesday night. My guess is because it almost reached 60°F during the day, a sign that spring is just around the corner. Our D-Quad common area is jam-packed with students playing foosball, drinking in lounge chairs, and blasting the song *Drive* by the Cars. It is not lost on me that it is 60°F on the day Boston's Larry Bird scores 60 points, that the Cars band hailed from Boston and that the word segment 'hail' is in the new Soviet Premier's first name. Not that any of this means anything. My brain enjoys connecting things, looking for patterns that are meaningful, or otherwise.

This is probably otherwise.

I am very happy with the commotion; it takes my mind off of the fact that I had been brutally attacked not much more than 48 hours earlier. The Hawaiian-shirt-wearing dog with the sunglasses on the beer poster in the hallway seems happier today, but it might just be the splatter of guacamole dip that has found its way onto his face.

Paul has returned from wherever it was that he had gone for several days, and he does not like the noisy distraction. As I sit with Jeff on the peripheral of the party, Paul slams the door to C2D1 closed behind him. The sounds of *Tom Sawyer* by Rush waft out from under the door frame:

> Though his mind is not for rent,
> Don't put him down as arrogant
> His reserve, a quiet defense
> Riding out the day's events
> The river

"Paul has been in a dark mood lately," Jeff comments, watching my face for some type of reaction.

"I know."

As midnight approaches the party begins to clear out, the process is expedited by the Residence Director who offers to write up anyone who is still making noise when she returns in ten minutes.

A few of the scattering party-goers complain about her, but no one takes her up on her offer.

Jeff and I are preparing to return to our own rooms when I happen to glance out through the common area window. It looks at first as though some – likely drunk – college student has climbed the tree outside the window to get a better view of the party. My guess is he is about 25 feet up in the tree. *'That would be quite a climb'* I think to myself, trying to get a better look to see if I know who it is. The reflection and glare from the lights inside the room make it difficult to see even when I shift my location a few feet. I sit down onto a chair, to lessen the effect, and I can now see the person out in the tree. He isn't perched on a branch at all; rather he is tied to the tree and drenched in blood. He hangs there naked and it looks to me as though the tree's branches are reaching into his body.

Dear God.

I feel my jaw drop open, and I rise out of the chair, my heart rate quickens.

"What's the matter?" Jeff asks.

"It's him!"

It is Tommy. His mouth hangs open, and it appears as though the skin on both sides of his mouth has been cut. Dark blood oozes out of it and runs down his chin dripping like a slow, leaky faucet onto his battered chest. His hands are stretched out and it looks like most of his fingernails have been painted ... no wait ... ridged sections of flesh are showing where his nails should be. His genitals have been sliced almost entirely off and are hanging from his body by a very thin piece of skin; blood is leaking out onto his thighs and dripping down his legs. His toes look damaged, and I can't make out one of his eyes. It is either missing or rather damaged so badly that I can only see some red meat in the back of the socket. It looks like animals have chewed out sections of his arms.

I want to scream, but I am afraid that the effort will make me spill my dinner all over the floor.

"Chris?"

Yet, in spite of all of this, it remains the pulsing tree limbs entering his abdomen that are the oddest part of this horrific spectacle. They look almost like thin, malleable, rubber hoses ... like ... like ... his intestines!

Those are his *intestines,* emerging from a huge slice in his lower torso, that are wrapped around the tree!

"Why," I scream as loud as I am able to, "Why would it *do* that to me?!!!"

Jeff furrows his brow trying to understand who it is – or what it is – that I am reacting to.

"Jeff, it's out there, in the tree!" I am in near hysterics for the second time in a month, "It's trying to scare me by mutilating its appearance! It is so horrible! Why would it be so cruel? Why is it so evil?!"

"Where do you see it?" Jeff asks placing a hand above his eyes trying to block the light from above.

"There, outside the window!"

I point but now only the lonely tree remains, no leaves – no horrific-looking dying man – just a tree probably patiently hoping, as I was, for the return of spring.

Almost losing my footing as I run out of the quad and down the steps that lead to the first floor, I take up refuge in the dorm's Main Lounge. The mundane and casual movements of the luckily ignorant people walking near me are comforting.

My first goal is to calm my nerves so that I can *breathe* normally. My second goal is to clear my head of the image so that I can *think* normally. My third goal is to get the hell out of Geneseo as soon as I can, so that I can *live* normally!

"If you cannot get rid of the family skeleton, you may as well make it dance."
— George Bernard Shaw, *Immaturity*

24. Momma's Boy

The ride home, with some college students who lived on Long Island and were willing to drop me off along the way, was surreal.

While we were discussing our favorite all time movies (it was a five hour ride for me, almost eight for them) the passenger in the front seat said that she *loved* horror movies ... all of them. She said that she had recently seen *Friday the 13th: The Final Chapter* and that it was a bit of a disappointment. The driver agreed and said that the first movie in any series was typically the best.

"Do you watch any horror movies?" she asked looking back over the seat towards me.

I was in the back seat, leaning forward most of the way, as my scratches were starting to heal, and the friction when leaning back against the chair made them itch.

"Nope," I replied trying not to get too deeply drawn into this particular conversation, "unless you count *King Kong* or *Godzilla*."

"No," she smirked, "We do *not* count *King Kong* or *Godzilla*; those aren't horror movies, those are ..."

"Monster movies," the driver chimed in.

"Right, those are *monster* movies," she completed her thought, eying me with suspicion.

"Then, no I haven't," I replied with a sheepish grin, "sorry."
She continued to stare at me in disbelief.

"What?" I asked, lifting up my palms.

She tilted her head to one side, which made me very uncomfortable. I wondered if, from now on, every time I saw a person tilt their head I would think of the ghost. I hoped that I had not been that badly affected by it. She held her gaze a while longer.

"You're f***ing *hiding* something, aren't you?"

"Hey, he doesn't like cursing," the driver interceded on my behalf.

Six. I'd heard the word used in my vicinity six times now, three times in that last month. I wondered if it was just college-aged students, or if the whole world was starting to lose its civility.

"Sorrrry," she sarcastically apologized to *him*, and then returned her attention to me.

"You were *attacked* weren't you?"

I shot her a nervously quizzical stare, the kind I gave my father back in grade school when he asked if my homework was done, and it wasn't.

"Let me guess, he got you in the back, didn't he?" Her face was 'set in stone' serious. She did not blink. Her mouth was drawn back and straight. The driver looked at me via the car's rear view mirror, to gauge my reaction. They were both watching me.

I heard a faint ringing sound in my ears. My heart rate was already increasing. How could she possibly know that? She lived in a different dormitory and I hadn't seen her – even once – in almost two full months, since before the haunting had even begun. My head began to race through the possibilities: She had spoken to either Jeff or Paul. No, not Jeff, definitely not Jeff, he was afraid to talk to girls. Paul? No, she definitely was not his type, plus she had a boyfriend. Beth! Maybe Beth had told her about … I stopped the guessing game, it was getting me nowhere. Maybe I should just try the truth.

"Yes," I replied calmly and clearly. "I *was* attacked on my back, and I had no clue it was coming."

They both burst out into tremendous laughter. For a good two minutes they had laughed, and when they happened to make some brief eye contact with each other, they would laugh all over again.

I was at a complete loss. How was me being attacked at all funny?

"No clue it was *coming*," she started to laugh again.

"Good one," the driver added, looking back at me again through the thin horizontal mirror, this time with a smile on his face.

Finally, as she gasped for air between laughter induced coughs, she turned to me and said, "I didn't think that you knew what I was talking about at first. So you *have* seen a horror movie! You look just like him, the guy who got the spear stuck through his body while he was doing his girlfriend on the bed. SPLOTCH!"

"That was *Friday the 13th Part 2*," the driver offered for the sake of clarity.

"Doesn't he look just like him though, with the wavy blond hair and the-always-smiling and everything?"

"Yeah, I can see that," the driver concurs with some hesitation.

I had almost made a critical – and as it turned out – totally unforced error.

My visit home, discounting the unsettling car ride, was pleasant and largely uneventful, save for some high drama of the positive variety with the Sargent Warriors of the Good Fellowship Dartball League.

Above: The 1984-1985 Sargent Warriors Dartball team photo.

The league was established back in 1935, during the Great Depression, and was designed to get young men off the streets, out of the bars and into some good, clean competition. I had begun playing darts when I was only thirteen. I was technically too young to play, but as the team was a player short, my dad penciled my name into the lineup over the vocal protests of the team captain. Three consecutive home runs later I was a regular. After twice leading the twelve-team league in home runs, I had gone off to college.

Now, I was given a chance to play with my team in Playoff hunt. The team yearbook described the results.

...

He hadn't shot a dart in five months. What was he instructed to shoot for?

"I think I'll leave it up to Chris," replied manager Vito Jr.

The 19-year-old with the golden hair had a golden opportunity. He made the most of it. He collected seven hits, two of them home runs, in a three game sweep that was to become that start of the Warriors' pennant drive of 9 consecutive victories.

...

The visit was a much needed return to normalcy: I visited with my family and relatives; went on a few runs with my dad; took some time to reflect on past fun I had growing up with my sisters; and ate pretty much every morsel of food in the house. The opportunity to sleep in my own bed, surrounded by the many comforting artifacts of my childhood, helped in temporarily grounding my emotions.

I also, as briefly and nonchalantly as I could manage, mentioned that I had stopped running for the college, might be failing one of my classes (possibly more), and that, oh yeah, there was probably a ghost in my room.

These statements were met with silence. I always had a fairly odd sense of humor, so I'm not sure if anyone thought that I really meant what I was saying. When I was seven years old, I watched around fifteen minutes of the "movie of the week" (with actor Scott Glenn) about living gargoyles in which one of the horrifying winged and beaked creatures rises up from the foot of a bed in a motel while the protagonist is sleeping. He wakens and tries to fend it off. The scene was much too scary for me and I turned the channel. My preference back then was for something more suitable such as *The Land of the Lost.*

"Run Chaka, Run!"

That night, as I lay in bed, I wondered if a person really would be able to react that quickly to an unexpected threat. As my dad (who boxed as a youth and was a high school track runner) was likely the most able to do so, I decided to try that on him. Walking in silence, I made my way into my parents' bed room, whereupon I found both of them asleep. Considering the situation with great care, I opted to take my place next to my father's side of the bed, rather than down at the foot like the gargoyle had done.

There I stood; my face suspended mere inches above my dad's. I was a little, puffy-haired, wide-eyed gargoyle in pajama bottoms.

I am unable to recall how long I stood there, or the precise moment that my father's eyes flicked open, but I do remember the compelling sight of a fast-moving, clenched, fist stopping just a hair's width from shattering my face. And my dad's great relief when he realized he had not mistakenly killed his only son. My mom yelled a lot, and then I went back to bed.

Gargoyles were over rated.

Now, as she brought me some cleaned clothes, my mother pulled me aside at the base of the hallway steps.

"Are you OK?" she asked me with a concerned look in her eyes.

"Sure. Why?"

"You just seem ... different."

"Running is a Family Affair!" A photograph from *The Daily Mail*, Catskill, N.Y. dated August 9th, 1982. **My father had hopes that all of his children would be athlete-scholars. My mother wanted us to be good people.**

My mother had discontinued her higher education to get married and have a family. I was born not long after. She was as devoted a mother as one could imagine. She would make my lunch for school each day; wash my laundry; buy me clothes; check my homework; and go to every track race and cross country meet that I ran in ... no matter how far away it was, and whether or not she herself was feeling well. My favorite memory of her was reading the book *Goodnight Moon* to me when I was young. Eventually I knew the words so well that I would correct her, without looking at the book, when she would misread a word, or accidentally skip one. In fact, after the first few readings, I didn't look at the book all the way through because I was looking at her instead. I would watch her read to me. The understanding that somehow I 'lucked out' having her as my mother, was something that I understood from a very young age.

I could never lie to her.

"I don't know, Chris. You look the same on the outside," she continued, watching my face for any brief change in expression, "but you are a completely different person on the inside. Are you *sure* you are all right?"

For the first time in my life, I lie to her.

"I'm fine, mom."

"It's easier to dismiss ghosts in the daylight." – Patricia Briggs, *Dragon Bones*

25. The Great Compromise

I wasn't quite sure what to make of the fact that a pile of Jeff's books was sitting on Paul's desk as I walked into C2D1 after the long trip back from my parents' house. Nor was I able to surmise what the reason would be for Paul to be washing his bed sheets at 11PM on a Sunday night before classes, as his mattress was stripped bare.

Placing my duffle bag on the ground, I was surprised to see Jeff carrying a large basket of clothing into the room.

"I suppose you are wondering why I am bringing my things in here," Jeff shares, "Paul and I have decided to switch rooms. Ed said he was fine with it."

My lack of a verbal response – or lack of celebration – must have raised some concern in Jeff as he added, "Are you going to be OK with this?"

In truth, my emotions on the switch were mixed. There was no doubt in my mind that Jeff and I had grown far closer together as friends, than Paul and I were at that time. His demeanor was much more positive and his approach to life much more cerebral and artistic. Moreover, his assistance during this time of crisis seemed essential for me safely meandering through it. In many regards, the move was a decidedly positive one for me.

Still, there was a distinct sadness inside of me. It was the sadness of a valued friendship being lost amongst the floating ashes of the great fire that was the C2D1 Haunting. It was the sadness of not having had an opportunity to speak to Paul before he had opted out of my life. And it was the sadness of the choice being made by those around me, without a single word of warning, because they must have felt that they knew better than me.

My pride was sorely injured.

Before the ghost had intruded, I had been the 'golden boy'. Now, just one month later, I was still unique, but I had now become some type of dangerous curiosity.

Gargoyles sitting atop ancient Parisian structures now seemed more welcoming. And as overrated as I knew them to be, at least they seemed to be able to ward off evil spirits. I seemed only to attract them.

What had once been approving glances of admiration had become cautious scans of derision. Where conversations had once revolved around my fast running, they were now almost solely about what I was running *from*.

Worse still, word was now spreading fast about 'The Ghost Boy of Geneseo'.

In spite of all this, I could not deny the objective reality of the situation: Jeff was willing to move *into* C2D1 at a time when virtually everyone else was moving *away* from all of the terror that was swirling around me. I would not have to be alone.

This was enough for me to accept this change, this great compromise: I would accept being recast as a victim, as long as I would not have to do so alone.

As we settled into the loft, Jeff lamented that the clock was displaying a time well after 1AM.

"So how did all of this happen?" I asked, hoping that I was prepared to hear the answer, "the whole room change thing?"

Jeff explained to me that he and Paul and Ed had discussed the move several times during the weekend. Paul had insisted that he needed to "get out" of the entire Tommy situation and he felt that moving into C2D2 with Ed would be one step closer to his goal. According to Jeff, Paul *was* actually trying to balance his desire to leave with concerns for my safety as the move was discussed. The choice obviously pained him, as Paul never said more than a quick 'hello' or 'how's it going?' before he left ... this time for good ... a short time later.

As of this writing, almost a full thirty years later, I have not seen or spoken with Paul since he quietly exited Erie Hall. In 1994, some nine years later, a personal friend of mine, Alan Lewis, managed to track Paul down. He was living in a suburb of Rochester less than an hour's drive from the college where the horrific events had occurred.

Lewis reported that while Paul was initially reluctant to speak about the events of 1985, that eventually he agreed to do so. In the course of the conversation Paul confirmed having seen the golden orb floating above my head as I slept; the ghost with the tilted head looking at him from the bottom of the loft; and watching me wrestle for possession of my pillows – that were suspended in the air – against some unseen force.

Furthermore, he shared something that shed great light on his abrupt departure. He revealed that the ghost warned him – on two occasions – "clear as day" to "leave Chris alone."

Paul wasn't about to wait for a third warning, thus the lightning fast move out of C2D1 that weekend in March.

. . .

Jeff, for his part, was also keeping secrets.

At my behest, he agreed to switch loft 'sides' that first night. Since he was still in the process of unpacking, I felt that the slight change in location would help to ease my mind and put some distance – no matter how slight – between what had been and what currently was. I would be taking the location that Paul had slept in, and Jeff would be taking up residence in my former spot.

While Jeff would not notify me of this until we were part of an Extreme Haunting Survivors panel (with Bill Bean) at the Sands Hotel in the fall of 2013, his first night in C2D1 was a terrifying one. He revealed for the first time how he had been held down in the bed, by what he described as a 'shadowy figure' kneeling on his chest. It had left him temporarily paralyzed and gasping for air before it eventually let up. Jeff decided not to share this with me then, as it pointed to a distinct possibility that Tommy was back in C2D1. Jeff's thinking on the matter was that such knowledge might very well have shattered my faith (as it appeared that Fr. Charlie's blessing had not been completely effective) and have served to lessen my newfound sense of security in the room. I suppose that he concluded that while it was important to be correct in one's knowledge, it was more important to be kind or helpful with its application.

As well, my mother must have shared her concerns, about my alleged change in personality the previous weekend, with my father. I knew that he was disappointed by my update to begin with.

A few days later a letter came for me in the mail. This was the first time that my father had written to me, separately from the rest of my family members, so I knew that it must be important.

Printed out on old-fashioned lined computer paper, the letter was cautionary in its approach, reminding me of the importance of "stability."

```
                                                          A PERSON
 ENTERING A FIELD THAT MIGHT DEAL WITH EMOTIONALLY DISTURBED
 INDIVIDUALS MUST BE A PARAGON OF STABILITY. YOU SHOULD BE THE
 PERSON THAT OTHERS SEEK INFORMATION FROM. WHATEVER YOU MIGHT
 BELIEVE OTHERS WILL DEAL WITH YOUR INFORMATION IN A SKEPTICAL
 WAY UNLESS THEY ** FEEL  SEE  TOUCH  ** THOSE THINGS YOU DO.
 IF THEY DO NOT, YOU AVAIL YOURSELF TO CRITICISM OF STABILTY .
 NOW ON THE OTHER HAND A BRIEF NOTE ON PHILOSOPHY--TO SEEK IS
 TO FIND. TO DENY IS TO ADMIT THAT THERE MAY BE. THUS : SEEK
 AND YE SHALL FIND THOSE THINGS THAT DO NOT EXIST, FOR YOU
 SHALL CREATE THEM IN SPIRIT OR FORM, IN REAL OR IN MIND; AND
 IF IT IS ALIVE AND EXISTING IN MIND, THEREFORE IT WILL BE REAL
 FOR YOU, EVEN IF NOT FOR ANYONE ELSE. BELIEF THEREFORE IS THE
 KEY.
```

```
 I AM ALIVE NOW IN YOUR MIND AS YOU READ THIS. BUT DO YOU KNOW
 OTHER THAN FAITH OR BELIEF? AND IF YOU READ THIS 50 YEARS FROM
 NOW WHEN I AM DEAD WILL I EXIST ANY MORE OR LESS THAN THE WAY
 I EXIST IN YOUR MIND NOW? DO NOT BELIEVE AND I DO NOT
 EXIST,BELIEVE AND I DO.
```

Above: A sampling of the letter that my father sent to me in late March. My initial reaction to the letter was mixed. I was proud that he cared for me and embarrassed that he felt I might be having some type of breakdown.

I shared the letter with Jeff when I had the chance, and he felt that it was a very positive gesture. In his estimation, most parents simply did not bother themselves with issues as sensitive or complicated as this, and if they did it was usually just to issue a quick condemnation or rebuke.

Fair enough.

Doing my best not to irritate the thin scabs on my back, I continued wearing oversized shirts during this time period. This no doubt fueled the flames of gossip in and around Erie Hall that I had become 'skeleton thin' (no pun intended). In actuality, I *had* lost between 12 and 15 pounds over the last few weeks, but the irony was that my efforts to lessen the physical discomfort caused by the haunting, only served to make them more noticeable to those around me.

Finally, in late March – around the time of my twentieth birthday – I made *the* frantic call home to my father.

Since the priest's blessing, Tommy had been getting alarmingly bold. He was now appearing in broad daylight, and at locations *outside* of Erie Hall. I saw his head protruding out of a wall of reference books at the college library where, not surprisingly, a few seconds later a half-filled shelf of books fell to the ground near my feet. It was time to leave.

I next caught a glimpse of him through the shower's mist at the college athletic center, where I went with increased regularity following the attack in the dorm bathroom.

He was observing again, watching me wash inside the steamy room, from the doorframe that connected the locker room to the showers. The weight of his stare felt oppressive, almost controlling.

As before, I felt as though he was longing for me; longing to be in control of my legs, my lungs, and my life. I shot occasional glances his way, just to let him know that I was aware of his presence but that I was not willing to adjust my actions because of it. Here again I noted that he looked like a young Caucasian male. Whether it was me adjusting to his presence or him allowing me to see him with greater accuracy, I could plainly see that he looked to be about my age, just a few inches taller, with a wider frame, but not as athletically built. The hair on his head looked to be a medium brown, he was clean-shaven and actually not (without all of the wounds and gauges) unattractive.

But then the eyes; how they stared with a desperation that I had never seen before. And the breathing, the rhythmic pained breathing that I could faintly hear over the spraying shower water.

He is waiting.

Only the knowledge that the locker room was fairly busy kept me from panicking. Chillingly, as I was in the process of getting dressed

afterwards, I was approached by an acne-faced student (with a rather concerned expression) who asked me if I knew who had been standing by the showers while I was in there. Examining his face to make fully sure that it had not been him watching me in the shower, I shook my head and told him that I hadn't seen anyone.

"Well, if they come back, I'm calling the campus police," he said tightly re-securing the bath towel around his waist.

A part of me wanted to stop him, right there, and tell him what I had been experiencing since that fateful day in February.

To find out – since he had actually *seen* Tommy as I had – if we had any other similarities aside from being two athletes who had somehow found our way to this tormented place; a place that the local Native Americans had called 'Chenussio'.

I chose to say nothing.

The ghost was also making his presence known across Erie Hall, and in dramatic fashion.

When Beth did not show up for a set appointment she had made with Jeff and I, we found her lying on the floor of her room in a state of panic.

As I helped her up, she claimed that she had heard the ghost calling my name, "Chrissss," and that she had yelled for it to stop. It would not. Before she was able to run for help, she apparently had tried to hit it, and then she collapsed on the floor where we had found her an unknown duration of time later.

Judy, her roommate, told us later that night that she had been feeling abnormally cold breezes in the room and that she felt as though she was being "watched" in the bathroom when no one was there. She mentioned that she planned to talk to her pastor about it when she returned home.

Early on the in the prior semester, when my life was still as golden as the autumn sugar maple leaves, I read an article in the university newspaper (October 5, 1984) by a student named Craig Norris. It detailed the construction of the college's first all-weather running track. As an avid and competitive runner the piece's subject matter naturally drew my interest. While the cost of $318,000, paid via the State University Construction Fund, seemed a bit steep, Norris pointed out that the new track would benefit both the college's varsity runners (we currently had to train at the local high school's cinder track) in any weather conditions and casual joggers who wished to run on their own, and could use it at any hour of the day. In this way, Norris wrote: Many people feel embarrassed or stupid running around the campus by themselves in front of their peers. The new track will give these shy people an alternative to waking at 4 a.m.

When I first read the article, I wondered why someone might be embarrassed by the healthy action of running. What could possibly be so disconcerting about having one's actions known?

The ghost had since taught me otherwise.

Being forced against one's will to face the scrutiny of others, whether it is due to one's physical conditioning, financial status or mental state can be a devastating experience.

Now, five months later, Craig Norris (who had lived in C2D2 of Erie Hall the year prior) approaches me as I quickly attempted to enter my dorm room and mentions to me that his roommate, Curt, was claiming that he was hearing voices in his head. That he had 'heard' my name in his thoughts.

Craig wonders if I have any thoughts – or advice – on the matter.

Not sure as to how to effectively deal with my own situation, I politely decline any involvement. It is quite honestly a simple reaction to my own fear of not being able to meet the expectations of others. What help can I possibly be to his roommate, when the fact stands that I cannot effectively - in spite of a host of efforts - aid myself? Why should I risk further failure, a further erosion of my faculties? I have quickly been transformed into that shy student who sneaks off to run at 4 a.m. so as not to be seen by others that Craig had so aptly described in his article.

It can be argued that my inactivity led to disastrous consequence.

I happened to see Curt, on one occasion, shortly after Craig had interceded on his behalf. I had been gazing out of the window of the room that had become my voluntary prison, enviously watching those who had been blessed by dull normalcy. The dull normalcy that allowed them to smile effortlessly, to not worry about surviving each and every day, and to avoid wracking their brains with the necessity of questioning every sound and movement that whirled around them.

Curt exited the building.

As he passed beneath my second floor perch of isolation, his steps seemed heavy, his shoulders hunched forward, he wore a look of misery. I intently followed his form as he solemnly made his way down the walking path towards the college union. I felt a profound sadness in my chest as he exited my line of sight. Perhaps it was born from a feeling of guilt. Or maybe it was that I sensed, somehow, that I would never help him.

That choice was forever taken from me when he chose to end his own life.

...

It seemed to me, that in light of the vicious attack that I had recently suffered, the ghost's increased range of appearances and the recent distress of others in the dorm, that the blessing – while largely effective in its original purpose – had only made things worse ... for everyone.

It was time to call home.

"Dad," I breathed nervously into the pay phone's receiver, "I'm in trouble."

The phone call was an awkward one. My father had been a science teacher before he became a building principal, and while possessing a fine sense of humor and being a creative-minded problem solver, he was an empiricist at heart. He had invested a lot of time and a lot of money in me growing up, and he did not particularly enjoy the possibility that I might be frittering away my vast potential with nonsensical stories about a ghost. I could hear it in his voice.

Finally, after several minutes we found that we were at loggerheads, so my father said: "Fine. I want you and Jeff to go find the biggest, meanest, strong-looking guys you can. You bring them into your room. If *they* see anything, I'll come up there."

Deal!

Outside the common area window Jeff and I could see a group of about five or six guys, some of whom we recognized from Erie Hall, playing a makeshift game of soccer where grass normally grew.

It was now a large swamp of mud from the combination of the melting winter snow and their activity.

I explained to a slightly incredulous Jeff what my father had requested, and then we set out to collect what were the unknowing subjects of our grand experiment. So sure was I in the existence of the ghost, and in its desire to interact with me – just to be near me – that there wasn't the slightest hint of doubt in my mind that this normally questionable test would work.

Four of them, two covered with mud, and all of them six feet in height or taller, agreed to follow us back: Luke and Brian from C2D3, Don from across the hall, and someone who Jeff described as 'a rugby type'. All we said to them was: "This is going to sound very strange, but we want to show something absolutely amazing in our room."

Whether they assumed there would be a keg filled with beer, a stolen final exam answer key, or some hot chicks lying half-dressed on my bed, it didn't matter to me. All I cared about was what their reaction would be when the *real* surprise showed up.

They were immediately annoyed when we reached the doorway of C2D1. Whatever it was that they had expected to see, was not there.

"What's going on?" asked Don, who had a cloth bandana tied around his spikey-haired head, asked. He and his friend were obviously 'playing it tough'.

"Just wait one minute, you'll see."

There was still no doubt in my mind.

Jeff was maintaining the appearance of outward composure as well, save the nervous shaking of one of his legs. I was pretty sure that he was becoming increasingly concerned about what would become of our belongings – and us – if the four unwitting test subjects happened to grow angry.

"Dude, why did you bring us all here?" the rugby player in the light blue tie-died shirt asked, with more than a hint of irritation in his voice. Brian and Luke looked at each other, they had no clue what was going on either. They decided that it was time for them to go.

As the four were standing up to leave, I felt the temperature in the room chill at a rapid rate. I made strong and direct eye contact with Jeff and mouthed, "It's here."

Jeff nodded that he understood.

Brian, making a face similar to one that he might have made if he had just discovered that he had tracked dog poop on a brand new carpet, turned to me with and asked:

"What's *grabbing* me? Something is on my *leg*!"

The others are now caught between the choice of finding the cause of his sudden case of delirium, or giving in to their fear that something 'wrong' is occurring.

They chose door number two. Don, who turned left, and Luke who headed to the right, were the first to bolt out of the room.

Brian by then was becoming red-faced and frazzled

"What *is* this?" he implored.

"The ghost" I answered, deciding that there was no longer any point in concealing the truth with the level of activity as high as it was.

The 'rugby guy', who seemed to be friends with Don, attempted to leave the room. As he did so, Brian seemed to break free of the thing. But when the 'rugby guy' took a few steps towards the door, he then stopped and started shaking *his* arms and legs as though he had become caught in a large spider's web.

"F***! This is too freaky!" He yelled, as he threw his large arms into the air over his head and ran out of the quad.

That's seven, I sighed.

Brian walked slowly back to C2D3, shot us both a look of extreme displeasure as he rubbed his left thigh, and slammed the door behind him.

I thought to run up to him and say, "You want to see something really scary?" and then drop my shorts like he had weeks earlier, but I didn't think that either one of us could be as scary as the ghost.

It was tempting though.

None of them ever asked us another question, ever made a snide comment, or even spoke to either of us again. They chose to avoid us ... and the ghost that had grabbed them.

Our mission thus accomplished, I yelled out into C2D1, "You need to go away now! Do you hear me?"

"How did you know that he would show up," Jeff asked as he jotted down details about the most recent incident.

"He has been following me around," I replied, making sure I didn't see him so that I could finish the next part of my statement, "he is a lot like an abusive boyfriend or girlfriend. He is physically aggressive to the person that he views as his property, but protective about them at the same time. As those guys grew angrier, the ghost's fear that they would 'get to me' before he did forced him to react."

Jeff nodded his head in approval. This further underscored his belief that the ghost could be talked to, reasoned with, perhaps even ... made public.

I still wasn't so sure about that.

The temporary manipulation of a potentially dangerous soul was one thing, trusting it not to attack again, was something completely different. It was a risk that I was not willing to take.

Even more disconcerting was that in my zeal to win my father's respect ... and help ... I had permitted Tommy to re-enter C2D1.

There was no formal invitation back into room, as I wanted to keep my promise to Fr. Charlie, but there was a tacit acceptance given. This is why I shouted for the ghost to 'go away', as a reminder that he shouldn't be there in violation of the blessing. It was all just a house of cards that I was building on, and I knew it, but it was better than having nothing at all.

With Jeff standing beside me for moral support, I made the call to my father. I shared what had happened. There was silence on his end for about ten seconds.

"I'm on my way."

He arrived that night, completing the five hour car ride in almost exactly four hours. He carried with him a baseball bat; a crucifix with a vial of holy water imbedded in its back; and a handgun. He wasn't there to fool around.

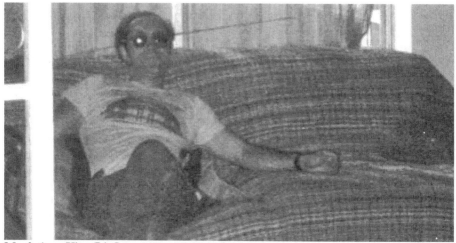

My father, Vito Di Cesare Jr., relaxes on the old brown couch in room C2D1 in the fall of 1984. Six months later, he would be keeping a tense vigil over me.

Whoever had been bothering me, whatever kind of intimidation or hoax was transpiring, he was going to put a stop to it tonight.

Jeff was beside himself with anguish as his parents had pulled up in their bulky (and to Jeff ... "embarrassing") Dodge Caravan to take him home for the evening.

"Sac-re-mént!" he exclaimed, "It would have to be now!"

I hadn't slept for more than three or four hours at a time since the moment that I noticed the figure standing over my right shoulder as I ate the Hot Tamales. So, after we had some dinner uptown at my favorite eatery on the planet, Aunt Cookie's Sub Shop, my dad told me to get some sleep.

Armed and ready, he placed himself at the foot of the loft, scouting as I would have imagined General Anthony Wayne did before the battle against the British at Stony Point in July of 1779.

I must have slept through the entire battle.

In the morning, I awoke to find my father sitting in the same location he was in when I fell asleep some eight hours prior. He looked exhausted, but gave me a slight smile when he saw me looking over at him.

"Are you OK?" I asked him.

"I'm fine. Why don't we go for a run before I head back?"

There has been much written about the loneliness of the long distance runner, but that was never the case for me. Running – even during the harshest of practices and in the hardest fought races – was still largely a social event for me. If I wasn't running with my teammates I would run with friends like Gene Piaquadio Jr. while in high school, and Paul and Jeff during my college years.

But my favorite runs were the ones with my father. He had been training me since I was eleven years old, and even though he had long ago put away the stick, he was still the primary reason that I ran ... I wanted to make him proud of me.

I recall with great clarity, and welcome cheerfulness, a race that my dad and I had run in the summer of '84.

It was appropriately called "The Miracle Mile", a mile-long footrace down a main thoroughfare in Poughkeepsie, New York. As a distance runner and one who preferred to run negative splits (the second half of the race faster than the first) I was accustomed to letting other runners take the early lead. But in a 'short' race like the mile, losing several seconds at the start could cost you a chance to win.

My dad, seeing that I (and Gene Jr.) had lined up in the second row, barked out: "Chris! Gene! Get in front of them!"

He then specifically pointed to a group of four runners who were stretching carefully at the starting line.

"They're too slow!" he announced above the pre-race clamor.

Gene and I turned to each other, and he whispered, "I think your dad's going a bit crazy. I don't want a fight to start."

"Chris! Gene! Get up here with me. Come on!"

Sheepishly, we both funneled past the runners who were now known to the gathered throng as the 'slow' ones, and took our place in the front row. I worried that the man with the mad mustache might be lurking nearby, but couldn't help but be amused by my father's boldness.

I didn't know the half of it!

The starting gun sent the large pack of runners sprinting down the smooth, cool, morning-lit asphalt. I jostled my way, with Gene at my right shoulder, into the lead pack of five high school runners. It was as good a place as any to analyze who the competition would be without being drawn out at too quick a pace to maintain.

"Who is that guy out in front?" asked a laboring, black-haired runner who was proudly wearing his school colors. His tan, thin legs were turning over at a pace that caused his step to stutter every few strides.

He wouldn't be able to race at the current pace much longer.

Neither would his friend, who with his red hair and freckled skin was sure to suffer in the summer heat once the shadows from the buildings no longer protected us. He was already drenched in sweat as we hit the quarter mile mark in 72 seconds, now a good ten yards behind the leader. It was going to take a sub-5 minute mile to win.

"Look at that guy!" The freckled runner remarked with an incredulous tone as he wiped his brow of sweat.

I glanced up ahead.

It was my forty-one-year-old father! His legs were ferociously pushing against the hard surface of the road, torso straight, and arms pumping like mad.

"Does anyone know who that is?" asked the dark-haired runner, who seemed so psyched out by the prospect of being outsprinted by an old man that he began to shake his head back and forth.

"I have no clue," I offered weakly.

Gene pulled up a bit closer to me and, with a worried tone, asked me "What on earth is he doing out there by himself?"

"Winning" I said with a stone face as I struggled to take additional amounts of dry summer air into my expanded lungs.

As proud as I was that my father was embarrassing a group of runners a full generation younger than him, there was no way I would live down my pops beating me after I had represented New York at the National AAU Junior Cross Country Championships in Kansas less than eighteen months before, right?

I threw in a surge using my powerful thighs, churning like the pistons of a steam locomotive.

Steady.

Only Gene was able to stay with me as I began to close the gap on first place. Each stride brought me a little closer to the ageless wonder. 2:21 was his time as he passed the half-mile marker.

Four seconds later, an eternity in a short race, Gene and I moved through the same spot. We were now on target to run a 4:50 mile. But still not fast enough to catch my dad the way he was now running.

I had a choice to make: work still harder and go for the victory, or simply maintain and let my father make history. Could you imagine that? At Labor Day picnics or games of darts for decades, my father could regale the gathered with the tale of how he beat all the young horses that fateful summer day in the 1980's?

It would be the stuff of legend.

Of course, if that did happen, then for the rest of my natural life I would be forced to answer questions about how a forty-year-old beat me. Was I out of shape? Did I run foolishly? Did I lack the natural talent, or the intestinal fortitude to win the race? If I ever admitted, in a moment of pride or weakness that I had let him win, it would destroy the mystique of the wondrous accomplishment.

No. It was best that I just challenged the old man, 'mano-a-mano', and let the chips fall where they may. No games.

I continued to push the pace. A quick glance over my shoulder revealed that aside from my friend none of the lead pack was able to go with us. The black haired runner, wearing his school colors, was now running in fourth place a good ten seconds back.

Gene looked back as well, and seeing as there were now just three runners with a chance to win, he decided that it might as well be him.

He pushed ahead of me and now led the charge to catch my dad. I preferred it that way. It was a much less personal issue for me now, as I was no longer trying to pass my father, I was only trying to stay with Gene.

At the ¾ mile mark Gene managed to pull even with my dad, as I hung off his left shoulder one step back. I think my father sensed at that point that he might have pushed the pace too quickly and too early, but it didn't stop me from being proud of the man. No one else's father that I knew could do what he was currently doing.

He said nothing as we both moved ahead, focused instead now on a strong finish, trying to hold his now-aching body together enough to finish third, ahead of the high school runners that he really had no business beating.

Gene looked about as Italian as one could look: olive skin; long, dark hair; a teenage mustache, a strong nose and deep brown eyes. In contrast, I looked like I had just stepped off a plane from Norway or Sweden. Just throw some wooden clogs on me and put me to work in a windmill. We were great friends, and our running style and strategy were often similar. But we both knew from our countless training runs that at that time I was the stronger and more experienced racer. If I wanted it, the race was mine.

I wanted it.

"Break five," he breathed when he saw me start to increase my turnover and my stride length.

"I'll try," I answered.

I was a notoriously bad hot weather runner, and I could already feel the sunburned skin on my shoulders, ears tops and neck. And in the growing heat I knew that being a stronger runner or more experienced runner meant diddlysquat if I ended up passing out on the curb from heat stroke.

Instinctively, I moved to the far right corner of the street (even though it meant running a few additional steps) to take advantage of the shade provided by the buildings that still blocked some of the late morning Sun's rays.

That did the trick.

My body instantly cooled, I was able to push myself across the finish line with a solid, but not fast, time of 4:47. But it wasn't bad considering the 85°temperature.

Gene, looking drained but satisfied, crossed the line in second place, also under five minutes, in 4:57 with my dad chasing him across the finish line with an amazing age-considered time of 5:01. The gaggle of astonished teenagers was still yards behind.

Did I mention he was forty-one years old?

After the race I apologized to my dad for beating him, and he replied that he would expect nothing less from me.

We were equally proud that day.

   ...

Now, as we ran down the college walkways, up onto the shop-laden Main Street, and then down around a portion of the cross country course, very little was said. When two athletes are 'in sync' there is not much that *needs* to be said. We had trained together well over three thousand times, in the driving rain, under the scorching sun, and through the frost of winter.

This was something sacred.

The morning passed far too quickly, and as he was packing his duffle bag and retrieving his car keys he composed himself, looked at me, and said: "You know that you can always turn to me. You can turn to your mother. If you need help, just call."

And then came the coup de grâce: "And, Chris ... move out of this room!"

key —
I'll be home around 2 pm. I'll be down soon

Dr. Cader   Rm. 4
Wed. 5-6
Thu. 11-12

"I shall not commit the fashionable stupidity of regarding everything I cannot explain as a fraud."— Psychiatrist Dr. Carl Jung (1919 address to the Society for Psychical Research in England)

26. The Good Doctor

For more than a quarter century my father did not share with me what he had witnessed that night. It wasn't until 2012, when he was asked to share his experience for the television show that *SyFy* was planning to make about the haunting, that he finally decided he would share his recollections. He felt that it was important, in spite of his natural level of discomfort with the topic, to back up his son.

Like the rest of the world, on Wednesday, June 27th, I anxiously watched the television to see what he was willing to say about that night in Geneseo. The Jarrett Creative Group had gone through great pains to ensure that he, Jeff, Beth, Craig, and I recorded our testimony at separate times. They wanted no collusion. In fact, many of us had not talked to each other since the days of the haunting, so it wasn't all that difficult.

My father revealed that there was a 'presence' that emanated from my closet (check) and that it was so disturbing (check) that he wasn't even sure he *wanted* to know what it was (check)!

All those years later, he was still able to summarize what were key components of the haunting in room C2D1, and with just that one night of exposure to it.

My dad took a lot of heat after the show: "How could he just leave his son there like that?" "Why didn't he tell his son what he saw?" "Why would he shoot his gun in the dorm room?"

I called him right after the show aired (missing some of the party being thrown at a local Italian restaurant for me). It was important that I thank him for his bravery and, finally, ask him why he had refused to talk about the events for so long.

"I thought about that night from time to time," he said, "but what was I going to do? I couldn't shoot it, or fight it. I realized, like I said for the TV people, that the answer had to come from inside you. I believed that you had what it took to endure the situation, even to come out on top, a better person because of it. Still, you were my son, I worried about you. That's why I suggested that, if you could, you should change your room."

Additionally, he pointed out that he never fired his gun that night.

...

So what *was* I going to do about the ghost? If the answer was supposed to come from me, as my father believed as he drove back home yesterday, I certainly didn't know what it was yet.

...

10:45PM, Erie Hall room B2B2 – Linda is lying across her bed near her window, which is closed. She is having difficulty moving her legs, claiming that the ghost is holding her down and "sitting on" her. Only moments earlier she sent for Jeff and me to assist her in getting Tommy out of her room.

I glance about the room which is swirling with a light gray mist that is at its most dense near Linda.

Approaching Linda, my arms outstretched in the manner that had worked before, I ask her – as she is now close to tears – if I can put my hands near her.

She nods her head in the affirmative.

Jeff raises his camera and takes a photograph as I approach her. I am conflicted by his decision to snap the photo. While I recognize its definitive scientific, psychological and paranormal research value, I am concerned it was taken without her consent. This is a very personal moment.

I peer over my left shoulder, "Jeff ... did you want to ...?"

Jeff lifts his head from behind his camera, a slight look of confusion etched across his intelligent face.

Then he understands.

"Oh. Linda, you wouldn't mind if I take a few pictures ... would you?"

"No," she offers with a nervous laugh, "if you guys can get *rid* of this thing, you can do whatever you want."

In spite of the memory of my own recent attack, I begin to talk to Tommy. I ask him to leave. In my head (and I am still unsure as to exactly how I can hear him) he refuses.

It is 10:52PM.

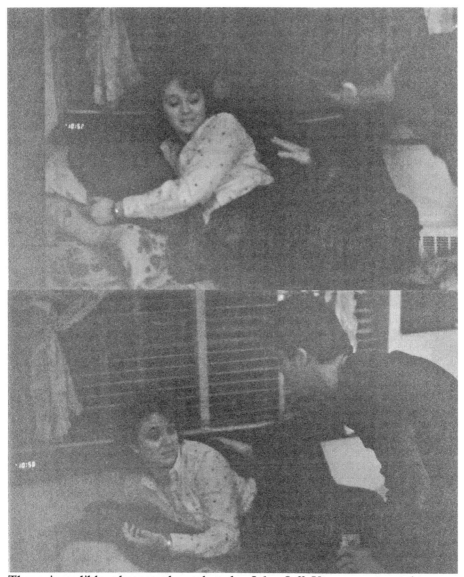

These incredible photographs, taken by John Jeff Ungar, capture the raw emotion that an extreme haunting can have on its victims and offer a real-time glimpse into the C2D1 haunting as it was occurring.

Six minutes later, at 10:58, the misty energy is now departing.

I make a verbal promise to the ghost that soon – not now, but soon – I will try to help him.

I do this even though I suspect that helping him might mean hurting me. But I think I have convinced him that he wants me, not Linda, and that was my primary goal. He wasn't going to hurt my friends; I am not going to *let* him.

I was the 'Ghost Boy of Geneseo'.

...

Still, an exact plan eluded me, and I did not know where to find one.

Sitting up in the loft later that night, Jeff revisits the idea of meeting with the parapsychologist, Dr. Casler. While he warns me that the result might simply be a theoretical discussion and not the resolution to the haunting I am so desperately seeking, I understand that it will be worth our time. Plus, I don't want to bother the priest again; he has already done his part.

The meeting was set up by Beth, who was visually pleased by the fact that we were finally acting on what had initially been her idea. We had missed the first meeting that she set up, several weeks prior, as I didn't want Fr. Charlie to think that we were hedging our bets with him.

Now there is nothing to lose.

...

We had our sit down meeting with Dr. Lawrence Casler in his office on the college campus. I was a little embarrassed – and much honored – that a busy man such as he was, remembered that we had missed our first appointment with him. He admitted that he wasn't sure if the initial phone call (made by Beth) had been a hoax, or if maybe we were in some kind of trouble when we did not show, and he was quite pleased to see us in the flesh.

Dr. Casler impressed me as a man of great intelligence right away. His mannerisms, his eye contact, his rate of speech, his verbiage ... all bespoke a man who took his work, his studies, and his theories very seriously.

He in turn was very fascinated by us. A slight smile crossed his thin lips, he marveled at how he had traveled all over the country looking for cases such as ours, and here we were, right at his very doorstep!

I shot a quick glance back at Beth, who was sitting behind us in a chair by the wall. Her hands were folded and she was wearing a proud smirk. She had done it ... she had brought together teacher and students, helped her friends, and (hopefully) done everybody some good in setting this meeting up.

As Dr. Casler, captivated by the level of detail in the journal notes, turned page after page, I noticed that Jeff was also quite enthused by this informal summit. Ever a creature of ideas, this is what *he* needed, this was *his* validation. That a learned man of science, a published author, a noted scholar was finding value in his efforts was gratifying for him beyond measure. The level of satisfaction that I took from winning a foot race was mirrored now in him, at that moment. I was happy for him. I was happy for Beth. I was happy for both of them.

Looking down at my sneakers, I lifted them to make sure that I had tracked no mud into his office. A soft chuckle – which I quickly disguised by clearing my throat – inadvertently left my mouth as I thought to myself: *Wow, trying to cover up your tracks already are you Chris?*

I didn't belong here.

Dr. Casler asked Jeff what he wished to be called.

Jeff was unsure of what he was referring to, and repeated back, "What do I wish to be *called*? Do you mean, what is my name?"

I could see that Jeff was startled over the prospect that he had made such a minimal personal impression on the psychology professor, especially in light of the fact that he had just pored over the detailed pages of more than months' worth of his efforts.

I smiled.

I understood immediately what Dr. Casler was asking, and why Jeff was responding in the way that he was. That is only because I had no vested interest in winning this learned man's approval. With what had transpired, I already knew that I won't *have* to. That is what alarmed me.

I wanted to leave.

"For my papers, my archives, how would you like me to record you? What name would you like me to use?"

"Jeff … Jeff Ungar is … fine, yes … that's good." Jeff stated in an absolutely uncertain tone. I had never seen him this nervous before, not even when an undead creature was assaulting his friends or when he was working through a 10-page paper the night before it was due. I tried not to smile too much.

As Dr. Casler began to jot down some notes of his own, Jeff abruptly leaned forward in his chair, and offered: "You know what? I've reconsidered. I would prefer to be called 'John Jeff Ungar'. Is it too late to change that for the record?"

"It is absolutely *not* too late," Casler replied, now wearing a largely unnoticed smile like my own.

Jeff sat back into the chair and emitted a genuine sigh of relief. He felt good about his choice. Every photographer worth their salt was careful to list the camera that they had used, the location the image was captured, and the film type when preserving or displaying their work. If Jeff was now to become the official 'chronicler' of this haunting it was important to him that he be – listed correctly … and from the start: John Jeff Ungar.

It was going to take me a long time to get used to that.

Jeff had called it correctly, the night before, when he cautioned me not to expect any concrete answers in regards to ending the haunting. In fact, much like Jeff himself, Dr. Casler was now advocating that we acquire additional forms of evidence ... perhaps a tape recording of the ghost's voice.

Jeff smiled, nodded his head and allowed himself a quick, "Yes!"

I could feel my hands start to tremble from a combination of anger and fear. To prevent my reaction from being noticed, I place my hands under my thighs, and sit on them. It was still damp enough outside that I could pretend that they were cold, if anyone asked.

Understanding, going in, that Dr. Casler would not be able to directly assist us in bringing the haunting to a close was acceptable to me. Nevertheless, my assumption was that we would at least ascertain ways in which to lessen the haunting's effect. It seemed to me that redirecting our approach to 'evidence gathering' only risked further perpetuating the whole horrid ordeal.

When he noticed my body posture, Jeff visibly tempered his enthusiasm.

Good.

Beth reminded Dr. Casler that his next class was scheduled to start, so we began to close the meeting. He instructed Jeff and me that I should be the one to take the lead in these efforts.

"Chris, you appear to be the focus of the entity's attention."

I said nothing, but I did acknowledge his statement with an affirmative nod.

"Let's go," I whisper to Jeff, "I want to leave this place, *now!*"

Jeff finds himself in the unkind position of having to decide between inquiring what was currently bothering his good friend, and bidding a proper adieu to Dr. Lawrence Casler, Ph. D. He chose the latter of the options. I was quite thankful, as I figured it would make my escape a quicker one.

That still didn't stop Dr. Casler, his intelligent eyes scanning me from behind his shining glasses, from calling out: "Oh, and Chris, I'd like you to come back and talk with me. Just you; when you get the chance."

I *knew* it.

. . .

Less than ten minutes into the meeting with Dr. Casler, I knew that his primary interest wasn't necessarily in the ghost at all. It was in me.

When Jeff presented the photograph of the ghost to him, he barely considered it. Inspecting it for no more than five seconds, he placed it to the side of his desk in front of him. I am not even sure if he saw the skeletal image in the background. Instead, he asked: "What made you two decide to take this photograph when you did?"

He wasn't looking for static moments, or photographs for that matter, he was looking for causality, and for *meaning*.

What did it mean that this young boy was seeing a ghost? Under what conditions did it manifest? How had the event affected their belief systems? What did it mean that many other college students were now experiencing this purported phenomenon? What was going on in the minds of these young students, who were clearly horrified by, and completely invested in, the ordeal?

But, perhaps most importantly, how was it that this ordinary boy – with no outward inclination towards it – was able to manifest all of this? Had he been successful in unlocking some portion of the human mind; perhaps he had been able to pierce, to see beyond, some long taboo veil?

Jeff, Beth, Linda, and I gathered in room B2B2 for the experiment. My concerns over the psychologist's true intent aside, I had made a promise to the ghost – who by now everyone was calling Tommy – and I was intent on trying to keep it. What might occur if I broke my word was not something that I cared to consider.

As Tommy had most recently manifested in Linda's room, all involved felt it was the most logical place to start.

Jeff had procured the Sears Roebuck SR2100 tape recorder, the one that Tommy had turned on twice, from my desk drawer. A great fear ran through me: *Had the ghost planned this all along? Is this, what had taken us almost two months to decide, what he had wanted from the start? Had we played ourselves into his hands?* If so, then we would be no match for him when the 'end' of all this occurred. I, Chris, was fearful for all of us. But the 'Ghost Boy of Geneseo' couldn't afford to be.

The significance of what we young college students were about to do cannot be understated. Just twenty-five years removed from the work of Sir Friedrich Jorgensen, regarded by some as the 'father' of the EVP (Electronic Voice Phenomena) we were going to try to speak with the dead. We had no hand held active recording devices, no infrared motion sensors, and no EMF meters. There was nothing for us to depend upon but our own instincts, a 35mm camera, a tape recorder and a shared desire for understanding …and survival.

I glanced about the room hoping beyond all hope that I wouldn't see him smiling down at me as if to say, "I win."

Mercifully, there was no sign of him.

Jeff, in what to this day may very well be the most focused intellectual effort I have ever witnessed, moved from location to location locking windows, securing drawers, measuring distances, gauging temperatures. There was an understanding that he was now working under: he had seen enough to know that Tommy would come when I called him; now it was up to *him* to ensure that it was recorded properly. The more controlled the environment, the more valid the results would be.

Dr. Casler had lent his academic and professional credibility to Jeff's preference to gather more data, and he was now an inspired man on a mission. Additionally, our social support network had grown with the help that we were now receiving from Beth and Linda (and somewhat from Ed).

I was very well aware that Jeff had both logic and reason on his side. Additional data, photographs, eye witness accounts, and voice recordings were all viable means on the road to understanding what exactly we were dealing with at Geneseo.

Moreover, it could potentially lead to breakthroughs in society's understanding of the paranormal as a whole. Imagine being able to talk to the spirit of a dead relative; being able to ask them questions about what the 'Other Side' was like; or even globally-transforming topics such as: what value could be placed in the world's great religions? What about self-determination?

Jeff, Dr. Casler, and Beth ... all of them ... they were absolutely right. But I had the most powerful motivating force ever to grace mankind with its presence driving my thoughts: Fear.

I didn't want to risk having my eyes gouged out, my genitals sliced half off, my fingernails pulled out, and my abdomen sliced open ... because that is exactly what I thought might happen if I failed in what they wanted me to do: deal with a demon who seemed much smarter than I was.

I already had felt his wrath (my back was still not close to healed) and his intentional transformation on that tree just one week prior was ample warning to me that this haunting was a lot larger than we understood it to be.

We all cheer when tyrants fall, but rarely are we the ones who are tasked with the responsibility of making it occur. The brave men and women of the armed services are honorable enough to perform the risky – potentially deadly – work that the public lauds from their recliners as they watch their sports, soap operas, and music concerts, all the while asking what else can the government do to make life better for them.

Don't get me wrong, I didn't mind taking another hit for so noble a cause, it's just that in this case, I wasn't even sure I knew how to fight the battle.

The tape recorder is ready. I begin ...

"Hello Tommy. I kept my promise ... I'm here. I'm trying to help you. If you'd like to say anything, I'm leaving this box on, right here, for approximately 15 minutes. All you have to do is speak; it will pick up your voice. At a later time, I can hear you on the tape, and hear what you said. In this way I can speak to you. I'll come back tomorrow, around the same time. If you have left any questions for me, I'll answer them. As I said [deep breath] I'm trying to help. In order to help, I must know what your purpose is and why you are here ... the remaining time is yours, Tommy. Go to it."

I took care to be respectful.

With the tape recorder still recording, we all leave the room. Jeff turned out the lights, and locked the lone door to B2B2 behind us.

He pulled up a chair collected from one of the common room's tables, wedged it under the door knob, and then sat down in front of it. He hands me the key. No human being is getting in, and no human being is getting out.

That shouldn't pose a problem for Tommy.

"Ghost on Tape" by artist Kerry Lyon (2014)

Beth and Linda accompanied me back to C2D1, I was not enjoying the direction that things were heading, and they obviously saw that I was suffering. I understood that leaving with them did pose a certain 'risk'. Both of them had previously expressed an interest in possibly dating, in fact, one of them even devised code names for our written communication in case they were intercepted by her then boyfriend. I was 'Steven'.

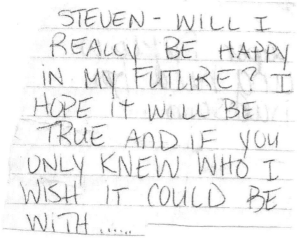

Both young women were highly intelligent, humorous, attractive, and stacked with positive qualities. Most of the guys in the suite would have jumped at the chance to date either one of them. Under more normal circumstances, even with my extreme dedication to my running, I might have dated them as well. But the cold, hard truth was that I just wasn't ready for a relationship at that time. My faith was being sorely challenged, my academics were suffering to the point where I had gone from the dean's list to almost failing, and my body was still trying to recover from the month-old marks that now ran down my back. For some, it might have been the perfect solution: finding a moment of love amongst a crisis, a veritable wartime love story. For me the thought of adding the risk of a failed relationship was too potentially destructive. Even though I had turned twenty years of age only two weeks before, and was well known for gallivanting around the dorm in my birthday suit (perhaps to the point of obnoxiousness) I had yet to be with a woman.

Almost no one knew that.

When I eventually confessed that to Paul, late in the fall semester, he seemed in near shock. To him my situation was analogous to purchasing an expensive sports car and then never actually driving it! What was the point of being involved in a naked shower party with a bunch of hot college girls, if you simply dried off and walked away from it empty handed when it was all over? And while he ultimately respected my decision (or at the very least my level of willpower) it seemed largely counterintuitive to him.

Look, I knew the parts were OK.

I received my first awkward indication when a friend challenged me to skinny-dip as we swam in the above ground pool behind his house.

Being that he was tall and lanky and I was one of the shorter boys in our grade, he likely assumed that the experience would prove an embarrassing one for me. I had read a lot about lions and other wild cats while growing up and this seemed a lot like a primal male dominance kind of thing to me.

It also seemed highly inappropriate and the kind of action that might bring with it a multitude of un-welcome consequences.

But after stalling for what seemed to be about ten minutes using a series of weak excuses (my parents would be upset, what if someone sees us, what if I can't get my suit back on in time) I uneasily gave in to the pressure.

I had to do it if I wanted to be cool like he was.

Inching my bathing suit off, I draped it with care over the thin vinyl siding of the pool. It took three adjustments before I felt certain enough that it would not fall down to the ground, far out of reach and usefulness. My friend had already tossed his jean shorts out of the pool with a recklessness that was completely foreign to me. They just sat there in the grass, ostensibly as carefree as he was.

We hit an old volleyball (that looked suspiciously like one that had been missing from my house) back and forth until it too landed out onto the vast, soft, grassy no-man's land.

Trying my best not to look at my friend's body (it was very hairy in certain spots), I watched as a large green-eyed horse fly walked around on top of the scuffed volleyball, constantly cleaning its legs. I couldn't be sure if the fly's eyes were actually green or if it was merely the reflection of the lightly waving grass near him.

"What's the matter?"

"Nothing" I said, shifting my gaze down through the water's depth at my own unclad body, now tinged a cool blue by the rippled reflection of the pool's walls. I wiggled the toes that I saw at the bottom of the pool to make sure they were my own, as I still felt somewhat disconnected from reality, or at the very least, normalcy.

What helped at that moment was the decision to think of him as my brother. I didn't have a brother, but if I did we would likely have shared a bedroom for many years, and gotten dressed and undressed alongside each other in it. An activity such as this would be no more out of the ordinary than sharing a Paul McCartney and Wings cassette tape or a Steve Garvey baseball glove.

Yes, that's it, we were brothers.

Once the initial shock of seeing someone other than me naked (and at such a close range) for the first time had passed, I found the experience to be an exhilarating one. It actually bothered me that I had never thought of this skinny-dipping thing myself. I felt so 'free'. There was no way that Aquaman, the Submariner, or *any* ocean-dwelling humanoid would ever want to wear clothes, I now reasoned.

The fact that neither of these comic book heroes actually existed did not intrude into my new-found logic.

This was my first experience with any manner of intentional public exposure, and I liked it …a lot. It would serve as the precursor to my immersion in the upstate waterfall years later; my first true taste of that Arcadian Ideal.

Then things got uncomfortable.

As the water settled a bit, my friend decided to use his private as a periscope.

"I bet you're afraid to do this."

I was.

For several minutes he chugged around on his back, kicking his long, thin, legs with his little man proudly pointing up to the sky. I looked over at my beckoning bathing suit; fresh droplets of water were still dripping off of it. It would be very easy to throw it back on, jog home, open up a baseball book and forget this ever happened.

It would be the smart thing to do.

It would also be the cowardly thing.

To skulk back home, crestfallen, because I hadn't been brave enough, or man enough, to pull my weight with one of the 'big boys' was not an acceptable outcome. He had an expensive leather jacket that we all got to touch on the school bus, and a real pocket knife (that I was afraid to touch), and he said whatever he wanted, whenever he wanted, and to whomever he pleased (except to his old man).

This was a test.

Glancing about as nonchalantly as I could (which looking back probably meant not nonchalantly at all), I effected the necessary change so that I too might have a workable periscope. Then, as though in some subverted Norman Rockwell painting, I joined him in chugging around the perimeter of the pool at a comfortable pace, but one that (likely due to my conditioning) was faster than his.

Eventually, when I pulled even with him he ordered in a slightly tense tone, "Wait!"

So I slowed almost to a stop, moving my arms and hands in a rapid back and forth motion in order to keep me both afloat and stationary, which was not an easy task. But it was what the cool kid, the one who I once saw ride a motorbike over a large dirt jump (while I was in the process of reading the 'C' volume of the encyclopedia) wanted.

I watched with some apprehension as he looked first at his periscope, then over at mine, and then back again at his own.

I didn't understand what the concern was and it worried me.

They looked (surprisingly) similar to me, a 'brother-like' match if you will, with the sole exception that mine reached a bit higher into the breezy, blue summer sky. To my innocent way of thinking, this was probably a bad thing as I understood that stealth was the key to victory in submarine warfare.

But apparently my rebellious friend wasn't thinking about actual submarines.

He emitted a soft grunt, stood up, and flinging his long, flowing, 'hippie-length' hair off of his forehead, hopped out of the pool using just one arm.

I was impressed by that: just one arm!

Then, with a casualness to his movements that would have you suspect he was all alone in his room (and not outside, in an open field and near a busy highway) he bent over (ugh, more unexpected hair) and tugged his damp, frayed, denim shorts back on.

In sullen fashion he walked (the way I walked when I had to go to the dentist) into his house without saying so much as a single word.

Confused, I reluctantly slipped my bathing suit back on. With my bottom now safely out of public view, I bounced around for a few minutes to keep body warm, hoping that he would come back out and tell me that he had heard his phone ringing.

He didn't.

Eventually, feeling quite unwelcome, I climbed out of the pool (using the dangerously uncool safety feature commonly referred to as a 'ladder') and walked home, with the skin on my shoulders gently burning in the hot summertime sun ... and a quiet smile on my youthful face.

He never invited me back over to swim.

Later that same summer, while visiting my grandparents on Long Island, an attractive girl who lived down the street invited me to relax for a while in a hammock that was suspended between two large deciduous trees, probably Oak.

To illustrate my emotional immaturity at the time, I recall worrying over whether or not I had left my *Hostess Twinkies* Darrell Porter, Ross Grimsley, Bobby Murcer panel of baseball cards in a safe place (my grandmother's kitchen counter top).

She had me quickly fearing for my life.

Wearing what must have been a practiced look of anguish, she said that I looked very ill. Of course once she claimed to be a doctor, I caught on. After all, no self-respecting doctor would treat a patient without proof of insurance. How could I pay her?

My heart thumped as I watched the rich, green leaves swaying gently in the summer breeze from my vantage point on the hammock, as she adjusted my clothes in order to perform my surgery.

But like the calm before any storm, it was too brief.

I'll never forget how wildly her mother screamed to her out the back door, "[name], what are you doing? Put him away! His family 'are good people' and I don't want them thinking anything bad about us!"

For the next few years I thought about her every time we drove by that house! I was her Bucky Dent and she was my Farrah Fawcett. We could place our respective posters side-by-side on the wall above our couch and hold hands and kiss ... and stuff. Mostly stuff.

I don't think I ever saw her again, she likely moved on to someone who had money, or at least a car. But I was left consoled by her mother's comments; I liked the fact that people thought my family 'were good people'. Good people didn't take advantage of other people ... even when they could.

Yet both of those 'journey to adulthood' forays had ended with a static awkwardness, and I still had no clue what do with a woman if I were ever to have one. My parents prohibited me from seeing R-rated (or worse) movies, and I was far too much of an upstanding citizen to try to figure out how to steal the *Playboy Channel* signal on the cable box whenever I heard the squeals of what may or may not have been pain or joy.

I certainly had no way of telling.

Then there was the sheer morality of the moment. I had been taught that virginity was a state of grace, a gift that should be given only to someone that you truly love, someone who you were willing to spend all of your days with. Sex before marriage, by default, was a huge 'no-no'. And even if I – in the wake of the turbulent sixties and early seventies with its anti-establishment, pro-feminist movements – had been at all intrigued by this new age of sexual revolution and freedom, I knew that my family was not.

Still, if not for the ghost, and a growing belief in life after death, I might have been further tempted to explore and test those boundaries. For if 'Tommy' was around, I reasoned, so might my great-grandparents, and great aunts and uncles, and whoever else! I did not want to risk their spirits 'seeing' me do something immoral to their way of thinking, to cast aside the values and principles that had created who I was.

All of these things played a role in my decision to remain celibate.

The girls and I sat around for about five minutes.

I was lying on top of my loft, enjoying the fact that I was with living, breathing company. Beth was sitting almost directly below me on the old brown couch underneath. Every once in a while we would shoot each other quick glances through the space that separated the loft and the wall. The one that I had reached down through a month earlier to get my pillow, the one the ghost wanted to take from me. Linda was sitting, and smiling, at Jeff's desk as she inspected his many books, drawing utensils, and wall art. She expressed her regret at not being able to draw quite as well as she would like, but shared that she was proficient in many other areas of arts and crafts design.

I couldn't help but feel some pangs of loneliness, as though I were alone in a small crowd; a prisoner of some self-enforced exile.

Eventually, probably just to lighten the mood, one of the ladies suggested that we play a quick game of Truth or Dare. I had heard of it, and knew it was often associated with things that got a person into trouble.

The idea initially had little appeal to me.

Being forced to share my most intimate thoughts and experiences was not my idea of an effective way to relax under the current conditions, nor did I want to get arrested for doing something stupid, which I did seem prone to at times.

As it turned out, the 'dare' part of the game was actually pretty cool. At one of the ladies' request I re-created my 'Ice Skate' Dance; the one that had gotten me written up by the Residence Director just a few months prior.

It was December 10th; I was blasting Adam Ant's song "Strip" on Paul's stereo, jumping on and off of the loft, and running through the windowed hallway chasing some screaming girls wearing a pair of white ice skates around my neck. Yes, pretty much just ice skates.

TO: Chris Decesare

FROM: Stephanie Cioffi, R.D.

DATE: December 10, 1984

Re: Student Conduct Interview

After some nervous and sincere pleading, I was able to have the write up reduced to a noise violation (akin to playing music too loudly or screaming too loudly at a party) as long as I promised not to do it again. I promised with head bowed and eyes wide open like a puppy that had just peed on the carpet ... again.

Jeff, who just so happened to be studying at that time in the same area, was called down as well, and he sat in the chair next to me, one leg nervously shaking up and down the whole time.

He was absolutely mortified.

We hastily fled the RD's office, Jeff warning me that I'd better not get him caught up in any of my antics again. As we turned the corner, I gave him an impish smile.

"Chris!"

I raced up the stairs, mooning him the whole way.

Corners are important.

Accordingly, *this* time the Ice Skate Dance was done in the relative safety of my own dorm room, Adam Ant's song "Strip", accompanying me at a modest volume. And I made sure that the ladies removed some of their clothing as well.

Fair is fair.

Our fifteen minute diversion soon became a thirty minute delay for Jeff and when we realized that we had completely lost track of time   I commented, "Jeff is gonna' kill us!" We gathered up our clothing and turned the stereo off.

As we hurried through the glass enclosed foyer that connected the B and C buildings collaborating on the creation of an effective alibi, I realized that I hadn't laughed that much in weeks. Neither, apparently, had they, and there was talk of adding a third girl. The following day this typed slip of paper was taped to my door:

-Chris:Shall we make it four?

We never did.

Jeff was standing in front of B2B2, an anxious look on his face, when we finally returned to him. As Jeff could not leave the doorway of B2B2 (thus possibly invalidating the experiment should someone have entered the area) in order to get us, he had no choice but to wait it out.

"You *do* realize what time it is, right?" he remarked as I placed the room key into his eager palm.

Beth, Linda, and I made fleeting eye contact with each other, but none of us were able to phrase a sensible reason as to why we were late. Beth was unable to contain a short burst of laughter as Jeff anxiously unlocked the door.

The cold draft that blew out of the room immediately washed away the feelings of happiness and joy that I had been experiencing. I couldn't wait for all of this to be over … forever.

Jeff began to list, out loud for all of us to hear, the many changes in the room from the way we had left it: the desk chair had been pulled out (like it had been in C2D1 when Paul noticed it); the tape recorder's position on the desk had been moved a few inches from where it had been placed; the room's temperature had dropped 6°F; and the closet door in the room … had opened.

We gathered around the desk and listened as Jeff first stopped the recording, then rewound the tape, and finally hit 'play'.

The tape, from the first instance that we all heard it, had a rhythmic throbbing to it. This was no doubt due to the recorder itself. Dale Kaczmarek in his publication *Field Guide to Ghost Hunting Techniques* points out that: Many cassettes and digital units have built-in condenser microphones and while they are good for normal use, thy should probably not be used for EVP experiments as the sound of the motor and pulleys can often be recorded on the tape and can be impossible to separate from the ghost voices.

As sound as that advice is, we were oddly 'fortunate' in that the ghost's wailing voice – once it began to speak – would be so clear and so distinct, that when it breathed into the recorder there was no mistake as to what it was, even with the internal sounds of the recorder: a voice.

It was odd hearing my voice on the tape as I was leaving Tommy the instructions. I couldn't help but wonder which was more accurate: the way my voice sounded to me when I spoke or the way it sounded on the tape?

For the first few minutes the tape recorder had only captured varying levels of static, the soft beat of the tape spinning in the old device and the occasional and recognizable squeak of the large door opening and closing in the common area of the building, about fifty feet away. In retrospect, given the mind numbing boredom that might have resulted had we left the recorder on for hours, I was thankful that Jeff had decided to limit the taping to approximately fifteen minutes.

But then, more distinct sounds could be heard. Sounds made very close to the device's imbedded microphone. Having brought no papers, or surfaces to write on, I scooped up the cover of the cassette case and began to record what I was hearing and what the 'count meter' read as I heard it.

At '099' I heard what sounded like a draw(er) or window opening. I watched as Jeff moved around to the front of the desk, only to point out that the desk drawer had indeed been opened a few inches.

Markers '202' and '225' brought with them sounds that I associated with guttural noises. These were disturbing, but not all together very compelling. I began to lament where I found myself: kneeling on the floor, in a dimly lit room, listening to static (and barely audible grunts). Why couldn't I be like the majority of the Geneseo college students and be doing *anything* else?!

'247' yanked me right back into the moment ... I could make out the sounds of a person talking. A lump in my throat formed because I recognized the voice ... it was the voice that I had heard coming from the C2D1 closet ... and pushing through Paul's headphones. It was the same voice that had called, "Chrissss" when I was working on my paper.

It was Tommy.

'253' happened right after, and it was *far* worse.

"Hellllp ... meeee ..."

Dear God. I dropped to the floor, shaking my head back and forth, trying to cover my ears ...

Jeff was pumping his fist in the air celebrating the impressive accomplishment. We had captured what today would be called a 'Class A' EVP. Back then I simply called it 'horrible'.

"Turn it off!" I yelled, "Turn it off!"

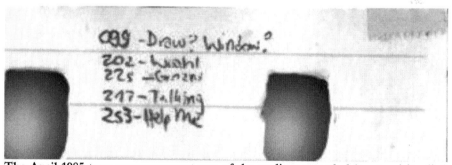

The April 1985 tape may represent one of the earliest recorded 'post-spiritualist' EVP – electronic voice phenomena - recordings in New York. In 2010, the cassette's audio data was transferred to CD format by members of the *"Please, talk with me"* production crew with an eye towards its long-term preservation.

Jeff immediately stopped the cassette tape playback. He looked thoroughly perplexed by my reaction.

"Don't you get it, Jeff? Don't you get it?"

I left him no time to respond. "The thing wants my help! I offered to help him, and now he wants my help!"

"That was the goal, wasn't it?" Jeff replied correctly.

"Jeff ... I don't know *how* to help it!"

The room was silent.

Beth and Linda sat cross-armed looking very afraid, spooked by the voice they – we *all* – had heard on the tape. I wished that we hadn't gotten them involved. The only sound that could be heard was Jeff tapping his pencil on his leg. There we sat four young people who had crossed into a place where none of us had expected we would. We were communicating with a spirit.

Tommy had called my bluff ...

The following Thursday I found myself back at the door of Dr. Casler. Alone.

I had no choice as I saw it. My hand was being forced by everyone around me. If I could no longer control my destiny, then I felt that I should learn more about the one being foisted upon me.

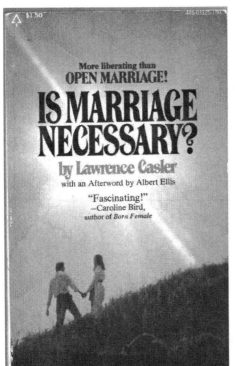

Dr. Casler had written a book in 1974 entitled, *Is Marriage Necessary?* in which he argued that many people got married because they wanted to avoid the social stigma of not being married, not because they benefitted from – or were satisfied with - monogamy. He wrote an article in the December 1969 edition of *Psychology Today* in which he proffered that love was a 'disease' as it propagated an unhealthy dependency rather than individual maturity.

Casler had also apparently gained a measure of notoriety for his studies regarding nudist camps in the late 1960s as well. Among his findings, as recorded in the June 1969 issue of *Psychology Today,* were that male nudists did not get erections when they viewed the naked body, and that the body can become deconditioned as a sexual stimulus.

As much as I loved to run around in my birthday suit, had I been aware of any of this that April morning in 1985, I would not have been found knocking on his office door ... ten minutes before his office hours began.

That would have been a shame, because I was about to learn a lot from him.

As I had imagined, Dr. Casler was pleasantly surprised to see me. He recalled my name immediately and asked me to take a seat.

His subject had arrived.

In the mold of any decent clinician, he did not ask me how the experiments were going or about any of the evidence that had been presented to him the week prior, he asked me instead if I had any questions for him.

I wasn't about to waste this opportunity, nor was I going to pull any punches. I wanted answers, and if he wanted anything from me, I would get my answers first.

"Why," I asked him, "is all of this happening to me?"

"If what you are claiming is true, regarding seeing and hearing a ghost, then I would suggest that you are sensitive; sensitive to your environment in ways that most of us are not."

"So what you are saying is that, in a perfect world, everyone would be able to use their latent sensitivity to see ghosts?"

"I don't know if I would consider everyone seeing ghosts around them *perfect*, but it certainly would be fairer. There are certain people, those with severe emotional instabilities, that I would prefer not see ghosts."

I sat quietly for a moment, reflecting on his words. He was implying that all of this ... the ghost, the sensitivity ... somehow fell inside the natural order of things, or perhaps at its very edge.

"Then tell me, if you can, how things like ESP or ghosts or precognition are able to be explained through the laws of nature. Science can't explain them."

He was studying me, I could feel it. It wasn't bothering me though because I could tell he was pleased with how I comported myself through my extreme level of discomfort, and by the quickness and depth of my responses.

He liked exercising minds, his own included.

Leaning back slightly in his chair he issued me a challenge: "How can you prove a boat, that you cannot see, is in the water?"

Just relax, I silently counseled myself, *stay calm*. This riddle would have less real-time effect on me than choosing my breakfast cereal did that morning. It was just concept, not application.

Consider your options and make your choice.

Then it struck me!

"The wake; a moving boat leaves a 'v-shaped' trail behind it! Even if the boat had already passed from your line of sight, you could logically still account for its existence, and know that it is still there in the water because of its effect on the environment around it."

Dr. Casler smiled for the first time. Leaning forward onto his desk, as though he were about to reveal a trade secret, he said, "That same boat also displaces the water in front of it as it moves forward. A person who is very sensitive can see the water level rise before the boat actually gets to them."

"Precognition," I respond to demonstrate my understanding.

He relaxed back into his chair, and began rifling through his desk drawers. When his hands collected what he was searching for – a neatly stacked deck of cards – he stated, "I want to try an experiment."

"No, I'm good," I countered placing my hands in front of me like some type of social shield.

The professor removed his glasses in order to clean them, and looking at me out of the corner of his eye he asked me what I was afraid of. "I've already failed at enough things this semester, and I don't want to embarrass myself in front of you, too."

"Let's just do a few," he replied in a soothing tone, "if nothing happens we'll just stop. What do you say?"

He had quickly turned my own logic against me ... there was in fact nothing to lose in attempting whatever it was he wanted to attempt.

Each card was blank on one side and had a shape on the other. The object was for me to determine what card he was holding up to his forehead, as he concentrated on it. Once I had offered up a guess, he would then proceed to draw the next card off the top of the pile, which sat face down in front of him on the desk.

The experiment moved with greater rapidity than I had expected, and by the tail end of it, I was simply calling out 'circle' and 'wavy lines' and 'square' ... whatever ... at random. When we finished Dr. Casler did not say anything for quite some time.

"Did I get them all wrong?" I asked.

He looked up, adjusted his glasses, and replied: "Actually, yes *and* no. Your answers were incorrect for almost every single card."

Failure; I knew it.

I had warned him not to do the experiment. *Well that was a grand waste of time.* Without looking up, he began to make a series of straight-lined pencils strokes on his paper and said: "But what I am seeing here is a very strong case of positive step progression."

"Is that good?"

"Well, it is inherently neither good nor bad; those are labels that I try to avoid using. What it *is*, however, is extremely rare." He held up his sheet of paper to show me his marks, "You managed to predict the next card, the card on *top* of the deck, accurately in five of the first seven cases. That is a remarkable result."

Apparently, I really was somewhat sensitive.

Oh, crap!

Jeff often said that ghosts were attracted to 'sensitive' people, just like Lorraine Warren had said in her lecture. I had a flashing neon motel sign that read 'Room Available' above my head. Now the question was: How do I turn it 'off'?

"The path to paradise begins in hell." – Dante Alighieri.

27. Resolution

April 12th, 1985. I sit alone in C2D1 watching the misty rain that has washed away the snow that had fallen earlier in the week.

The temperature has climbed in the mid-fifties. This was the kind of weather that I used to love running in.

I watch as the other students open their umbrellas as they leave for some destination that I think has to be better than where I am. The soft tapping of clear, fresh rain creates a living tapestry on the outside of my window.

New Zealand's Rod Dixon had won the 1983 New York Marathon in this type of rain. He overtook Geoff Smith in the last few yards by running the tangents, zig-zagging across the roadway in straight lines, cleverly chopping off distance from the course. Smith, who had bravely led the race for over ten miles, stared down at the long blue line that ran down the middle of the road, not knowing that Dixon was closing in behind him, and that he would snatch victory from him with the finish line in sight because he, Smith, had run the whole distance.

I wonder who I would have been in that scenario, the cleverly creative Dixon who had won, or the bravely honorable Smith who had lost.

Wiping away the fog that my warm breath had created on the window, I can see the bones inside my fingers lit up by the light streaming into the room. People spend so much time on their appearance, countless hours of their lives, all the while hidden inside is their skeleton. When their bodies are consumed by the earth, only that – now invisible – skeleton will be left visible … until time eats that away too.

I'm not sure why Tommy appeared as a skeleton in the photograph. He didn't look like that when I had taken the shot. Dr. Casler suggested that the ghost might have been in the process of forming (from orb … to shadow … to skeleton … to full appearance) and that had I waited a bit longer to take the picture, he might have appeared as though having flesh.

Still, I worry that there might be more to it than that. The skull and crossbones had been a symbol of death for many centuries.

The song, *Nightshift*, by the Commodores is playing as I turn on Jeff's boom box. There is something healing about the song, the sounds of it make me feel … better. I even remarked to Jeff – a week or so earlier – that whatever sound was used in the song (maybe an open 'E'), it seemed to have a calming effect on Tommy, who I could sense around the edges of the room, as well.

The song is climbing up the charts, so I have the opportunity to listen to it often.

At the time I have no idea who 'Marvin' and 'Jackie' were, and I thought that the term 'nightshift' was being made in reference either to people working the midnight shift, or to a comedic movie that I had once heard reference to. [Looking back now all these years later, an ode to the departed Marvin Gaye and Jackie Wilson, and reference to the 'nightshift' (being Heaven or the concept of a connected and positive afterlife), I further understand how the song might have been both appealing and healing … to anyone … during an extreme haunting.]

The sound of passing laughter from a group of female students, outside my window, shakes me from my peaceful moment.

Looking out across my room, I see Tommy's face – pushing through the wall – approximately three feet from what is now Jeff's closet. Blood leaks from his mouth as he silently moves it. I close my eyes. I am reminded that I am still, essentially, a prisoner in my own room.

According to Albert Camus, nothing was more despicable than respect based on fear. Apparently he never had to face what I am facing.

…

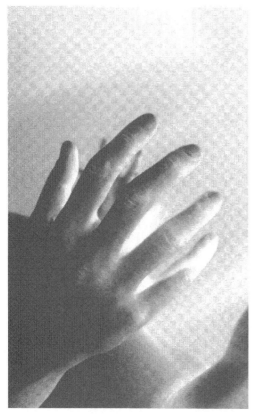

The dream was horrific. Resembling Michelangelo's *Last Judgment* fresco, I watched as people I knew – one by one – were falling into the burning fires of hell below them. They would call out to me, asking for my help, begging for assistance, as their skin began to melt away. All the while, I sat strapped to the darkness, unable to grasp their hands or allay their fear of the pain that surely awaited them.

I wake up with a start, breathing heavily, and sweating to the extent that my forehead, neck and torso are soaked. At the moment I glance over, the clock switches to 3:33.

Make a wish!

…

My fingers and toes are ringing with numbness, even when I move them, and my throat is parched to a sting. Not knowing what it is, I wipe some recently-crusted blood from the corner of my mouth. Damn. This *has* to end.

The room seems to echo with a nauseating silence, and I cannot fall back asleep. Shortly after 4AM, I decide to get up and start my day a few hours earlier than I planned.

The hallway light had been turned off, so when I push open the heavy wooden door, my tired eyes are immediately blinded by the bright light that pours out of the bathroom.

As they adjust, I can see that the bathroom has an occupant.

Standing by the sink on the right, wearing a pair of dark sunglasses and a towel, Craig Norris is shaving his face … at four in the morning.

It was typical 'atypical' Craig.

My first thought is that he has come back from a long night out on the town, but that would make too much sense. It turns out that he and a friend are going to be heading out for a sunrise hike in the next hour.

Craig is the most intense person that I ever met. He is so intense that he sometimes scares people away. Not that he ever seems to mind, it's all too easy to get bored talking with the same person for too long anyway.

I recall that in the fall I had seen him sitting in one of the cushioned chairs in the common area. As three of the ladies from the A building walked past – yammering on about which name brand jeans were currently the 'ones to wear' – Craig hopped right into their conversation and lambasted them from paying extra for a pair of jeans in order to advertise for someone else.

"They should be paying *you* to wear them! You're doing *them* a favor!" he smiled as they scurried off to the safety of anywhere else.

Craig Norris was the most intense, and fascinating, person I had ever met. He would approach perfect strangers in the college hallways in order to comment on their conversations, and he once advised me, "Never walk the same way to class, if you do, you'll never break old habits or experience new things."

I haven't seen much of him since the first few weeks of the fall semester when he and Ed and Jeff had been 'tripled up' in C2D2. Craig found a new location to live in by October.

Why he is now in the D-Quad bathroom, and why he is wearing a pair of sunglasses while shaving at four in the morning, I cannot say.

Being too tired to walk across campus to shower, and not sure that I could gain access to the building at this time of night even if I did, I decided to roll the dice and take one here.

Welcome home.

Craig being here was actually a bonus, in as much as if I am attacked again, at the very least I would have a witness.

The warm shower water soothes my entire musculature. I breathe out a huge sigh of relief.

Craig must notice this because, to my vexation, moments later he sticks his half-shaven face past the new (and still useless) replacement shower curtain, and asks me if I am OK.

"Yup, I'm good."

"You don't seem good."

Why is this happening? Why am I being questioned in the shower at four o'clock in the morning by a guy who doesn't even really belong here and is wearing sunglasses?

"I'm sorry if I don't seem good," I grunt, pulling the skimpy shower curtain in between us.

"Everybody is talking about your ghost," he says, "You need to do something about it."

My ghost? I need to do something about it? How dare he!

"What? Are you saying all this is my fault? That it's some kind of ... poltergeist?"

My reactionary question is actually borne of my own fears from early on in the haunting. The movie *Firestarter*, starring Drew Barrymore and David Keith, had hit the theaters less than a year prior, and had brought the concept of poltergeist activity to water coolers and mall food courts across America.

Poltergeists were suggested to be a form of psychokinetic energy, often manifesting in teenagers who are going through puberty, or who are unable to deal with the frustrations or pressure of life as they move towards adulthood. It was purported that the young person displaying this psychic feat might actually be unaware of being its source. Jeff has effectively demonstrated several times that leaving one's mind open to any and all explanations could be useful, but I can see no obvious proof that these phenomena originate within my own mind.

The now-scabbing lines that run down my back from neck to waist seem proof enough to me that the source remains external. I hope that Craig does not notice them.

Craig sticks his head back into the shower stall.

"Honestly, Chris, I don't know *what* it is. Jeff thinks it's a spirit that followed you home from one of your long runs in the country side. Paul thinks it's definitely a lost soul who has its sights trained on you. But it doesn't matter who is right or wrong if the people around you – if you – are constantly suffering. Does it?"

"No."

"You need to stop running from this and deal with it. If you don't, you're going to run from everything in your life. This is a chance to become the person that you are supposed to be. You can't rely on others to do it for you. Your dad isn't going to be able to help you through this, the priest either. You are going to have to take care of this, my friend."

Looking at his face, now covered with droplets from the shower spray, I can see his eyes.

At some point in time he must have removed those ridiculous glasses. They are not filled with anger, or judgment, or any tinge of disappointment. His eyes are filled with concern.

Still facing him, I reach back, turn the water off, and ask: "What should I do?"

"What do you want to do?"

"I want to face it."

"Then *do* it."

. . .

I am going to face whatever it is. I am going to face Tommy. Craig instructs me to leave my clothing behind. He feels that this might be a chance for honest communication and that clothing is not honest. He says that it would be like wearing a mask.

"You go in the way God made you. You bare both body and soul to that thing. Talk to it, and get this done."

"There is only one thing that makes a dream impossible to achieve: the fear of failure." — Paulo Coelho, *The Alchemist*

Although I am uneasy, I trust Craig. I trust his ideas. I trust the concern in his eyes. Whether he knows it or not, this notion plays into my concept of every person, and everything around us, being part of a 'Whole', the Grand Design. Just as the cold rushing water of the waterfall seemed to fill my body with a sense of renewal, I am hoping that I can, in turn, do something that will help whatever it was that has been plaguing us all as well.

If I live.

Closing the door to C2D1 behind me shuts out the light, as well as my only physical connection with the living.

The night – and the darkness – belongs to him. It is 4:30AM and I am standing, seemingly alone, in the middle of my room.

The residual droplets of water from the shower, that had only recently warmed me to my core, are now instead stealing away my body heat. Silent beads of chilled liquid are running down my neck, my back, and my legs from my still-soaked head of hair. I cannot help but to shiver. I also cannot help but think back to the day I thought I would die, forty days ago.

Amazingly, forty days and forty nights had gone by since March 10th, when I had studied that one mind-restoring drop of water, the one that clung to my wrist in hopes of hanging onto me forever. Now, I had to hope that I could convince this dead thing that was haunting us that it too could not hold on forever, that it too would need to 'let go' of me.

There is but one candle in the room, it isn't even mine. Beth or Linda or Judy must have brought it over on one of their visits to make the room smell nice for one of our last minute parties, probably the one for Valentine's Day. The kind of parties we had before things became terrible.

My wet fingers are slippery and cold and make it difficult to light the candle; the drops of water from my bangs nearly put the flame out once it is lit. Carefully placing it on the floor in the center of the open area as close to the center of the room as I can figure, I kneel down beside it. The hard floor hurts my knees. The slight curl upwards of my toes also makes me recall the only too recent shower attack and its aftermath.

I do not want to die here.

The 'Our Father' (Lord's Prayer) rolls off my tongue with such a practiced ease that I am left wondering if I had rendered it completely ineffective having not concentrated at all on its delivery. I decide to say it a second time, carefully pronouncing and emphasizing each word ... with obvious intention this time.

That's much better.

"I know you can hear me," my soft voice eases through the still room, "I can sense you all around. You are being invited back in this room ... against the priest's blessing."

My ears listen for the slightest hint of movement as my eyes scan intently around the dimly lit room. I want to avoid the panic that can be induced through surprise. There were too many times when I had awoken to see that dead face in mine.

Running had taught me that preparation can reduce the effects of such surprise, I want to be prepared.

The squealing of the heavy wooden bathroom door tells me that Craig is leaving the area. I wonder if he is the last person that I will ever see, and if he will remember this day. *God, protect me ... please.*

The waiting continues.

I am fighting against the strong impulse to run. It would be so very easy to grab some clothing from my dresser (or not) and to take a well-needed rest in the common area. I can cover myself with a couch cushion I reason. It would be better than staying here!

Don't be a coward.

The fire atop the wick of the candle is snuffed out as liquid wax engulfs it. I smell the wisps of smoke in the air as the room darkens. Only a scant amount of bluish light, an extension of the moon's gaze creeping through the window's blinds, remains to help me see into the shadows.

The base of my neck and the top of my ears are the first areas to notice the plunging temperature. The chill breeze that advances closer from the area of the closets would certainly have blown the candle out had it still been lit.

Not wanting to be seen in such a weak and submissive pose, I stand as I prepare for his imminent arrival ... his first and hopefully only ... 'formal' visit. Standing, the cold now washes over my front causing my chest and thighs to tighten. The water in the corners of my eyes is cold against the lids when I blink.

I can see him.

The dark gray soft-edged shadow – which is distorted and elongated – precedes a darker, more defined human shape. It slides across the wall to my right, disappearing behind the loft's front edge. After taking a quick, tense step in that direction ... I am stopped in my tracks by the sight of a face, eye level with my own, mere inches to my left.

My solar plexus heaves, as I draw in a nervous breath and steal back several feet. It is not moving. It just stands there, wet blood on its face, neck, chest ... arms glistening in the faint light like dim blue stars in the heavens. Standing bare, as I am, as I had seen him on the tree, it begins to open its damaged mouth.

Stomach acid runs up into my own mouth, but I swallow it back down my stinging throat.

"Help me ... Chrissss."

The words, and the voice that speak them, are so familiar to me now. In contrast, however, with a form attached to them they are slightly less haunting and infinitely more powerful. They have moved from the realm of the potential to the world of reality. It is time to speak my piece, while I still have the chance to.

"I have no idea why you had to choose me. You know I didn't want any part of this. I was happy before you stole my sanity, and you damaged my faith."

I try to invoke some level of measured anger in my voice, but can only share sadness.

"Pain ... soooo much pain," he rasps out of this mouth, "made ... missstake ... "

His suffering is real; both the terrible wounds to his body and the anguish in his voice are testimony to it. I can discern what I think are tears running down his cheeks and down past where a part of his nose should be.

"Who are you, where are you from?"

I do not invoke the name of 'Tommy' as I face him, as it occurs to me that it might not be correct. I do not want to offend it or to make any kind of mistake with it so close.

Its head moves forward unnaturally on its neck, and the face contorts wildly. It is gasping for precious air that is clearly not traveling easily between its mouth and lungs. With a wail that sounds like it comes from a parent who has lost their child, he cries out: "Dannnnnvillllle ... "

My hands clench into nervous fists and I turn my hips slightly ... towards the room's door.

I am ready to run, but he does not attack.

His face and shoulders are broader than mine but he doesn't look as physically intimidating as I had worried. His hair, though matted down with what looks to be blood, is darker.

"Why are you here?"

His head tilts more to the side than I have ever seen before and he shares, "Missssstake ... made ... was wrong ... ssssso wrong."

A guttural coughing sound accompanies the sudden convulsion that spews more blood down his face. As I cover my own mouth, I am thanking God that there is no foul, rotting stench in the air. Rather, the air around him smells crisply clean and fresh like an ice chest. The dark blood that I anticipate will have spattered the floor and my frozen feet is nowhere to be seen. The ghastly site of his intestines spilling out of his body, and his half-severed other parts, are also not visible. It is as though everything below his rib cage is currently someplace else, represented now only by an electrically-charged swirling mist. I am encouraged to stay.

"You asked for my help, and I am going to give it to you. You need to leave. You can't stay here. You're hurting my friends. You're hurting me. You have to let go and believe that you can find forgiveness."

The figure is still, save for some labored breathing. With ears that I cannot see, I know that it hears me. I feel sad. I feel sad for *him*.

"You are taking my very will to live, and if you do that, you will never find rest. There has to be someone out there who loves you."

He extends a gnarled but youthful hand out towards me. I do not receive it; instead I pull both arms behind my body and clasp my hands together. Never in my life have I been so vulnerable, or so correct. I cannot allow him to fool me, or himself. His way will not work.

"You have to go; you just can't stay here anymore. I am sorry."

At the moment he groans an ever more pitiful sound, the candle suddenly erupts with a high flame, and fearing the carpet will catch fire, I crouch down to blow it out.

It is then that a wave of grief sweeps over me. I burst out into tears because I know that his soul has gone ... and I don't know if it will be in a better place.

"The only way to find true happiness is to risk being completely cut open."
— Chuck Palahniuk, *Invisible Monsters*

28. "Horror Cannot Outlast Hope"

When Jeff returned the following day, with the temperatures soaring to a record-setting 75°F, he immediately inquired about the changes. The same changes that I too had noticed several hours earlier when I opened my eyes after a long and restful sleep.

In what would have constituted an unacceptable safety risk, less than seven hours prior, I had been sleeping on my back – my hands clasped behind my head – one of my feet protruding out from the bed sheets. On this morning, though, there was no fear of the ghost breathing in the warm breath from my mouth into his, or of his ice cold fingers running along the relaxed muscles in my foot.

The ghost was gone.

I cast off the bed sheets and hopped down the loft's ladder. The dark sense of foreboding, that had survived even the priest's blessing, was no longer present. *Maybe it had worked*, I thought to myself, *maybe I had truly sent the ghost away!*

Opening up the blinds and curtains, the bright late-morning light streamed into the room, I smiled the smile of victory, of a race well-run. My anxious fingers unfastened the 'seemingly eternally locked' window, and the warm spring air smelled of life. It seemed as though my life had been restored to me.

The thought that all of this had been an unreal nightmare wandered across the landscape of my mind, like it always did. And like it probably always would. To appease my curiosity, I unlocked and opened the door of C2D1, and slid open the heavy bathroom door. I turned my body to the left … there they were, the remnants of the three long scratches. It had happened.

I ran through the most recent events, wondering how on earth the horrid ordeal had finally come to an end. Then I remember: Craig Norris. Craig had butted his nose into my shower, and his advice into my subsequent actions.

I had to smile: it figured that the man who was known for thinking outside of the box would help me find the key to opening mine. Also, because he had made off with my favorite pair of running shorts, the ones that I had left on the floor of the bathroom the night before.

But even if, in the worst case scenario, Craig had just wanted to score a laugh at the sight of me walking bare-assed across the hall or that he simply needed an extra pair of running shorts for his hike … his plan had worked beyond my wildest expectations.

"What happened," Jeff asked as he dropped some items he had brought with him from his home on his desk, "why does everything feel so different in here?"

I watched as he summoned forth the talents of all five senses in an attempt to determine the multitude of possibilities. It was an aspect of his personality – the desire to understand – that I hoped he would never lose. It had helped to save my life, and I was thankful to him for it.

He squinted his eyes, switched his mouth from side-to-side, and then announced, "The room feels like it's back to normal."

As I was working on a project, and as I wanted to get a rise out of the normally unflappable Jeff Ungar, I did not answer.

"All right," he continued, "if you are not going to tell me, then I guess that I just won't know."

He unpacked his belongings, adjusted his collared shirt, and sat himself at his desk thumbing impatiently through book after book. I could feel his polite level of tension rising. He opened up his spiral notebook, and began twirling his pencil between his fingers.

Still, I said nothing.

Wait for it.

"Oh, come on! This isn't fair!" he kindly protested, "You're *really* not going to tell me?"

I then unleashed my widest, toothiest, grin and he understood that I had just been teasing him. Holding a comic book that I had just begun, I offered, "What do you think of this?"

"Hmmm. These two lads look familiar. They look like *us*," Jeff remarked seemingly pleased with the quality of the artwork, "what is it about?"

"Cool. It's good that you can tell it's us. We have just been transported through a dimensional vortex, and into a dark abyss."

"Does my character at least have some inkling as to what is happening," Jeff asked immediately invested in the potential of the piece.

"You get to observe as I get tossed around by the energies inside the vortex," I replied, hoping to get another rise out of him.

"How typical," he grumbled with a smile on his face, "Once again I can only watch the exciting stuff."

"Exactly," I continued "Notice how most of my clothes get ripped off?"

"You do realize that the scenario in your comic plays out in similar fashion to the whole ghost situation, right?"

"I do."

The comic was my first attempt at dealing with, trying to explain both to me and others, what had happened during those terrifying ten weeks. It was just a start, but it was a safe and very important first step in what would become a lifetime journey for understanding.

"Have you seen the ghost, lately?" Jeff astutely asked, "You seem noticeably more relaxed now."

I placed the comic, which I knew I would never have enough understanding to finish, down onto my desk. Then I began sharing with my roommate – the person who would be the Best Man at my wedding only four years later – what had occurred the day prior.

...

Over the next few weeks – my last at Erie Hall – I rededicated myself to my academics, and was able to obtain a passing grade in all of my classes. Jeff marveled at my ability to plan, create, and edit a ten page paper in one hour's time.

"I have no choice," was my honest reply.

But the haunting had left indelible footprints. Footprints that even I, at the center of the haunting, would not know of for decades. Several newspaper reporters arrived on campus around this time, investigating stories of a 'boy who could talk with ghosts'. With the haunting now finally over (as far as I could tell) I didn't want to take the risk of talking about it publicly. My fears were that it might prevent me from moving on with my life and potentially lead to a rash of 'copycat' incidents in which someone else might actually get hurt.

I chose to make myself 'invisible' to the newsmen. Whenever a reporter found his way to my vicinity I would hide behind trees, crouch behind mailboxes, and sneak around the corners of buildings.

Corners are important.

Interestingly, I almost did talk with one reporter, a man from the *Democrat and Chronicle*, as he sincerely seemed interested in the people behind the rumors. But I turned around on the college walkway right in front of Erie Hall as I was about to introduce myself.

I wasn't ready yet.

Jeff was with me on several occasions when people pointed at me and announced to their curious friends: "Look! There's the ghost boy, that's *him!*" Or when a random person would come up to our door and either accuse me of worshipping the devil or ask me, "If you are Jesus, then who am I?"

Much of my spare time in the days following the haunting I spent reading about Geoff Smith's recent victory at the Boston Marathon, where he had hung on to win (for the second time) in the intense heat while battling severe leg cramps. He had set out at a world record pace, but the conditions just weren't conducive to running fast times.

I also tried to return to competitive running shape. Losing the fifteen or so pounds that I did during the haunting (while not necessarily a healthy thing) did make running easier than I had originally anticipated, and without the physical and emotional drain of the ghost dragging me down, I found that I was just as fast as I had been the prior autumn. It was a relief knowing that the haunting had not stolen that from me as well.

The weather had been nice all week and Jeff, perhaps sensing that I needed the emotional lift, told me to put on my NCAA shirt (that he knew I was extremely proud of) and some running shorts so that he could test out a new camera lens and take some shots of me running on campus. I was more than happy to oblige.

"Because this is what I believe - that second chances are stronger than secrets. You can let secrets go. But a second chance? You don't let that pass you by."
— Daisy Whitney, *When You Were Here*

Other than the fact that the impromptu photo shoot aggravated the cuts on my back (for which Jeff later apologized profusely) I found the exercise refreshing.

Still, there was a part of me that feared I would never be 'normal' again. I wanted to be 'normal' again. I had been alone in a crowd for far too long, and was no closer, in spite of months of hardship and suffering, to understanding why it had all happened. I continuously asked myself, "Why me?"

I had no desire for the possibility that it could happen again, and surmised that there *must* be some way to prevent it. As mentioned previously, Jeff had developed quite a few interesting theories as the haunting proceeded. One of the more unusual ones that he felt was a possibility was that, as he put it, I had an 'unusually tight-fitting skull'. This then might have led to additional or excessive pressure on select portions of my brain. That pressure in turn might be the cause of whatever either attracted Tommy to me, or at the very least, allowed me to see it. As comically absurd as that concept might sound to a reader three decades later, it demonstrates the lengths to which we strove for answers and, in light of the fact that we had no clear solutions, it was one possibility that I dared not discount. In fact, upon reflection, the theory might not be as odd as it first seems. The brain sends messages back and forth via synapse. Fast-moving electrical charges jump from synapse to synapse when we think. If the distance between synapses was reduced, then perhaps the thought process or other faculties of the brain would be in some way quickened or enhanced.

Then there was the possibility of physical DNA in terms of musculature. If you were to take a survey of those who knew me in high school and ask them which physical characteristic most stood out to them, they would have all said my legs. One of my track teammates once joked, "My God, it looks like your muscles have muscles. It looks like you have two thigh muscles on each leg!" One teammate even took to calling me 'Tree Trunk legs'.

My body's muscles were able to do amazing things, and they grew in an unusually rapid rate with any type of regular exercise. And this was without lifting weights or taking any type of anabolic steroid.

I had a talented athlete friend whose girlfriend had stunningly long and beautiful legs, and when he took to complimenting my legs instead of hers, she grumbled, "Why are you looking at a guy's legs and not mine?"

"His are nicer" was the humorous reply.

All through my childhood and into adulthood at times I could perform above anyone's expectations ... for a while. No one my size hit a ball farther than me, but later my wrists would ache to the point where I could no longer hold a bat. No one could throw a dart into the center of the board with more precision, but eventually, like my knees, my shoulder wore out and it was too painful to sleep on it much less throw again. Even when not regularly exercising, the pain from a casual massage was too great for me to enjoy them. After a long run just touching the skin (which would be often 'radiator' hot) on my calves or thighs would hurt; this at the age of nineteen and twenty. No sports physical or physician was able to explain this.

Perhaps this aspect of my physiology played a role in any ability I might have developed or inherited? Or in what seemed to be the ghost's consistent determination to constantly be near me whenever I was undressed. Were these potential bursts of energy what initially drew the ghost to me? Was this an electrical (or EMG) issue? Was this energy what the 'faith healers' or Reiki (life force) practitioners used? Did wearing clothes somehow reduce or weaken this effect?

But those same notable, strong, well-defined, muscles were likely the reason I never became a world-class distance runner. While they gave me uncanny endurance, they were 'over-sized' and heavy for a long distance runner and placed a great deal of pressure on the joints and connective tissues. I was constantly pulling muscles and getting minor injuries because my muscles were large, and my joints – my knees, ankles, even my wrists – were frail.

Everything would come crashing down, for good, in the late fall of 1985 when I sustained an injury while out on an over distance training run. I was about six miles into my run on the old dirt roads in the Livingston County countryside, when a large dog decided to chase me. I turned and braced myself (as no human who has already run six miles can out-sprint a dog) and put my hands out to protect my head and neck. The impact from the speeding dog sent me to the ground, with a loud 'popping' sound from the area of my knee, when my foot got caught in a rut in the dirt road. The huge dog was friendly and simply licked my sweaty face when I landed, but as I made my way back to the college, near the beginning of a bridge that crossed a dark stream on route 20A, my knee just gave out. The next morning it had swelled like a balloon filled with air.

Above: The Bridge (at left) where my knee gave out after a large dog had knocked me off of my feet. I had to walk the final two miles back to the college.

I was on crutches for a while and by the summertime was getting back into decent shape, but from then on, every time I tried to pick up the pace enough to be competitive I risked tearing my knee again. And no 33:00 10K was worth that.

Another theory Jeff had offered was that I somehow 'picked up' the ghost on one of my long runs in the Geneseo country side. This concept was terrifying to me in that it suggested that I might not be safe anywhere, and I much preferred to think of the ghost having been attached to the room (or building) itself and not me! Yet there could be no questioning that both on the day of the shower attack, and the day that I badly hurt my knee, I had run the exact same route, along 20A. And that information would prove quite useful in the years to come!

During the haunting itself, I along with most of those involved, felt the best guess as to why this all happened was that I had unwittingly found myself in a room that was haunted beforehand, and that for some reason as yet determined (fate, bad luck, location or proximity, similar backgrounds, that gift that Lorraine Warren seemed to sense) the ghost had attached itself to me. Smart money was also on the possibility that some college student, or perhaps the relative of one, had hung himself while despondent somewhere nearby.

In any event, I decided that it might be healthier to put the whole ordeal aside now and then, rather than allowing it to consume my every waking thought.

John Jeff Ungar succeeded in lightening our spirits while we visited Fallbrook.

In what was an apparent celebration of Arbor Day, Jeff, Beth, Linda, Judy, Ed, and I made a trip down to Fallbrook. The laughter, the joking, the running water, the fresh air made it feel as though ... for the first time in a very long while … my body was healing. I watched as my friends climbed the rocky slopes, hopped across some large stones that made it possible to cross the running waters, and helped each other around protruding brush. "This is how life is supposed to be." I thought to myself.

The notable contrast between the months spent in a cold, dimly lit, whispering, haunted room and the sound of my friends' laughter amongst the smell of sprouting grass in the mild spring air was further accentuated in my mind when I noticed the cover of the May 13th issue of TIME magazine when we got back to town which read: Reagan in Germany, "Horror Cannot Outlast Hope". The news stations the prior week had apparently been awash with the planned trip the president was taking to Germany for the G7 summit, but I had been involved with 'other' things.

I quickly plunked down two dollars on the stationary store's counter top, and brought the magazine, with a photograph of President Reagan carrying a large ceremonial wreath in a cemetery, back to C2D1. My brain, suddenly hungry for information, tried to absorb every detail: In what was intended to be a gesture of reconciliation between two nations that had been rivals during World War II (The United States and Germany), the President gave a speech at what had been the Bergen-Belsen concentration camp during the Nazi regime. Reagan spoke: "Above all, we are struck by the horror of it all – the momentous incomprehensible horror … Here, death ruled."

Glancing about my now warm and sunlit college room, I thought about the likelihood that whoever lived in this place the next school year would have no way of understanding the suffering that had taken place during this one. And why should they be forced to? Better that they make their own memories, positive memories, which could help serve to bury the unspeakable past. Why should death be allowed to rule here either?

I closed my eyes a moment to recall lying face down, naked and bleeding, on the cold floor so near to where I now safely sat. It was not difficult to imagine my young corpse amongst the many. The despair of those moments was still as fresh and real to me as the scratches that would line my back for several more months. I hoped that the millions of frightened human beings, guilty of no crime other than being who they were, did not know the despair I had. Yet, I also knew otherwise. I let my eyes tear up. There was no shame in mourning the painful loss of hope when one most needs it.

"We are here because humanity refuses to accept that the freedom or the spirit of man can ever be extinguished," Reagan had said, "We are here to commemorate that life triumphed over the tragedy and the death of the Holocaust – overcame the suffering, the sickness, the testing and, yes, the gassings. We are here to confirm that the horror cannot outlast the hope."

I folded my hands and said a quiet prayer for the millions lost, understanding that they may not hear it, nor recognize any worth in it if they did. They suffered far more than I, and as I lost hope, as the ghost named Tommy had lost hope, that wasn't the point. Rather, my prayer was that people wouldn't forget them or the hopes and the dreams that they once had. Jeff had saved me because he cared about me. I had attempted to save Tommy because over time I realized that I needed to care for him. Now I was praying to whatever higher power that might be out there that we, as a species, care for one another, even if just a little more than before.

May 15th, 1985 was the last day that Jeff and I lived in Erie Hall.

The following year we would move to a new dormitory (Wayne Hall) which was as far away from C2D1 as we could get and still remain on campus.

The last day at Erie Hall: Saying goodbye to Linda and Beth.

Beth and Linda were present to see me off, as was Paul Davie (a talented guitarist who would, on occasion, play alongside the Rolling Gumbys). I can still recall Paul saying that he thought my father looked like the actor Alan Arkin. It is interesting how the brain recalls some things and forgets others. For some reason, I never forgot that.

Underneath the broad smiles and sincere hugs there was a palpable sadness in saying goodbye to Beth and Linda, 'the girls' as Paul and I had called them. The truth of the matter was that I had grown closer to them than I had to any non-related female to that point in my life. And there was a sense that (in spite of that) this was likely going to be a long-term farewell. I suppose it came down to the fact that we all needed time to defuse, to reflect, to heal before we could think about furthering our friendships. It is my belief, all these years later, that the decision to move along on our own separate paths was a mutual one, made out of an intense respect for each other.

Still, I knew I was going to miss them for a very long time.

It should be noted that before Jeff and I left that May, we sold the loft. Two male students, sophomores I think, were excited to have it, and we watched as they eagerly took it apart, and then industriously carried it out of our lives piece by piece. There would now be one less reminder of the haunting for us to tolerate.

The long dreamed of ride 'back home' reminded me that I had been present for the arrival of the Iranian Hostages when they landed at Stewart Airport, only three miles from my family's home. I was able to see them, and wave to them, as they made the escorted bus ride from the airport to West Point … after 444 days of captivity.

That was January 20th, 1981, the same day that Ronald Reagan was being sworn in as the 40th President. I was able to make out some of their faces as they waved back to us through the dark tinted windows. One word related to their expressions came to mind: relief.

That was precisely how I felt as we headed south on Route 390, finally on my own way back home: relieved.

"Yea, I shall return with the tide." — Kahlil Gibran, *The Prophet*

29. Avoiding an Encore Performance

Being a die-hard fan of Elvis Presley, I noticed that he would never give an encore. He sang his heart out, cast a few scarves out into the audience to the adoring throng, and then said "You've been a fantastic audience, adios, we'll meet again". A few minutes later came the immortal "Elvis has left the building" pronouncement.

In much the same way, I too was looking to avoid an encore performance, although mine would most likely have a few less screaming forty-year-olds.

Jeff and I made sure to stay in contact during the summer of 1985.

Among the items discussed was where to live during our final year at college, certainly not Erie Hall. One of our mutual friends, Don H., was moving over to Wayne Hall on the south side of campus (the farthest on-grounds location from Erie Hall) and Jeff recommended that we follow suit. Listening to his advice during the haunting had largely worked, so I was not about to second guess his latest offering.

But first, I had the warm summer months to enjoy.

I learned a few things. One was that I would have to keep a shirt on as much as possible in order to avoid having to continuously explain the long, but fading scratches down the length of my back. Luckily the fallacious reputation of me as a ladies' man allowed me to teasingly suggest to my wide-eyed (and envious friends) that they were caused during a particularly wild physical encounter with a ravishing college girl. It wasn't my nature to mislead, but it saved me the potentially arduous and very emotionally-painful task of taking three hours to share the 'ghost story'.

When pressed, as expected, for the sordid details of the encounter, I quickly changed gears and joked that the truth was I had been attacked by a rabid wolverine while running naked through the woods. Maybe she was trying to protect her babies? Who knew? Wolverines were crazy after all, right?

The laughter from that response typically got me off the hook. I knew I wasn't ready to share my experience yet; it was still too fresh of a psychological wound.

In late June, my family took a week-long vacation to Virginia Beach and Colonial Williamsburg. It was there that I learned that my forced involvement with the paranormal was not going to end with the C2D1 Haunting. While standing in the room where the Williamsburg Declaration was signed (at the 1983 G7 Summit hosted by President Reagan) my mom thought it would be nice to take a picture of me there. I put on my best forced smile and posed.

As I waited for the picture to be taken (which when my mom was involved could last for several minutes, "Is my flash on?") I heard what sounded to be an old grandfather clock chiming three o'clock. Being that it was eleven in the morning, this seemed odd. But it wasn't out of the realm of possibility for some high school volunteer charged with setting the clocks properly to have shirked his or her responsibility. At this point, I heard a faint woman's scream to my left. My best guess was that they might be acting out someone being put to the gallows down the reconstructed street. That guess was proved incorrect when I saw a ghostly apparition of a long-haired woman in a flowing gown, run through the room (between my family and I) screaming as though she were on fire.

Click.

"OK, Chris, thanks. I think I got it."

I had heard that before!

When I excitedly asked if anyone had seen or heard the clocks or the screaming I got the 'uh, yeah, right' look from everyone.

Several weeks later the pictures, which had been sent out to be developed came back. My mom was the first to notice the white circular clock shapes floating in the air which seemed to indicate three o'clock. Then, she saw the swath of white, wispy, cloudlike matter passing in front of me as I stood arms to my side with a pat smile.

And just as with the skeletal apparition photo some five months prior, the photo was passed around eliciting looks of both fear and wonder. What did it all mean?

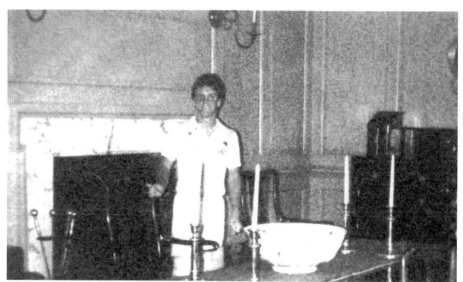

More evidence of the paranormal was not what I was hoping for on what was supposed to be a relaxing family vacation.

On a much welcomed positive note, I was once again able to thrust myself back into my running. The late summer and early fall of 1985 would mark the best physical conditioning of my life, and I again began to think of pursuing my marathon aspirations. Once back at Geneseo, Jeff accompanied me on some of my runs and showed a natural talent for the distances. It wasn't uncommon for Jeff to hang with me at a 5:30-5:45/mile pace with little training. He parlayed that talent into a bronze medal performance at the 1st Annual Geneseo Olympiad mile run. Where, there too, he was able to 'hang on to me' for a decent amount of time until I pulled away from both him, and a runner named John Antonucci from Ontario Hall, to win the gold. It wasn't the Olympics that I had hoped to win someday, but it would mark the only one that I would ever win.

Still, even in the blessed throes of health and success, I couldn't fully relax my mind. Although I vowed to never step foot again into Erie Hall (and I would not for over a quarter century) I would see it from time to time on a training run, or while visiting a friend and it would seem to silently stare back at me as though it were waiting for me. And every time I walked over the Route 20A crosswalk to get to class, I would recall reading about the young student who had been hit by a car there the year prior. I also recalled each time that I had read about it in room C2D1, in Erie Hall, and memories of the haunting would roll back into my thoughts.

Why was I so frightened to go back there? The rationale behind my fear was this: What if the ghost was still there? What if its disappearance was all about the levels of static electricity in the dry winter air? What if I had not helped him to find rest? What if he were there now, watching out of a quiet window, waiting forever for my return? What if he were hurting people? What if I had failed?

I wondered if I had survivor's guilt.

Jeff and I did our level best in room 312 of Wayne Hall to turn negative associations into positive ones. We used the tape recorder that the ghost had spoken into to create some hilariously entertaining songs. One humorous duet was titled: "Then He Was". The inane lyrics went something like this:

Now he is,
Then he was,
Woke up in the morning, sun overhead,
Worked 'till 5, then went to bed
They say there is a Heaven,
They say there is a Hell,
Buy your bonds
Then quickly sell
Now he is,
Then he was

Typically Jeff would sing in a Bono (U2) or Ultravox-inspired fashion, and I would warble like an adolescent-sounding Elvis Presley. We both knew that the songs had no professional value, but we had a blast making them. During one recorded session Jeff recited a poem about a wandering barbarian minstrel, and I could be heard laughing uncontrollably for the entire duration, about forty minutes. After the sheer terror of the prior school year, I needed the cleansing laughter. Jeff and I even had the opportunity to guest-host for a night on the college's radio station WGSU. I think I just laughed the whole time then as well.

"I'm not afraid of death; I just don't want to be there when it happens."
— Woody Allen

Making these humor-laden tapes forced us both to recall an event the year prior that we had apparently and independently agreed to place out of our minds: what we had referred to as the 'Forsaken Thing'. In truth, its very existence had been almost completely suppressed for me since we made it.

It was in December of 1984, a little over a month before the Warrens arrived in town, and the haunting would begin. Jeff had been telling me about some conspiracy theory he had heard about. Apparently, if the rumors were correct, if you played a particular Beatles song backwards, it says: "Paul (McCartney) is dead."

As a rabid Elvis fan, I felt it my obligatory duty to dismiss the Beatles almost outright, so to me I could not care less whether or not the then current Paul McCartney was a real or fake one. But I liked the idea of a recording having more than just a musical purpose. So I began to make sections of pre-recorded voice snippets for use in our role playing. When Jeff (or Paul or others who role-played) reached a certain part of the story arc, I would play a voice sample for them as a clue. It gave the gaming a bit of a multi-media feel and provided the players with something to look forward to above simple die roles and ability statistics.

Prior to one particular session, I wanted to share an NPC's (a non-player character controlled by me) sorrow. I tried to think of the best way to project that feeling to the players. The best example of despair I could think of was found in the *Bible* in Matthew 27:46 when Jesus cried out in a loud voice, "Eli, Eli, lema sabachthani?" which translates to "My God, my God, why have you forsaken me?".

So, being the rocket scientist that I was, I groaned those words into the tape recorder, as slowly as I could. The result was pleasantly horrifying to my needs (although nowhere near as horrifying as Tommy's voice would prove to be several months later).

That night, I played that taped portion, and the players were predictably aghast.

Perfect.

Perfect, that is, until several seconds later, when Paul's stereo (the same one that the ghost would phase through, and whose headphones it would speak to me through) which had been turned off, emitted a loud, almost deafening, 'popping' sound that sent everyone in room C2D1 running scared as can be into the safety of the hallway.

Jeff had warned me in advance not to play the clip, and as he hastily made his way back to the safety of his own room, notebook and character sheets tucked safely under his arm, he now lamented, "No one ever listens to me!"

That would be our last Dungeons & Dragons session until Wayne Hall when I spent over two hours developing what I thought was a very compelling character: An albino wood elf who could 'see' the future in his dreams, but was also physically blind. Because he had no physical sight he had great difficulty trying to share the content of his visions with those in his party who sought to make use of them. When I rolled for his attributes, his charisma was 'off the charts' which added to the character's nuanced development: thus he was stunningly attractive, but found no value in that.

Cool, right?

Except he fell off of the horse he was riding and snapped his neck on a rocky beach a mere four minutes into the campaign!

"So much for him seeing the future," quipped one of the players.

I quit.

Wanting to move beyond simply physically surviving (unlike the blind elf) the haunting, I decided to risk sharing some of the details of the events with someone new: a girlfriend.

I met Lorraine Bowles in Wayne Hall at a Friday the 13th dance (what else) the second weekend of the fall semester. She was an adorable, high energy, fair-haired girl who seemed to share my love for life. It helped that Lori was politically conservative like me and a naturally gifted runner to boot, though perhaps less zealous in her approach to both. We walked to classes together holding hands the whole way and singing Prince's hit song "Take Me with U" aloud, without a care as to who might hear us. And she proudly attended all my home cross country meets, cheering with abandon and offering me a heartfelt embrace at the conclusion of each race. She also became a willing accomplice in my good-natured attempts to tease the intensely socially shy Jeff Ungar.

Lori and I would lie in wait on my bed. Whenever we heard the Residence Director's voice approaching down the hallway we would nonchalantly request that Jeff open the door, using one excuse or another. Each time that he did so, I would quickly pull down my shorts and Lori would then 'mistakenly' lift the bed covers up off of me so that I just so happened to 'moon' the RD when she walked by.

"Why is this door open?" she would demand of Jeff who had typically just opened it. This would immediately send Jeff into a comically nervous frenzy, aghast that he had unintentionally led to the woman's (who he worked for as a dorm Night Host) displeasure. Lori and I would laugh until we cried.

Soon he learned to simply tell us to open the door ourselves.

Smart.

With that activity effectively halted, I unilaterally decided that Jeff needed a girlfriend as well. Unlike Erie Hall where there was a shared phone in the common area, in Wayne Hall the rooms had their own phone. Making use of this, I began the practice of dancing naked in our dorm room window, facing the 'girls' dorm. I held aloft a hand-written cardboard sign that read, "Jeff Ungar" with our phone number on it. Our phone would ring, but Jeff would stoically refuse to answer it. It turns out that on my own I was not nearly as effective as I was with Lori's creative assistance. The unsuccessful ploy served only to earn me some scattered female applause at the dining hall from people who now thought my name was Jeff.

This benefitted no one.

"A day without sunshine is like, you know, night." — Steve Martin

By mid-October, I felt close enough to Lori to share my secret: that I had been the unwilling focal point of a severe haunting just one year prior. My reasoning was that the bond of attraction between us was so strong that it could withstand her thinking I was a little 'off'. I was pleasantly surprised, as I was with Jeff the year prior, that Lori was far more intrigued by the possibility of a haunting and thus concerned for my well-being than being offended, or put off, by it. Her reaction was hugely gratifying and served to help me put my mind to rest over whether or not I could move on with my life after the haunting, even if I didn't fully understand it.

We dated for several years before the reality of a long-term, long-distance relationship took its toll on both of us. As she would share with me decades later, "We were young, in love and without a plan." It was the first serious relationship for both of us, and I think we both emerged as better people because of it.

In late January of 1986 I woke up from an intensely vivid dream. In it I was standing on the roof of my parents' house, wearing a shining, skin-tight, silver suit. There was a large crowd of flag-waving onlookers pointing up at me and cheering. They were standing beside the tree where Joe S. had told me that his mother was dead almost a decade before. I was unsure as to what they were expecting me to do, but then my body began to warm and I saw flames swirling all about my feet. Nervous over the prospect of burning, I decide to leap down off of the gray-shingled rooftop, find some water, and abort the mission.

My effort, however, sends me racing skyward at a startling speed through the early morning light. The combination of my shining appearance and effortless flight has me envisioning myself as the Silver Surfer, a popular Marvel Comics character. I welcome the direction the dream is now taking. As the former herald of Galactus, Eater of Worlds, I would soar through the cosmos taking in the vast, cold beauty of space. The stars would shine as brilliant celestial Christmas lights in the teaming skies.

As the Earth's surface begins to fall away below my feet, I command myself: "Up."

But now I sense that the faces below me now are unhappy, and when I gaze back down to Earth one final time, my own mother is now in the crowd standing beside the red maple tree, crying.

Then all goes white.

Not silver, bright white.

I wake up drenched in a nervous sweat, my hands and feet tingling with energy. It is the first time, post-haunting that I awake in such a manner.

I do not like it.

Fearing the worst, I immediately rouse Jeff who, in a fashion not unlike the prior year, jots down both the details of my dream and my reactions to it in his latest of many journals.

He seems to think that it might suggest something.

I have no doubt!

"Something bad is happening right now." I tell Jeff with tears welling in my eyes. "I *know* it. A plane or something is going to crash soon, and I can't do anything about it."

"Maybe you can call someone?" Jeff counsels.

"Who do I call Jeff? What would I say? That a plane somewhere in the United States is going to crash but that I don't know where? And I don't know how? They might even think that I planted a bomb, how else would I know? Heck, they might arrest me for just making the actual phone call!"

Jeff agrees, and advises that I put the dream out of my mind for the time being, or, at the very least, until we can come up with a reasonable course of action to take.

Washing in the shower, again in a fashion not unlike the prior year, the fear returns. But it is a different, more mature fear now. I had survived the ghost's rampage half a year earlier, but I am now forced to question not just the present, but the future as well. I wonder if there might not be an end to this 'gift' of seeing, of knowing, that both Fr. Charlie and Dr. Casler had referenced. Thoughts of paying Casler another visit pop into my head, but I fear I will end up running in a giant 'hamster wheel' in some underground lab.

Jeff and I are stopped in our tracks in the dorm lobby as we make our way towards the dining hall for breakfast.

"Jeff, look!" I yell, pointing intently to the television screen.

"That's what I saw!"

Stone faced, Jeff nods in agreement.

The space shuttle Challenger is hurtling up towards the heavens down in Florida. My stomach begins to ache.

I can't swallow.

I want to start counting to ten.

I know that I won't even get to seven

The words "Roger, throttle up" are heard.

Then I know.

I know.

Jeff knows too.

My eyes begin to tears up, Jeff makes sure that I am all right then turns back to the screen with a grim resolve. I can't. Instead I witness the explosion in the reflection of Jeff's wire-rimmed glasses.

I mutter just loud enough for Jeff to hear: "Why would I be shown something that I cannot stop?" It is another frightening throwback to the dark days of the haunting. I lament, "Why can't I just be normal Jeff?

He has no answer.

Jeff and I stood in front of the television just like every other American that tragic morning, but perhaps for a different reason.

Sunday, April 20th, 1986. It is exactly one year to the day since my final conversation with 'Tommy' had taken place in Erie Hall. Perhaps in light of my Challenger dream, Jeff and I are discussing the concept of pre-determinism. There are some who accept as true that certain things are 'meant to happen'.

"Everything happens for a reason" they often say.

The protestant reformer John Calvin believed that all of our life's moments, and our ultimate fate, are contained in a Book of Gold. That it was impossible to escape one's own fate.

Some folks believe that astrology and numerology can also predict personality and outcome.

To test this theory, Jeff decided we should try to pick which of the runners would win the following day's Boston Marathon. I selected Australia's Rob 'Deke' DeCastella, who was running the race for the first time, while Jeff selected American Greg Meyer(s) who had won the famed race three years earlier in 1983. As a complete afterthought, I suggested that we 'really go for it' and attempt to guess the winning time as well.

I scratched in 2:07.51 next to 'Deke's' name and a 2:08.27 for Meyer as per Jeff's best guess. It was 11:35 p.m. and the marathon was just half a day away.

The next morning (it was rainy, windy, and cold) I hurried back from classes and turned on Jeff's boom box radio in the dorm room. I hit the cassette 'record' button so that Jeff could hear the live broadcast when he returned later in the day. I was hoping that I had not already missed the finish.

What I heard was sportscaster Brent Musburger's voice, and what he was saying sent a quick chill right up my spine: "And here comes Rob DeCastella of Australia! Rob DeCastella is going to win the Boston

Marathon in a new course record of two hours ... seven minutes ... (I gulped) and fifty ...one ... seconds!

When Jeff arrived back to the room an hour later, I reluctantly advised him that Greg Meyer had finished in twelfth place, but that spectacularly the 38-year-old Bill Rodgers (a four-time winner) surprised everyone by finishing fourth.

"Oh well," he offered, "I was just making a best guess anyway. I'm happy for Bill Rodgers. He's a class act. So, who won?"

I held Jeff's gaze for a moment, and then hit the 'play' button. Jeff's shook his head back and forth when he heard DeCastella's name, and he began to run a hand across his well-groomed goatee. When the time was announced, he jumped up from his desk chair, his mouth dropping open in a disbelieving fashion.

"No way! No way! That's not possible! How could you guess the winning time to the exact second? There is no way that is possible."

And then he said it. He said it as he pointed an accusatory finger at me, the line that he may never live down, and one that was decades later popularized in an X-Men film: "Hey, no powers!"

I jumped up and down on my bed in childlike celebratory fashion. Jeff could only pace around the room verbally questioning fate, a half-smile of amazement covering his wise-looking face.

Powers were cool.

...

Graduation Day was May 17th, 1986. In contrast to the often lonely, dark, frigid days that exemplified the haunting, the sun was shining brightly overhead and large crowds teamed about the college grounds. It was heart-warming and gratifying to be surrounded by my family, and relatives and my friend's families and relatives as well.

One of the highlights for me was watching my parents interact with Jeff's. I watched for any similarity of intent, personality and purpose between when they spoke to each other. After all, they had produced both Jeff and me. Our friendship had become so strong over the preceding eighteen months that I wondered if our parents, too, might have been friends had they met in college under similar circumstances.

With my Bachelor of Arts degree in Speech Communications now acquired (I had long before decided I wasn't materially-driven enough to pursue that vaunted law degree) I prepared to move on with the rest of my life.

Graduation Day, 1986: Saying 'farewell' to the place that changed who I was more than any other before or since. The balloon reads: You're one in a million.

Jeff and I would stay in touch for a number of years, until the rigors of career, family and distance intervened. But before we left our dorm room for the last time, we shared a moment of reflection together. What we had been through had been so unexpectedly traumatic, and so dangerous, that we spoke to each other now as if we were brothers. And I suppose, in some respects, we were.

As we sat alone in the now emptied and barren-looking room, I informed Jeff that I had asked for a 'sign'. A sign that all of this had somehow been worth it, that it was not just some random, perhaps meaningless, confluence of variables but that it had been for some purpose beyond ourselves.

He nodded silently in approval.

I told him that if one day, far in the future, when our hair was beginning to gray, we found ourselves walking along some sidewalk in a quiet little town, snow falling gently around us, both of us in dark coats chatting about the wonders of life, that then we will know that it had somehow been all worth it, maybe even meant to be.

We stood up, shook hands with a melancholy air of shared purpose, and then exited the room, closing the door tightly behind us.

"Usually, there is nothing more pleasing than returning to a place where you have endured hardship." – Tahir Shah, *In Search of King Solomon's Mines*

30. The Return

Back in January of 1985, when I watched the Warrens presenting their evidence, I leaned over to Jeff and whispered, "I could never do that." Now, over twenty-five years later, in the summer of 2011, we were standing on the stage at SUNY Geneseo, and getting ready to publically share the events of the C2D1 Haunting for the first time.

I had been wrong.

Yet the applicability of the situation was not lost on me. Noting this, I made it a point to share with the crowd that two decades ago I had been a teenager sitting in the back of the auditorium, listening to personal tales of the paranormal, and that my guess was that a young person sitting in the back of the auditorium as I was now speaking, would someday too, stand where I was, and share their story. That's how life works.

Jeff and I had arrived the day before and were provided with room and lodging from the college. As fate would have it, we were told that we would be staying in a dorm that went by the name of Erie.

Go figure.

I couldn't help but rub my hands together with a bit of a nervous shudder, as I walked underneath the window that I had so longingly stared out of in what seemed like an eternity ago. Pointing out the window to the members of the film crew accompanying us, I tried to remain in control of the growing fear. For them it was likely an exciting hands-on opportunity to connect the actual place with the events that they were recreating. For me it was like returning to the site of a great battle. I half-expected to see a few tombstones scattered across the college lawn.

Breathing in with full force, I stepped into the building. While some of the surrounding details had changed, the short walk to the Main Lobby felt very natural. I had walked this route several hundred times and even though my college textbooks had been replaced by a binder containing my speaking notes, and my body was no longer in shape to run mile after mile, if I squinted at my sneakered feet enough, I might have believed I was nineteen all over again.

Memories of the Toga Party, quick jaunts to the laundry room and of countless conversations rushed into my mind. The mere act of stepping into the building had me quietly awash with emotion.

The young woman at the check-in desk asked for my name.

"Chris Di Cesare. I lived here back in 1985."

She smiled a polite and disinterested smile as she looked through a stack of thin envelopes.

Her eyes temporarily widened when she located one with my name on it, then she presented me with my papers. My brain flashed back a quarter century to the girl at the Toga Party who had given us our name tags. She looked the same age, had a similar build and complexion, but she seemed a bit more innocent to me; much like the times themselves. I was wondering about the cyclical aspect of life as my own eyes read the marks on the envelope: C2D1.

"What?" I exclaimed aloud, "Are you kidding me? Do you know what room this is?"

The woman looked a bit nervous, perhaps anticipating that I was upset, and shook her head slightly in the negative. A slight smile was still affixed to her poised face.

"Oh my God, this is the room," I added not at all impeded by her apparent lack of understanding, "that we had, during the haunting back in 1985!"

. . .

It looked so non-descript, so sterile, so safe. The keycard (I had been expecting a key) had slid effortlessly into the modern door lock, and after a slight 'clicking' sound was heard, we saw our former room.

Decades of nightmares that contained the blurred motion of Christmas lights, maddening repetitive flashing clock numbers, frozen and bony fingertips tapping the side of my neck, and stares from the cold face of death mere inches from my own, had created a menagerie of horror in my psyche. A feeding frenzy of torn skin, blood beading to the surface, Nosferatu-type shadows scaling the wall behind me, and a freezing cage-like room assaulted my sense of stability.

But this lasted for only a moment.

The walls were freshly painted, the mattresses were new and clean and the furniture, stacked to one side of the room, was freshly polished and in good repair.

The old carpet that I stood on when the ghost had arrived was gone, replaced now with professionally waxed tile; the folding closet doors that would shake from the force of the ghost's presence were gone too.

Jeff and I exchanged a comforting glance, and then we tossed our varied belongings onto the two beds.

Back home again.

We were left alone in order to help us better acclimate being back at the 'scene of the crime', and to limit the number of distractions before our first major presentation. I appreciated the quiet time, and spent most of it gazing out of the window in an odd, and unintentional, homage to the past. Jeff was sprawled out across a bed reading the article written about us, the film, and the haunting in the local newspaper.

"Howard (the reporter) did a nice job on the article," Jeff shared as he gazed up over his wire-rimmed glasses.

His comments, as correct as they were, were simply a diversion to allow his eyes to look for signs of stress or discomfort in me. I nodded, and smiled. The nod was in order to express my agreement with his statement, the smile to express my thanks that he still cared after all of these years.

Jeff smiled back.

"Do you sense anything?"

"I sense that I have to go to the bathroom," I countered, not yet ready to begin a true 'exploration' of the environment.

Jeff laughed, wagged his head back-and-forth in mock annoyance, and returned to the paper.

"When you feel up to it, let me know," he said knowingly, "I don't think we should rush anything. Let's just play it safe."

"You don't think I should rush anything," I partially mimicked, "Is that an old age joke, my prostate is not enlarged yet!" I paused for effect, "I don't think it is anyway!"

Jeff chuckled again as I made my way towards the bathroom. Humor was my refuge, my sanctuary, and at times my salvation.

Walking a bit slower than I had a quarter century before, I slid the old wooden bathroom door open. Its shape and weight were both still very familiar to me. I notice my reflection in the mirrors of the bathroom, but now instead of seeing a young, naked, bleeding college student falling to the floor worried about death, I focus instead on Jeff's movements in C2D1 over my shoulder in the brightly lit room behind me. We were both proof positive that hardships could be endured under the proper circumstances and with the correct choices being made.

I turned the faucet of the sink, the one closest to the shower stall, in order to wash my face. Reddish, blood-stained, water poured out of it. If this moment were being filmed for a movie, screeching sounds and eerie special effects would be playing as the room began to spin with ever increasing speed around me. But I don't need those effects, as the feelings of dread and inevitability that they would encourage in an audience member, were already washing over me with great effect.

"Hey, Jeff?"

"Yeah?"

The water was now losing its reddened hue, and returning to a clear stream. I could make out what looked to be minute flecks of material in the ridges around the drain: rust.

"I'm glad that things here seem better now."

"Me too"

. . .

By now, there was no doubt in either Jeff or myself, that the events needed to be shared for public consumption. Seventeen months earlier, in what roughly coincided with the 25th anniversary of the beginning of the haunting; we had found ourselves walking along the quiet sidewalks of tiny Maybrook, New York, snow falling down around us, we in our dark winter coats, talking about the varied wonders of life.

Neither of us realized at that moment, that this was the sign that I had discussed as we were preparing to leave college. Too much time had passed, too many conversations had and too many jobs worked. Life had no doubt grinded out some of the hope and idealism of youth for both of us.

Jeff and I had fallen out of touch for almost a decade. It took a film project called *Please, talk with me ...* a look back at the 1985 haunting, to bring us back together again.

It wasn't until we had reached the set location, that we finally grasped it.

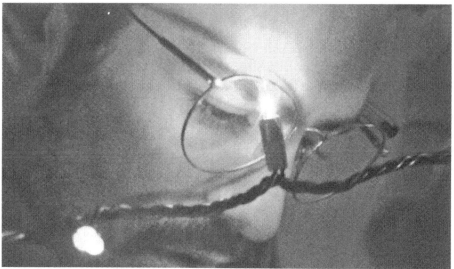

On Set: Actor Aaron Katter as J. Jeff Ungar on the set of the film *Please, talk with me ...* The film was produced by Bill Edwards and directed by Mara Katria. The independent film won Best Feature at Spirit Quest Film Fest in 2014, while Ms. Katria earned Best Director honors at the Wilson Film Fest the year prior.

Much like a train approaching from a distance, the sounds were soft at first, barely noticeable. But eventually the sound of the wheels on the track, the engine's roar, the horn blowing, it becomes impossible not to notice. And with every step that awareness grew. As we reached the bottom step of the nondescript shoot location, my mind lit up with recognition.

"Oh my God, Jeff," I exclaimed in a tone possibly unbecoming of a person of my age and station, "this is the sign! From college, remember?"

I could almost make out the spark of recognition in his eyes as he replied in a more measured but equally emphatic tone, "Wow. You're right! I remember that. I do. But what on Earth does it all mean?"

We were still looking for answers.

. . .

Hurricane Sandy devastated the East Coast, years later the effects of the ravaging storm can still be seen along vast coastline stretches of New Jersey, New York, and other states. As I stood in the darkened, powerless room watching the torrent of wind and rain assault the silent man-made structures all around me, I realized that sharing the events of the haunting was the smartest thing that I could have done. For like the tree limbs that would break that night, and the roofs that would be damaged, I too would eventually pass on. And it would have been a shame if no was left to tell the story of Tommy and the Ghost boy of Geneseo.

Daylight brought a welcome calm, free of the gale-force winds and blankets of rain. It reminded me of Erie hall and surviving the death-filled nights. My family was left intact: no injuries, no severe property damage, and no loss of life.

Others were not so fortunate. The damages from the storm (which at one point was a Category 3) have been estimated at over 65 billion dollars in the USA alone. Even more devastating was the loss of over two hundred thirty human lives as the super-storm tore its way across land and sea.

Thanks to the vision and hard work of many good people, I have been able to turn what had been the most terrifying weeks of my life into a springboard for assisting others. My appearances on television and radio programs, in films and at conventions – sharing the details of the ordeal – have placed me, if even for a brief time, in a unique position to help others.

Never was that more relevant than when I had the opportunity on November 24th, 2012, just three weeks after the storm hit.

I joined Steve Di Schiavi (*The Dead Files*); Joe Chin (*Ghost Hunters*); and John Brightman (Founder, N.E.P.R.) at the Irish Mist, a now-shuttered centuries old edifice in Troy, N.Y. for a paranormal fundraiser to aid the victims of Hurricane Sandy. The event was sponsored by John Tobin and the "Glory Haunt Hounds", a New York-based paranormal research group. We raised a good amount of money to help those, particularly in the hard-hit Brooklyn, NY area, who were still suffering from the storms effects.

2013: Jeff and I pose with Brian J. Cano from SyFy's 'Haunted Collector' as we pay a visit to the haunted Shanley Hotel in Napanoch, NY. The hotel's proprietor, Sal Nicosia, has spent years of his life repairing and maintaining the structure that has a reputation of being one of the most active sites in the Northeast United States.

In seeing the positive difference that I might be able help foster, I jumped head first into lecturing. There too, the reception was overwhelmingly positive. Unlike back in 1985, there was now an open fascination with the paranormal, and a strong interest in hearing about the C2D1 Haunting, the evidence collected, and the people who survived it. For that I am very grateful.

In 2012, the Rev. Tim Shaw (host of The Black Cat lounge on the Para X Radio Network), who was seated in the Geneseo crowd the first time that Jeff and I spoke publicly about the haunting, wrote the first book on it. Like the film it was a companion piece for, it was entitled *Please, talk with me*. The foreword was written by John Zaffis, the Godfather of the Paranormal from the long-running *Haunted Collector* series. It provided a well-organized and insightful overview from the perspective of a long-time researcher.

It was author/artist E.R. Vernor aka Corvis Nocturnum (*Embracing the Darkness; Haunted Prisons*) who inspired me to examine the decades-old events in even greater detail, and to commit myself to the process of serious writing. I had written essays, race analysis and a few 'Letters to the Editor' to my local newspaper over the years, but a 400 page book was something altogether different.

I begin many of my lectures with: consider what has been the worst moment of your life to this point, and then share it in detail. Because that is what every ninety-minute presentation I gave was, and that is what this book would represent; honest self-reflection and real pain.

Surrounding myself with old college photo albums and clippings, and drawing on some of Jeff's journal notes, and on the early research and writings of Alan Lewis and Steven Pomposello, I began the process of framing my memories and understandings of the past into written word.

I have heard it said many times that 'the *winner* writes history', but I hope that there is more to it than that. I hope that writers are those who honor the past, concern themselves with the betterment of society, and the structures and environments around them. That they desire to educate, inform, and inspire those who they are fortunate enough to impact. I hope that those who believe in something beyond themselves are those who do dare to write as we soar into the 21st Century.

...

Three and one-half years after the haunting, I was managing a B. Dalton Booksellers inside the Sunrise Mall in Massapequa (Long Island) New York. While dutifully placing the latest issues of *Time* and *Newsweek* into the magazine display rack, a customer walking by the store entrance caught my eye, and my heart.

My friends (many of whom developed an instant crush on her) claimed that she was a dead-ringer for actress Molly Ringwald who was at that time the queen of the coming of age movies like *Pretty in Pink, Sixteen Candles*, and *For Keeps*.

And at twenty-three, I was more than ready to come of age.

With flowing auburn hair, wild-colored eyes that seemed to match, a beautiful wide smile and curves that could derail a train, I was hooked. One of ten children, she was part Puerto Rican, part Irish and all consuming.

Oftentimes when she slept I would stare at her in the fervent hope that she wasn't just an impossible dream; Lord knew I had enough of an impossible nightmare.

She was patient and kind, nonjudgmental and grounded, and she tethered my ever-restless spirit with a loving acceptance.

Less than seven months later, Rita and I were married. Jeff was our Best Man, and Rita's sister, Alice (an opera singer), was our Maid of Honor. My maternal grandfather always had a weak spot for red-heads and when we got engaged, he made Rita promise to dance with him at our wedding reception. At that time I joked and warned him that it could be bad for his health. When he actually suffered a heart attack after dancing with her in the VFW Hall, it didn't seem quite as funny. We visited him in the hospital before leaving for our honeymoon in the Bahamas, and as would befit any red-blooded male worth his salt, he had no regrets.

Nor did I ... honeymoon.

"You know you're in love when you can't fall asleep because reality is finally better than your dreams." — Dr. Seuss

In the ensuing years, Rita (who had zero interest in the paranormal) and I would raise two amazing children together, a daughter Susan, and a son Matthew.

Fearing that what had happened to me at college, could someday possibly befall them (or anyone), I would tell them bedtime stories about a young protagonist who tried to beat the odds and survive against angry shadows, talking walls and wailing spirits. With each telling I would attempt to share with them some part of what I had learned back in the dark days of the haunting: study your environment for answers; seek out trusted friends for help; and never, ever, forget the importance of hope.

It was very gratifying for me when my children realized, years later while watching the SyFy show, that those bedtime stories were based on my actual experiences, and that they represented my earnest attempt to prepare them for anything, because I loved them so. They remain my greatest joy.

...

As to the question of *who* the ghost at Geneseo was, and what it might have wanted ... that would take time.

Jeff had been intrigued that the ghost said it was from "Danville" – which made enough sense at the time as Dansville, N.Y. was less than a half-hour's car ride from the college. The oft-mentioned tilted head seemed to signify to most a broken neck was involved, and smart money was on the ghost having been a college student who had committed suicide on – or perhaps near – the college campus, perhaps even in room C2D1 itself.

The year after the haunting, I did make one journey up to Geneseo's police station, and was even granted access to a file of information (under the unanticipated agreement of anonymity for all involved) where I found a compelling case. Police investigators are required to gather contact lists and related data such as addresses and phone numbers, when there is an examined death in the event others need to pick up the trail at a later date. Against Jeff's sound advice, I telephoned the boy's mother out of the blue and spoke with her about the loss of her son and its devastating long-term effect on the family as a whole. Some of the threads seemed to tie together nicely and she was pleased that someone cared.

And even though some folks still speculated that it might have been the troubled spirit of Gregory Bender, who died in a fraternity house party on December 20th, 1984, I knew otherwise.

It was my hope that this was 'case closed'.

...

Then, in late 2011, as I was preparing for the SyFy filming, my mother came across the most amazing discovery: A Lieut. Thomas (Tommy) Boyd had been killed just outside of what is now Geneseo in 1779, and along the route that I had run on a regular basis. Furthermore, it was one of my known maternal ancestors, Adam Hubley, who first reported his death!

Apparently Boyd, while serving under General Sullivan during what is often called the "Sullivan Indian Campaign", had been leading a small scouting party north, and towards what is present day Geneseo. He was warned by a Native American scout loyal to the patriot army that he would be walking into an ambush, but he chose to ignore the warning. After a large scale skirmish, Boyd and a soldier named Michael Parker were later captured and ritualistically tortured.

Others were dead as well.

Adam Hubley wrote in a letter to General Washington:

We moved up this plain for about three miles in our regular line of march, which was a beautiful site, as a view of the whole could be had at one look, and then came to Jenise river, which we crossed, being about forty yards over, and near middle deep and then ascended a rising ground, which afforded a prospect which was so beautiful that, to attempt a comparison, would be doing an injury, as we had a view as far as our eyes could carry us of another plain, besides the one we crossed, through which the Jenise river formed a most beautiful winding, and, at intervals, cataracts, which rolled from the rocks, and emptied into the river.

We then marched on through a rough but rich country, until we arrived at the capital town, which is much the largest we have yet met with in our whole route, and encamped about the same.

At this place we found the body of the brave but unfortunate Lieutenant Boyd, and one rifleman, massacred in the most cruel and barbarous manner that the human mind can possibly conceive; the savages having put them to the most excruciating torments possible, by first plucking their nails from their hands, then spearing, cutting, and whipping them, and mangling their bodies, then cutting off the flesh from their shoulders by pieces, tomahawking and severing their heads from their bodies, and then leaving them a prey to their dogs. We likewise found one house burned, in which, probably, was a scene as cruel as the former.

This evening the remains of Lieutenant Boyd and the rifleman's corpse were interred with military honours. Mr. Boyd's former good character, as a brave soldier, and an honest man, and his behaviour in the skirmish of yesterday (several of the Indians being found dead, and some seen carried off,) must endear him to all friends of mankind. May his fate await those who have been the cause of his.

Legend had it that Boyd had his stomach sliced open and his intestines nailed to a small sapling. He then expired when he was physically forced to walk around the tree until his full innards had vacated his body.

When I considered this, it changed my entire perspective on the haunting in general, and about the ghost itself: Could it be that Tommy wasn't trying to frighten or threaten me at all that warm night in March of 1985? Was he instead showing me who he was and what had actually happened to him? Was I simply too young, too frightened, and too unprepared to understand?

The more I read, the more the reported injuries seem to match: the severed head, the disemboweled body, the wounds on the arms and hands ... as well as the old, Revolutionary War-style clothing. I had great difficulty discerning it when I first saw the ghost, but via some internet searching I was now able to connect my initial impressions to historic wardrobe.

Even the information that he shared with me that early morning in April (that he had made a terrible "mistake," that he had been "wrong," and that he was "so sorry") made full sense in this new context, if it indeed was Thomas Boyd.

And now, slightly over two-hundred years after his torture and death, it seemed as though he might have found a sixth generation descendent of one of the men who he had fought alongside, and who had discovered his body, and who also hailed from Pennsylvania.

Research had revealed that Thomas Boyd was indeed from Danville (as the ghost had imparted to me in that dark, cold room): *Danville*, Pennsylvania.

The tree on which he was tortured was one that I unknowingly ran by dozens of times as part of my long distance training for the college, and the place where I recognized that my knee would be damaged permanently.

Maybe Jeff's preferred theory had been right the whole time. Maybe I did pick up the ghost on one of my long runs through the countryside. If true, it would certainly explain a few things.

But how will I – or anyone – ever know? And in the end proof of identity would not have changed the actions that I took at Erie Hall.

Whether or not that was the tortured spirit of Thomas Boyd, it is my hope that the ghost, or whatever it was, has found some sense of peace. That was my intention for him as I stood, alone, afraid, shivering, and naked, in that college room ... regardless of *whom* it might have been.

Tellingly, science still cannot prove 'love' exists either: At its core it is simply a series of coordinated and repetitive actions based on need, comfort and sensation due to some innate pair bonding instinct. I would posit that how we react to something (love, the paranormal, good or bad luck) and how we internalize it, helps to provide life with meaning, and not the rather specific attempt to define it.

Besides, if/when scientists do prove there are certain paranormal elements, you can be sure that the only things that will change are that they will be regulated and taxed.

While many people I speak with are saddened by the fact that these events were hidden in the shadows for almost three decades, there were some distinct positives in waiting so long before sharing our experience. For one, the passage of time has allowed us to reflect upon, and better understand the events of the haunting.

In my opinion, too many contemporary investigators work under the false notion that they can quickly skulk into an old structure, collect some fragmented and disjointed 'ghost box' sounds (likely emitted from a nearby radio station) capture a few cell phone images of floating dust particles, and then claim to have proven that they had some meaningful contact with a spirit that they can now easily identify.

Searching for answers remains essential for the progress of societies and for the human species as a whole, but in a world where provable and open verbal, written, and electronic dialogue can so often be misconstrued and misapplied, it is likely foolhardy to assume that one can fully understand a brief paranormal encounter, much less speak knowledgably about it.

Like most achievements of consequence, it takes time.

Had we 'gone public' with the haunting thirty years ago, it is likely – considering the amount of evidence that we had collected, and the sheer number of then active witnesses (well over two dozen) – that the C2D1 Haunting would be as well-known as the Amityville Horror events, or any other case for that matter.

But we were not seeking fame, or notoriety. And if we had, we might have very well made fools of ourselves, running full steam ahead with the story of an emotionally depressed boy who hung himself in room C2D1.

Being so young and naïve we might have fallen victim to what surely could have resulted in some type of cult of popularity, or maybe worse.

Even when considering all of my good intentions, my loyal friends, and my positive upbringing, if I contemplate what my impulses, urges, and interests were back then, I have no doubt that I would have ended up falling prey either to vanity (In this issue: The Ghost Boy Bares His Soul - and that's not all!), or ego ("On tonight's show we hear from a young man who it is said has pierced the veil between the world of the living and the world of the dead! He's going to share with our own [insert fake-looking reporter's name here] what the meaning of life really is!").

There would likely have been money, opportunity and fame - and a chance to change public perceptions on the occult as *Ghost Hunters* did some twenty years later - but there would have been no control.

No control over how the events were defined, no control for what would have happened to the college students who lived in that room in the years following, and no control over what has become the most important issue of all: the effort to understand (regardless of the level of success) what it all might have meant.

A young Chris would have soared towards the Sun like Icarus with those celebrated and coveted wings, but wings made only of wax, and he would have come crashing back down to Earth for having jumped far too soon.

Today, I feel no need to prove, only to share. To look for possible connections that might raise some interesting questions and thoughts for others to digest.

What did standing face-to-face with the apparition feel like?

It felt like I was watching a person drowning in a dark, cold lake, with the knowledge that I had a chance to save them, but not knowing if I myself could swim. Not knowing whether or not he would pull me under with him, and wondering if I weren't better off just walking away.

It would have been the smart thing to do.

It would also have been the cowardly thing.

In some ways, perhaps similar to the Hall of Famers in baseball, I no longer get up each morning with the burning fire of desire in my belly to step into the batting cage in the hopes that this is the day that I get that 'big hit'. Feeling that I still had to prove to the crowd, and to everyone I saw, that I deserved to be there.

For you see, whether I wanted to or not, and irrespective of how many people were (or were not) in the 'stands' on that fateful April day, I hit that ball with all of my might, and with every ounce of courage that I could possibly muster. And I didn't do it to impress the writers in the press box, or to better leverage that next contract negotiation, I did it in the hopes that others might believe that they can do it too.

Like Babe Ruth's "Called Shot" home run in the 1932 World Series, I can't prove beyond a reasonable doubt that it all happened exactly as they say it did. But I do know that in the grand scheme of things that it needs to be possible.

In a world often filled with loneliness, illness and violence, such inspiration can be a very powerful answer.

...

I was twelve years old, and I was hitting a ball in the back of my grandparents' house.   Pretending that I was Babe Ruth, I would try to smash the ball over the imaginary homerun fence that was equidistant to a small bush just beyond the far end of the home.   After a few false starts, it happened: the ball went soaring up into the crisp spring sky.   As it approached the artificial home run line, it hooked sharply to the left behind the red brick house.   I could not see where it had landed.   Was it fair or foul?   Was it a game-winning home run, or just a long foul ball?   Placing the bat down on the ground, I anxiously jogged over to the corner of the house ... and I turned it.

I didn't bother to pick up the ball, because the game had changed: my great-grandfather, who had passed away half a year earlier, was standing there.   He put a finger up to his mouth as though to say: "Shhh, you didn't see me."

But I had seen him.

. . .

Corners are important.

William J. Edwards is a member of Webster Masonic Lodge #538 of the Grand Lodge of New York and served as the Worshipful Master (leader of the lodge). He assisted the late George Peter, Past Grand Historian of the Grand Lodge of New York, with completing his book, *The Power and Passion of Freemasonry.* The book explores many Masonic topics including the history of Freemasonry in the Finger Lakes region of New York which included the Sullivan Campaign. Mr. Edwards was the Producer of the award winning film, *Please, talk with me.* The film is an authentic retelling of the C2D1 Haunting. He is an active student of Freemasonry and enjoys researching life's mysteries including the paranormal.

PostScript

All journeys have a starting point where the adventure begins. My journey with the C2D1 Haunting began in the early 1990's. I had the privilege of seeing the photograph of the C2D1 skeletal ghost and learning the details of the haunting from Alan Lewis. Alan was high school classmates with John Jeff Ungar and family friends of my future in-laws, all growing up in Webster, NY. Some claims of the paranormal are dubious and can be dismissed as fanciful or unfortunately even deceptive. However, in this case, Alan spoke with conviction and I could actually see the shape of the skeletal apparition. It was amazing! When one encounters stories of the paranormal, they can react in different ways. Some may believe, deny, be curious, or just indifferent. I was skeptical of individual claims but believed that there was something to the paranormal in general. Just one ghost had to exist for some form of life after death to be possible. As a child, I was intrigued by episodes of *"In Search Of"* and in college I started researching the paranormal with vigor, defining a personal framework of understanding. There just seems to be more phenomena in our universe than can be currently measured and proven by the scientific method. As Producer of the Award Winning Film, *Please, talk with me*, I had the opportunity to consult with Mr. Christopher Di Cesare on an approach to presenting the haunting.

This approach involved addressing three questions:

- Can one accept the concept that ghosts exist?
- If so, then how could you prove or demonstrate that ghosts exist?
- And if there is a ghost, then what are you going to do about it?

When confronted with a haunting one can struggle with the question, "Is it really possible for ghosts to exist?" In the 1980's claims of ghost phenomena were generally derided. Outside "New Age" book stores, ghosts or spirits were either viewed as non-existent by the scientific establishment or viewed as coming from a source of Evil by Christian tradition. Discussions about ghosts and the paranormal were to be avoided. If paranormal encounters did happen to occur, regardless of the evidence, sources such as alcohol, drugs or mental delusion were guaranteed to be the cause. Any larger phenomenon involving a group of people was dismissed as mass hysteria. In spite of this perspective, individuals seem to have experienced and continue to experience the presence of those who have died. In the case of Chris, he eventually accepted that a ghost was really haunting him. If one accepts that ghosts do exist, the **next question could be how to document evidence of the ghost.**

The book you have just read contains the *Surviving Evidence* of the C2D1 haunting. This evidence includes photographs, journal notes, tape recordings and the writings of those who survived the ordeal. The memoir **then retells the actions** Chris took regarding the ghost. It details how he found the internal strength to confront his fears and communicate with the ghost with the intention of helping it find peace.

The C2D1 Haunting is compelling.

Thirty years later people are touched in some way when they learn about the haunting and want to know more. I have been fortunate to attend a number of lecture events with Chris since the film premiere and a question that is often asked is, "So, who was the Ghost?"

The unfortunate reality is we may never really know who the ghost was or the reason for what occurred in that dorm room and around Erie Hall. But we can look at the evidence and try to find some further understanding.

The first place to look at is the *Surviving Evidence* from the haunting. What can the journal notes, witness conversations and writings inform us.

- Per the journal notes, Chris stated to John Jeff that he saw a teenage boy with brown hair wearing a yellow and blue striped shirt with navy blue sweat pants. Some early thoughts were that the ghost was of a young boy who committed suicide. The journal notes also state there was some possible paranormal activity in dorm room C2D2 the previous semester. The existence of multiple ghosts cannot be ruled out.

- At different times and locations, separate individuals including Chris, his roommate Paul, college classmates and Chris's father all experienced some aspect of the ghost. I would suggest that this rules out the idea of the ghost being mass hysteria. Also, as they were not desirous of seeing or experiencing the ghost, I propose it was not the result of intention or faith such as a poltergeist or phantasm.

- Chris and others independently began calling the ghost 'Tommy'.

- Chris and others heard the ghost calling out Chris's name.

- The ghost seemed to have some level of intelligence and interacted with the environment around it. Actions included moving or taking items, tugging at clothing, sitting in the loft resulting in creaks, a clock flashing 9:16 and the turning on of lights and audio equipment.

- At the toga party on January 26th, Chris recalls *"on this night I can make out just one lone person on the outside looking in. It is difficult to make him out... He is standing about twenty feet from the southernmost windows – at the edge of the darkness – and standing very still. I am not sure what he is watching."* In discussing this with Chris, he now believes that he saw the ghost standing afar watching.

- The photograph captured the image of the formation of a skeletal ghost where Chris stated it normally was found at night. This was next to his head while he tried to sleep.

- The ghost was passionate and intense and could respond with anger. By the actions of the ghost, it appears that it strongly desired to communicate with Chris. The ghost appeared to be possessive of Chris. His roommate, Paul, reported years later that that *"the ghost warned him – on two occasions – "clear as day" to "leave Chris alone."* In talking with Chris today, he does not feel its intent was evil. When we want something really bad, we want to possess it. Even if we end up hurting the object of our desire such as could be the case of a passionate, unrequited love. The ghost may have attacked Chris in the shower because he was angry at Chris for saying, *"The hell with you!"*

- The ghost expressed feelings of despair and regret. The audio tape captured the EVP of the ghosts stating, "Chris... help me, Chris..." In his final moments of the haunting, Tommy is finally able to talk with Chris. He shares, *"Misssstake ... made ... was wrong ... ssssso wrong."*

- As the haunting proceeded the ghost revealed more of itself. This could have been due to Chris improving his ability or the ghost wanting to share more of himself to Chris. I believe it is probably a combination of both.

What is interesting with this haunting is that our understanding continues to evolve and grow over time. It may be that multiple ghosts were being experienced in the haunting which would add to the complexity of the situation. As mentioned in this book, Chris initially thought that the ghost might have been a young man named Tommy who committed suicide on the campus. In 2010, while researching for the SyFy show *School Spirits*, Chris reevaluated his own understanding of the ghost and offered forth another potential identity for the ghost. Lieutenant Thomas (Tommy) Boyd, who was a soldier in the American Revolutionary War and murdered near Geneseo, NY in 1779 during the Sullivan Campaign against the Iroquois Confederacy.

The American Revolutionary War was fought during the years of 1775 to 1783. The causes of the war are found in the way Great Britain imposed a number of taxes on the American Colonies. To enforce the taxes, Great Britain increased the military presence in Massachusetts. Some colonists rebelled against these actions and started to form a resistance. The British military leadership was given orders to disarm the rebels of their supplies located in Concord, Massachusetts. This military action was the reason for Paul Revere's famous midnight ride. He raised the alarm of the invasion and notified the resistance that "The British Regulars are Coming!" This military action resulted in the first shots of the American Revolutionary War on April 19, 1775 at the battle of Lexington and Concord. Over the coming year tensions with Great Britain intensified to include a number of military actions. On July 4th, 1776 the Continental Congress adopted the Declaration of Independence from Great Britain. The colonies had declared their independence. However, the King of England, George III, would not let his subjects and their property leave without a fight.

Over the ensuing years, there are a number of famous Revolutionary War events such as Washington Crossing the Delaware River into New Jersey, the Battle of Saratoga where British troops are forced to surrender, Washington's dismal winter in Valley Forge and France becoming an alley against Great Britain in 1778. The year 1779 is of particular interest related to the haunting. Before exploring that connection there is another dimension to this story that involves the Free and Accepted Masons or Freemasons.

The Freemasons are a fraternal organization with documented origins dating to June 24, 1717 in London England with the official formation of their governing body called the Premier Grand Lodge. Records of individual Masonic lodges exist in the British Isles from the early 1600's possibly dating back to the Stone Mason guilds of Medieval Europe from the 1300's. The exact origins of the Freemasons are lost to time. Much speculation continues about their possible connection to the Knights Templar, The Royal Society or The Rosicrucian's.

The heart of Freemasonry is the ideals of Brotherhood, Service and Self Improvement through education. Freemasons are required to believe in God, whom they call the Great Architect of the Universe. They also believe in the immortality of the soul, that life does not end with physical death. Freemasons are linked in a fraternal chain of brotherhood charged to aid and assist their brothers in times of need while at the same time improving who they are and making a positive difference in the world. This self-improvement is accomplished by speculatively applying the stone mason's working tools to himself. As a stone mason erects his physical building, the Freemason erects his spiritual building utilizing Knowledge and Character. Freemasons have three degrees that members pass through in their initiation to membership. These are the Entered Apprentice, Fellowcraft and Master Mason or Third Degree. Phrases from Freemasonry have found their way into common language such being square (truthful), giving someone the third degree (intense interrogation) and being on the level (equality).

After its official formation in 1717, Freemasonry quickly spread in England and beyond. In the 1700's being a Mason was socially fashionable among the upper class. The implied social benefits of membership increased the desire for men to join the organization. New lodges were formed and Freemasonry spread across England, Ireland, and Scotland as well as to the European Continent. A lodge is what a local group of Freemasons are called who regularly meet and conduct business as well as hold social functions.

In this period of growth, Freemasonry came to the colonies with immigrants from England, Ireland and Scotland. There was no central Masonic authority and the ceremonies and practices of these early Masonic lodges evolved organically. The Premier Grand Lodge of England began appointing Provincial Grand Masters in 1730 to oversee Masonry in the provinces (colonies). The Provincial Grand Masters were not consistent with exercising their authority to oversee the affairs of the lodges in their province. In December 1730, future Patriot and Freemason, Benjamin Franklin in his Gazette mentions that "there are several lodges of Freemasons erected in this Province" referring to Pennsylvania.

In 1751, the Premier Grand Lodge of England split into two rival bodies. The Premier Grand Lodge of England, particularly in London, was aristocratic in nature. The Grand Lodge had made a few changes to the ritual. Due to these "innovations" they became known as "The Moderns." A number of Irish Immigrants were denied entry into the London "Modern" Masonic Lodges. In response, they established a new Grand Lodge called the, "Grand Lodge of Free and Accepted Masons According to the Old Institutions." They became known as the "Ancients." In 1760 the Ancients chartered their first lodge in the colonies in Philadelphia. A rivalry existed between these two bodies.

"Modern" Grand Lodge Masons living in the colonies tended to be wealthier property owners with ties to its aristocratic orientation. The "Ancient" Grand Lodge Masons were artisans and business owners. There is a general trend that The Modern Masons tended to be loyal to the King during the American Revolutionary War and the Ancients were revolutionaries. Professor Steven Bullock, in his book, **Revolutionary Brotherhood, Freemasonry and the Transformation of the American Social Order, 1730 to 1840**, explores in great detail the influence Freemasonry had on the American Revolutionary War and the early formation of the United States of America.

According to Bullock, General George Washington, a Freemason, encouraged his officers to become Freemasons. He states, *"At least 42 percent of the Generals commissioned by the Continental Congress were or would become freemasons. For the officers, Masonry's values of love and honor held particular attraction. It created an "esprit de corps", by forming bonds between men separated by local origin, religious affiliation and military rank. It helped create a sense of common purpose necessary for the survival of the Continental Army allowing them to eventually win the war."* During the Revolutionary War there existed a number of Military Masonic Lodges that traveled with the troops. The Grand Lodge of Pennsylvania Military Masonic Lodge #19 will be weaving its way into our understanding of the haunting.

By 1779, the focus of the war had shifted to the southern colonies. In New York City, the continental army sat in a standstill with the British army. Because of this stale mate, the battle in New York and Pennsylvania had moved to the frontier. In 1778, King George III had ordered the Native Americans who sided with the crown, to attack New York's Cherry Valley and Pennsylvania's Wyoming Valley. This was a bloody massacre and General Washington had to respond to these attacks. He developed a strategy for a campaign against The Iroquois Confederacy which was located in Central and Western New York.

The Iroquois Confederacy was an alliance of six Native American Tribes that included the Seneca, Cayuga, Mohawk, Onondaga, Oneida, and Tuscarora Nations. The Revolutionary War broke apart the confederacy with some tribes remaining loyal to Great Britain and others supporting the Continental Army. Intense animosity existed between the tribes due to the passions of war. The Seneca, Cayuga, Mohawk, Onondaga all sided with Great Britain and the Oneida and Tuscarora sided with the Continental Army. Major General John Sullivan and Brigadier General James Clinton were given responsibility for this campaign. It eventually included four brigades, totaling about 4,500 men with regiments from New Hampshire, Massachusetts, New Jersey, New York, Virginia and Pennsylvania. The campaign strategy was straight forward. Sullivan would gather three brigades near Easton, Pennsylvania and travel along the Susquehanna River Valley. An additional brigade lead by Clinton would travel from Schenectady along the Mohawk River

Valley to join up with Sullivan at Tioga, Pennsylvania. Once united, the combined forces would travel north into the Iroquois territory. The objective of the campaign was a scorched earth policy - destroy anything that might be useful to the enemy.

The campaign began on June 18th, 1779 with Sullivan leaving Easton Pennsylvania. Clinton eventually met up with Sullivan on August 22nd at Fort Sullivan, a temporary fort at the joining of the Chemung and Susquehanna Rivers near Binghamton, NY. During the campaign approximately 40 Iroquois villages were destroyed in the Finger Lakes Region of New York. The campaign successfully put an end to Native American and Loyalist attacks. It ended on October 3rd when the troops abandoned Fort Sullivan joining troops in New Jersey. Of particular interest is an event that occurred in September 1799 near Geneseo, NY.

On Sunday, September 12, 1779 Sullivan's troops camped at Foot's Corners in Conesus, NY. That evening Sullivan ordered Lt. Thomas Boyd to organize and lead an advance scouting mission to locate Genesee, the Seneca village from which Chief Little Beard ruled his nation. Sullivan had requested that Boyd take only a handful of men for the mission. Boyd insisted on taking approximately twenty-six men including Sgt. Michael Parker on the reconnaissance mission. Joseph Brant, The Iroquois Chief and British Colonel John Butler were in charge of defending the region. When the scouts set off, by chance and due to darkness, they missed encountering over 500 troops lead by Brant and Butler who were preparing a surprise ambush on Sullivan and his troops.

The next morning, the scouting party engaged in a brief gun fight with some Native Americans. One of the Native Americans was killed and at least one had escaped. Boyd now knew that the Native Americans would be aware of his presence – his reconnaissance mission was compromised. He sent some scouts back to inform General Sullivan what had occurred. Lt. Boyd also decided he should turn back from the mission. On the trail of their return trip, they came upon five Native Americans who quickly fled. The Oneida guide, Hon Yost, believed this was a trap and suggested an alternate route and warned Boyd not to chase after them. Boyd disregarded the advice of his guide and pursued after the Native Americans. It was a trap and his scouting party was led into the enemy who was waiting to Ambush Sullivan's camp. After an intense battle, fifteen in the scouting party were killed, eight men had escaped and Lt. Thomas Boyd, Sgt. Michael Parker and their Oneida Guide Hon Yost were captured by Brant and Butler. The ambuscade was in present day Groveland, NY. The prisoners were taken to Genesee Castle near present day Geneseo, NY.

Fortunately for those researching the Sullivan Campaign, written journals and letters exist from the participants documenting what occurred. Army First Sergeant, John Salmon, a fellow soldier with Boyd, documents the encounter upon their arrival at Genesee Castle:

"When Lieut. Boyd found himself a prisoner, he solicited an interview with Brant, whom he well knew commanded the Indians. This chief, who was at that moment near, immediately presented himself; when Lieut. Boyd, by one of those appeals which are known only by those who have been initiated and instructed in certain mysteries, and which never fail to bring succor to a 'distressed brother', addressed him as the only source from which he could expect a respite from cruel punishment or death. The appeal was recognized, and Brant immediately, and in the strongest language, assured him that his life should be spared."

This exchange between Lieut. Boyd and Chief Brant requires further explanation. Both Thomas Boyd and Joseph Brant were Freemasons. We do not know the specific lodge that Thomas Boyd was a member of however Grand Lodge of Pennsylvania Military Lodge #19 travelled with the Sullivan Campaign. In early May, Col. Thomas Proctor was ordered to join the Sullivan-Clinton Campaign. On May 18th he received a warrant from the Grand Lodge of Pennsylvania for Military Lodge #19. The book of minutes from the lodge does not exist however it is estimate that more than 150 men were made Masons during the campaign by the amount of money turned into the Grand Lodge of Pennsylvania after the campaign. It is custom for lodges to pay a fee to their Grand Lodge when initiating new members. General Sullivan and General Clinton were both Freemasons. It is believed that the Military Lodge was active almost every night when the army was encamped. Some of the lodge meetings were actually held in General Sullivan's tent! According to the research done by Past Grand Historian of the Grand Lodge of New York, George Peter, General Sullivan wanted to ensure that many of his officers selected for the campaign were Freemasons because of their character. Peter states, "There were not sufficient Chaplains hence it was Sullivan's belief that the leaders who were Freemasons would be concerned about proper respect and treatment of those casualties of battle and would administer solace and comfort to those wounded, sick and distressed men of his army. He wanted to be assured that those who died or were killed in battle would be given burial by men who believed in Almighty God."

Chief Joseph Brant was initiated into Freemasonry at Hiram's Cliftonian Lodge #417 in Leicester Fields, London on April 26, 1776. It is reported that King George III actually presented him his Masonic Apron. Brant was a civilized warrior. He was educated, loyal to the King and defender of his people. However, there is a long tradition among Freemasons endeavoring to maintain the ties of fraternal brotherhood across the lines of battle. While remaining loyal to their state, the tenants of Freemasonry can challenge a man to look within his heart to find the humanity of their enemy amidst the carnage and passions of war. In the real world, hatred and evil atrocities exist. One only has to look at the terror created by militant Islamic extremists in our present day. We do not all play nice in the sand box. Masonry teaches that all men are brothers of a common creator, the Great Architect of the Universe. Regardless of religious creed, race or nationality we are instructed to help aid and assist when possible. As Freemasons, we know that if we were in a different time and place, we would be celebrating the bonds that unite us rather than what at this moment must divide us. Joseph Brant was present at the massacre in Cherry Valley. There are historical accounts that when the attacks were made against the civilians, he actively tried to rescue and save them. There are also accounts that Brant had spared the lives of fellow masons. Years later, Joseph Brant's adopted nephew states, "that Brant used every endeavor to spare the life of Boyd."

Army First Sergeant John Salmon continues to report what happened next: "*After their arrival at Beard's Town, Brant, their generous preserver, being called on service which required a few hours' absence, left them in the care of the British Colonel, Butler, of the Rangers – who, as soon as Brant had left them, commenced an interrogation to obtain from the prisoners a statement of the number, situation, and intentions of the army under Gen. Sullivan; and threatened them, in case they hesitated or prevaricated in their answers, to deliver them up immediately to be massacred by the Indians, who, in Brant's absence, and with the encouragement of their more savage commander, Butler, were ready to commit the greatest cruelties. Relying, probably, on the promises which Brant had made them, and which he undoubtedly meant to fulfill, they refused to give Butler the desired information. Butler, upon this, hastened to put his threat into execution. They were delivered to some of their most ferocious enemies, who, after having put them to very severe torture, killed them by severing their heads from their bodies.*"

Mary Jemison, a "white" woman who was captured and adopted by the Seneca as a teen was present at the capture and torture of Thomas Boyd. Her memoir shares the following details about the torture:

"*Little Beard, in this as in all other scenes of cruelty that happened at his town, was master of ceremonies, and principal actor. Poor Boyd was stripped of his clothing, and then tied to a sapling; where the Indians menaced his life, by throwing their tomahawks at the tree directly over his head, brandishing their scalping knives around him in the most frightful manner, and accompanying their ceremonies with terrific shouts of joy. Having punished him sufficiently in this way, they made a small opening in his abdomen, took out an intestine, which they tied to the sapling, and then unbound him from the tree, and drove him round it, till he had drawn out the whole of his intestines. He was then beheaded, his head was stuck upon a pole, and his body left on the ground unburied. Thus ended the life of poor Thomas Boyd, who, it was said, had every appearance of being an active and enterprising officer, of the first talents. The other was, if I remember distinctly, only beheaded, and left near Boyd."*

On Tuesday September 14th, Sullivan's Army came upon the remains of Boyd, Parker and Yost. They were reinterred with military honors. It is reported the Boyd also received Masonic Burial Rites. In 1841, the remains were moved from the battlefield in Groveland and reinterred at Mount Hope Cemetery in Rochester, NY.

Unfortunately, it was not possible to perform a thorough ghost investigation in 1985 with the equipment and understanding available today. In my experience, connections matter. Sometimes observations help us to understand how the world works. My own belief is that we do not stop being human upon death. Some patterns of our human behaviors still exist and hauntings can be based upon an important connection. This connection could be the location of where the person lived or where they died, a family member or a close friend. It may be that the reason for the haunting is that some event occurred in or near the C2D1 dorm room. The other possibility is that there was a connection between Chris and the ghost, separate from the dorm room. Do any interesting connections exist between Thomas Boyd and Chris Di Cesare?

There are a number of personal connections between Thomas Boyd and Chris. As part of Chris's Cross Country Training he regularly ran by the "Torture Tree", the exact location were Thomas Boyd was murdered. The Tree is located within a few miles of the SUNY Geneseo Campus. Was there something unique about Chris that the ghost of Thomas Boyd could have felt a connection to? Amazingly, there is an ancestral connection between Thomas Boyd and Chris. The maiden name for Chris's mother is Hubley. Two of Chris's ancestors were in the Continental Army and actually participated in the Sullivan Campaign along with Thomas Boyd. They were Captain Bernhard Hubley and Lieutenant Adam Hubley.

Chris' great-great-great-great grandfather was Bernhard Hubley the second. Though from Pennsylvania, he was a member of the 8th Maryland Regiment and was serving on the Sullivan Campaign from July to October 1779. Adam Hubley is Bernhard's son and was among the army troops that found Thomas Boyd's body.

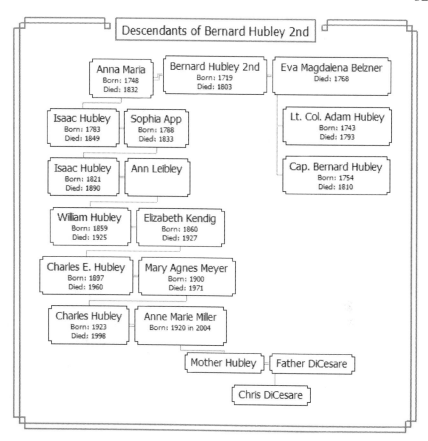

Descendants of Bernard Hubley 2nd

Anna Maria
Born: 1748
Died: 1832

Bernard Hubley 2nd
Born: 1719
Died: 1803

Eva Magdalena Belzner
Died: 1768

Isaac Hubley
Born: 1783
Died: 1849

Sophia App
Born: 1788
Died: 1833

Lt. Col. Adam Hubley
Born: 1743
Died: 1793

Isaac Hubley
Born: 1821
Died: 1890

Ann Leibley

Cap. Bernard Hubley
Born: 1754
Died: 1810

William Hubley
Born: 1859
Died: 1925

Elizabeth Kendig
Born: 1860
Died: 1927

Charles E. Hubley
Born: 1897
Died: 1960

Mary Agnes Meyer
Born: 1900
Died: 1971

Charles Hubley
Born: 1923
Died: 1998

Anne Marie Miller
Born: 1920 in 2004

Mother Hubley

Father DiCesare

Chris DiCesare

Note: Lt. Col. Adam Hubley was the child of Bernard Hubley's first wife Eva. Chris's family descends of Bernard and his second wife Anna. It is interesting to mention that Bernard's ancestor, Joseph Bernard Hubley (not shown) died under mysterious circumstances when he arrived in America in 1732. It is thought he was working on an exposure of the Jesuits and was murdered due to this research. His heretical manuscripts and research went missing upon his death. The name Hubley is thought to be adapted from "Oublie" which means To Be Forgotten.

What follows are excerpts from his actual journals from the Sullivan Campaign:

Sunday, Sept. 12th. — *... After arriving within half a mile of Kanaghsas, a small Indian village, which was previously destined for this day's march, night set in, and the main army being at least a mile in our rear, we received orders to encamp for this night, which was in the woods, and exceedingly ill calculated for that purpose, no water being nearer than half a mile. This day's march completed twelve miles. After we encamped, Lieutenant Boyd, of the rifle corps, some volunteers, and as many* *riflemen, made up six and twenty in the whole, were sent up to reconnoitre the town of Jenesse, having for their guide an Onieada Indian, named Hanyost, a chief of that tribe, who has been remarkable for his attachment to this country, having served as a volunteer since the commencement of the war.*

Monday, Sept. 13th. — *... Four men of Lieutenant Boyd's party this morning returned, bringing information of the town of Gaghsuquilahery (which they took for Jenese) being abandoned. Lieutenant Boyd having retired from the town of Gaghsuquilahery to wait for the arrival of the main army, which was detained longer than he expected, he sent back two men to know the cause. These two men had not gone far before they discovered a few Indians ahead. They then retired and informed Lieutenant Boyd, who immediately, with his party, gave chase, and followed them within about two miles and a half from the main army, where a body of savages, of at least four or five hundred, lay concealed, and probably intended giving the main army (the ground being favourable on their side) a fire, and push off according to custom, who immediately surrounded him and his party. He nobly fought them for some considerable time; but, by their great superiority, he was obliged to attempt a retreat, at the same time loading and firing as his party ran. The Indians killed, and in the most inhuman manner, tomahawked and scalped six that were found. Nine of the party have got safe in; but Lieutenant Boyd and Henjost, (the Indian already mentioned,) with seven others, are yet missing.*

Tuesday, Sept. 14th. —*... We then marched on through a rough but rich country, until we arrived at the capital town, which is much the largest we have yet met with in our whole route, and encamped about the same. At this place we found the body of the brave but unfortunate Lieutenant Boyd, and one rifleman, massacred in the most cruel and barbarous manner that the human mind can possibly conceive; the savages having put them to the most excruciating torments possible, by first plucking their nails from their hands, then spearing, cutting, and whipping them, and mangling their bodies, then cutting off the flesh from their shoulders by pieces, tomahawking and severing their heads from their bodies, and then leaving them a prey to their dogs. We likewise found one house burned, in which, probably, was a scene as cruel as the former.*

This evening the remains of Lieutenant Boyd and the rifleman's corpse were interred with military honours. Mr. Boyd's former good character, as a brave soldier, and an honest man, and his behaviour in the skirmish of yesterday (several of the Indians being found dead, and some seen carried off) must endear him to all friends of mankind. May his fate await those who have been the cause of his. Oh! Britain, behold and blush. Jenise town, the capital of the Seneca nation, is pleasantly situated on a rich and extensive flat, the soil remarkably rich, and great parts well improved with fields of corn, beans, potatoes, and all kinds of vegetables. It contained one hundred and seven well-finished houses.

Wednesday, Sept. 15th. *—About 3 o'clock, P. M., the business was finished, and the immediate objects of this expedition completed, viz., the total ruin of the*

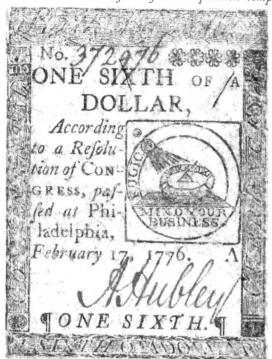

Indian settlements, and the destruction of their crops. The following is a part of the orders issued this day, viz.: "The commander-in-chief informs this brave and resolute army that the immediate objects of this expedition are accomplished, viz.: total ruin of the Indian settlements, and the destruction of their crops, which were designed for the support of those inhuman barbarians, while they were desolating the American frontiers. He is by no means insensible of the obligations he is under to those brave officers and soldiers whose virtue and fortitude have enabled him to complete the important design of the expedition, and he assures them he will not fail to inform America at large how much they stand indebted to them. The army will this day commence its march for Tioga."

What an incredible connection. Adam Hubley, Chris's ancestor, was among those who found the mutilated body of Thomas Boyd and ensured he received a proper burial. Adam Hubley was also a Freemason and member of Pennsylvania Lodge #29. Given my experience with Freemasonry, I expect that he would have had a close bond or connection with Thomas Boyd as Fraternal Brothers.

Chris is said to resemble his mother's family rather than his father's. Could he possibly appear like a Hubley? Chris is described as being psychically "sensitive." Dr. Casler's tests had found a very strong case of positive step progression. Lorraine Warren did not want her future revealed, something very private, to Chris in a similar manner as Chris had unknowingly done for his Uncle Jonny. His Uncle had died a few weeks after they shook hands. John Jeff believed that Chris was "sensitive to his environment in ways that most of us are not." Chris's great-great-grandmother, Maria Antoinette Ricciuti Fracasse, had been a seer who was renowned for her Tarot card readings. It is believed there may be a genetic predisposition for psychic abilities. It is my understanding that spirits can sense this ability. Lorraine Warren said "There is a Law of Attraction. Ghosts are attracted to compassionate or sympathetic people."

Did Chris's familial resemblance to Adam Hubley and his innate sensitivity motivate Thomas Boyd to become interested in Chris? Did he watch him as he regularly ran by the Torture Tree? Did he follow Chris back to Erie Hall and dorm room C2D1 after one of his long cross country training runs?

In discussing the haunting with Chris, he also mentioned several additional connections between himself and Thomas Boyd. If Thomas Boyd sensed these connections, could they have further emboldened him to passionately pursue Chris? Some of the connections include:

- On December 31st, 1775 Thomas Boyd was captured as a Prisoner of War and was paraded through the streets of Montreal. His prisoner exchange was in 1777. In his teens, Chris ran the Montreal Marathon (1979-1982) possibly on the same streets Thomas Boyd marched.

- Thomas Boyd was born in Washingtonville, PA in 1757. Chris was from Newburgh, NY which was just six miles from Washingtonville, NY. For his Communications Major, Chris remembers preparing and practicing five oral essays about high school race results that included reference to runners from Washingtonville, some of the best runners he competed against.

- Thomas Boyd grew up in Danville, PA. In 1985 Chris told John Jeff that Tommy said he came from "Dan-ville" which he may have incorrectly assumed was Dansville, NY which is a town located near Geneseo rather than Danville, PA.

- Chris commented that "The creature, wants to be young like me, to be able to run effortlessly across the land like me." The Boyd Family History states that when they were ambushed and Thomas tried to escape by following a fellow hearty solider named Murphy. *"Thomas justly supposed if any one escaped with their life, it would be Murphy, so he determined to follow him, but not being so fast a runner he was soon taken."* Another amazing connection. Perhaps Thomas was longing to be like Chris, who was a potential Olympian runner! If Thomas had only been faster, he may have escaped. Sadly near the location that Thomas Boyd was murdered, years later Chris experienced his knee injury, ending his Olympic dream.

The Family history also describes Thomas Boyd, "*as a young man of ordinary height, strongly built, fine looking, sociable and agreeable in all his manners, which gained for him many friends wherever he went.*" When Thomas and his older brothers John and William departed to join the patriots, their mother called out to them, "*I have one word more I wish to say before you leave me, and that is, whatever situation you may be placed in the face of the enemy in the defense of your country, always do your duty and never let cowardice cross your path.*" Throughout the haunting, Tommy could be described as being persistent and strong willed. These are certainly character traits attributed to Thomas Boyd.

Some aspects of the initial description of the ghost found in the journal notes do not exactly match Thomas Boyd at the time of his death. This adds to the complexity of this investigation and why it is important to peel back the different layers of obscurity to continue to find understanding. There are a number of factors that influence how we perceive and interpret visual information. Ask an investigator of a crime scene about the challenges related to conflicting eye witness accounts. Chris described the ghost as a young boy while Thomas Boyd was in his early 20's at the time of his death. It is common to mistake someone's age. For instance, when Chris was nineteen, he too was mistaken for a young boy by his dorm mates. The journal notes continue to describe the ghost as wearing a yellow and blue striped shirt with navy blue sweat pants. I have been able to locate an illustration of the uniform for Morgan's Riflemen, which was a yellowish shirt with navy blue pants. This is a similar description of clothing and what Thomas Boyd would have been wearing. Thomas Boyd was beheaded which would explain why Chris saw the ghost's head in an unnatural position. In mid-March of 1985, after the infamous shower attack, I believe the ghost finally revealed himself to Chris. He was situated outside his window in a tree with his body horribly mutilated. For years Chris was deeply disturbed as to why the ghost would show himself in this way. Particularly when he thought it was someone who had committed suicide. It was not until years later, while researching to aid the SyFy show, School Spirits, that he realized that his wounds were similar to those of Thomas Boyd.

When Chris had his pivotal communication with "Tommy", the ghost expressed deep remorse and regret. Thomas Boyd certainly would have had regret for making choices which resulted in the death of the men under his direct care and command. Could the relocation of his remains to Mount Hope Cemetery in 1841 contributed to him being a restless spirit? It is interesting to note that some historians believe that the actions of Thomas Boyd unknowingly thwarted the larger ambush planned for Sullivan and his troops. So in the end, his choices may have spared the lives of many by avoiding a larger battle. And if there had been a different outcome then the Native Americans retreating, it could have potentially changed the course of American History!

One reoccurring event that had intrigued me about the haunting was that the alarm clock in their dorm room, on different occasions, was set to 9:16. I felt there was some significance to those numbers. What could 9:16 mean? Was it the time of the ghost's death? Where there other meanings? Could it refer to a date such as of September 16th? Is that date important? Actually it is for two reasons. On September 16th Sullivan's troops came upon fifteen fallen men from Boyd's party and buried them. Secondly, Sullivan's army left Thomas Boyd on the afternoon of September 15th. Was Tommy sending a message that he has been alone since 9:16? And finally after 205 years of being alone, he finally found someone that reminded him of an old friend and also offered the opportunity of companionship – with someone who heard him when he called out their name.

"Tommy", I hope that this contribution to the haunting investigation has somehow helped you *Rest in Peace*. We may never be able to prove who the ghost of C2D1 was. However, given the amount of Surviving Evidence and the growing interest in this extreme haunting, I expect that the investigation will continue. And in time, it is my hope that this research and future research will aid in our further understanding of the events that occurred in SUNY Geneseo in 1985.

Additional Reference Material:

1. George Peter, The Power and Passion of Freemasonry, Cornerstone Book Publishers, 2012

2. Michael Karpovage, "Betrayed by a Mason? The Tragic Mission of Lieutenant Thomas Boyd"

3. Frederick Cook, Journals of the Military Expedition of Major General John Sullivan Against the Six Nations of Indians in 1779

4. James E. Seaver, Life of Mary Jemison, the White Woman

"You have peace," the old woman said, "when you make it with yourself."
— Mitch Albom, *The Five People You Meet in Heaven*

Photo taken by: Robert D. Edwards Sr. -- Lake George NY

"Alone in a Crowd" by artist Kerry Lyon (2014)

C2D1 Haunting Timeline

<u>09/03/84</u> - Chris Di Cesare and Paul A. move into Room C2D1, Erie Hall at SUNY Geneseo. They set up a loft.

<u>09/08/84</u> – Chris and J. Jeff (Jeff) Ungar meet in C2D Quad area.

<u>11/14/84</u> – Paul has a series of dreams and Déjà vu experiences, warns something catastrophic is about to occur.

<u>01/26/85</u> – Erie Hall Toga Party.

<u>01/30/85</u> – Ed and Lorraine Warren presentation at Wadsworth Auditorium, attended by Jeff and Chris.

<u>02/08/85</u> – Chris receives care package from his family.

<u>02/11/85</u> – Chris experiences strange creaking noises from loft, hears his name called inside the room, experiences drafts, cold spots, and closet doors opening without obvious cause. Chris' sweat suit unsnaps on its own volition. Chris too frightened to take shower. Later, Paul hears ghost call Chris' name in C2D1.

<u>02/12/85</u> – Paul is plagued by moving shadows. Chris sees moving shadows wash over his desk top. First sighting of what might be a ghost

– with a titled head - is made by Chris as he sits at desk in his room. Chris flees C2D1 in a panic to seek assistance, and runs to C2D2. Jeff agrees to 'journal' the events.

02/13/85 – Chris is heard shouting at Paul to turn the lights on, Paul refuses. Paul wakes Chris when he hears a 'hissing' sound in the room. Chris investigates, throws objects at wall where he sees a human figure, retreats to bed. Paul observes as Chris, who is screaming, engages in a tug of war (that lasts several minutes) for his pillows which remain suspended in the air. Later, Paul witnesses a gold orb floating above Chris' head as he sleeps, and sees a 'shadowy figure' standing on a chair looking at him.

02/14/85 – Upon waking it is noticed that Chris' chair has been moved, a picture frame taken apart, an alarm clock reset. Jeff conducts experiments for proof of ghost. Chris attempts to summon ghost (Tommy'). Gurgling noises are heard. Ghost passes through Chris. Chris panics. Chris' mattress can be seen with a human-shaped indent. Jeff continues takes numerous photographs of events, one photo is taken by Chris before he exits the room.

02/15/85 - Jeff leaves for family vacation in Florida. Chris wakes during night to find ghost near him and 'smiling' at him. Chris' ear, cheek and neck are cold and numb to the touch; he flees the room for several minutes to compose himself. Several hours later, as Chris sleeps, Paul sees a shadow figure – with a titled head - looking at him from the foot of the loft. He wakes Chris and with the information. Paul fears they will die. They decide to seek assistance.

02/15/85 – Chris and Paul walk to St. Mary's Catholic Church at 7 a.m. They are unsuccessful in their attempts to speak with a priest, but are given the phone number of Fr. Charles Manning of the College Interfaith Center.

02/17/85 – Chris and Beth Kinsman (from B building Erie Hall) flee his room while studying for an exam when they observe a pencil fall through the ceiling above them.

02/18/85 – Beth volunteers to assist Chris and Paul. Beth obtains the contact information of Dr. Lawrence Casler, a psychology professor.

02/21/85 – Chris' track coach calls to express his concern over lack of attendance. Paul reminds Chris of his earlier predictions, and says that his life is falling apart because of the ghost.

02/22/85 – While reading at his desk, Chris (shirtless) feels something 'freezing cold and firm' touch his right shoulder near his neck. He sprints to a corner of the room, and curls into a fetal position praying that God will 'take this ghost away'.

<u>02/25/85</u> – Jeff, back from Florida, has the roll of film from the Feb. 14th session developed at a 'one hour' photo booth. Notices the photo taken by Chris reveals a 'skeletal apparition'. Chris does not want to see it, but is persuaded by Beth - who also sees the form – to do so.

<u>03/02/85</u> – After a series of meetings between Jeff, Paul, Beth and Chris, it was agreed that Chris and Paul should bring Jeff's journal notes and meet with Fr. Charles Manning, while either Beth or Jeff would reach out to Dr. Casler.

<u>03/04/85</u> – Chris and Paul speak with Fr. Manning at the College Interfaith Center. After over an hour of journal reading and discussion, Fr. Manning agrees to assist. He will visit room C2D1 under the guise of a stereo repairman (making note of the events of Feb 12th) so as not to attract attention to the situation.

<u>03/06/85</u> – The priest arrives at 8 p.m. to 'bless' the room. Paul is not present. Jeff asks to be a part of the proceedings but is rebuffed by Fr. Charlie. Chris agrees to take notes in Jeff's absence. At the conclusion of the ceremony, Chris asks if the ghost can back in the room, and is advised by the priest, "Only if you invite him back in." Following the blessing, there is no activity reported for several days.

<u>03/10/85</u> – Following a long run outside of Geneseo, Chris is physically attacked, and wounded, in the dorm shower. Jeff, hearing 'some type of commotion', pulls Chris – who was found on the bathroom floor lying face down and bleeding from his back – out of the bathroom. Ed S. (Jeff's roommate in C2D2) and Beth confirm the wounds which are described as "Three long scratches" that traveled from his neck area to his lower torso. Chris refuses to go to the hospital. Upon seeing the wounds later that evening, Paul begins to withdraw from the friendships.

<u>03/12/85</u> – Chris (while talking with Jeff) sees the ghost outside the C2D Common Area, its body intertwined with a tree. He claims that the ghost looks 'mutilated and twisted' with an eye hanging out, nose missing and the stomach sliced open. Chris flees the room, with Jeff in pursuit, anguished over why the haunting had not stopped.

<u>03/14/85</u> – Chris is told by Craig Norris (Jeff and Ed's C2D2 roommate the year prior) that one of his friends is experiencing voices and paranormal activity in a nearby Erie Hall quad.

<u>03/15/85</u> – Chris travels home (Newburgh, NY) for the weekend to visit his family. He shares with his family a few minor details about the haunting to gauge their reactions.

<u>03/16/85</u> – Paul speaks with Ed and Jeff about changing rooms. Paul later reveals that the ghost threatened him to "Leave Chris alone." Jeff agrees to move into C2D1.

03/17/85 – His first night sleeping in C2D1 (in what had been Chris' bed) Jeff claims to experience a phantasmal paralysis, wrestling with a shadow figure that kneels on his chest. Jeff purposefully does not inform Chris of the incident who returns and questions the new roommate arrangement.

03/24/85 – Chris' father, Vito Di Cesare, concerned over his son's mental health, writes to him. He counsels for mental stability.

03/31/85 – Shortly after returning to college from a 20th birthday party at home with family at home, Chris calls his father to tell him that he was 'in trouble' and that the ghost was 'real'. Vito quickly drives to Geneseo, and spends the night in room C2D1, sitting at the edge of the bed. While revealing no details the following morning, Chris' father tells him that he loves him, and advises him to change his room as soon as he can.

04/01/85 – Students in the B2 area of Erie Hall, begin reporting 'ghost problems'. Jeff and Chris discover Beth, who was late for a preset appointment, unresponsive and dazed on the floor of her bedroom. She claims that she heard the ghost continuously calling Chris' name inside her room and that she 'lost consciousness'.

04/02/85 – Chris, Jeff and Beth respond to the pleas of Linda F., who claims that there is a ghost in her room and that it is holding her down and angrily grabbing her legs. Jeff takes a series of photographs showing Chris as he attempts to assist by calming Linda down and attempting to communicate with the ghost. "You want me, not her." He yells. The activity stops.

04/03/85 – Judy Y. reports that she felt an abnormal chill in the suite bathroom as she showered, as well as the strong feeling that she was being watched by someone that she could not see. She states that when she returns home, she is going to speak with her pastor.

04/04/85 – Chris, who showered regularly at the gym following the attack at Erie Hall, sees 'Tommy' peering at him through the shower stall doorway that leads to the men's locker room. Convinced that he was simply reacting to Judy's impressions, he attempts to shrug off the situation until the form eventually departs. As he is getting dressed, a flustered student warns that he saw 'some really strange-looking guy' watching Chris as he showered. He tells Chris that 'The guy stood there for quite a while', and that if he comes back while he is in the shower, he would call the police.

04/09/85 – Chris, Jeff and Beth visit with Dr. Casler. He marvels at both the amount, and the quality of evidence that the students have gathered. He encourages them to obtain audio evidence to go along with the photograph.

<u>04/11/85</u> – Ghost voice 'EVP' collected in B2B2 of Erie Hall. The gathered students (Chris, Jeff, Linda and Beth) hear the ghost on the cassette tape asking Chris for 'help'. While most are enthused by the growing amount of evidence, Chris is anguished, stating that he didn't know how to help the ghost, even if he wanted to.

<u>04/12/85</u> – Chris begins to withdraw from his friends, spending large amounts of time alone, on the couch in C2D1, watching people pass by his window.

<u>04/20/85</u> – Chris, after talking with Craig Norris about all of the people who were suffering due to the ghost, decides to enter C2D1 with a singular purpose: to get rid of the spirit. He goes into the room sometime between three and four a.m., under Craig's suggestion that it be done 'as God made him' (without clothing), with the intent of breaking the priest's blessing. Chris reportedly speaks with the ghost.

<u>04/21/85</u> – Jeff, not aware of Chris' efforts, notices a change in both Chris and the 'feel' of the room. Chris is hesitant to share any details.

<u>04/26/85</u> – Chris, Jeff, Linda, Beth, Ed and Judy all head out to Fallbrook to see the waterfall. To date, it is the last time that they would all be together.

<u>05/15/85</u> – Chris and Jeff move out of Erie Hall at the close of the Spring Semester.

Dark Culture/Philosophy

Girls Vampire Vixens and Satan's Sirens
Corvis Nocturnum and *Old Nick Magazine*
Introduction by Gavin Baddeley

Dark Moon Press brings you this collection of beautiful women from the shadowy underground world of the Gothic subculture, living vampire community and other alternative lifestyles. The author of *Embracing the Darkness: Understanding Dark Subcultures* shares the beauty found in this seductive and hauntingly beautiful world with detailed descriptions of types, and thoughts from the women he has met. Hundreds of gorgeous photos and photographers are in full color.

WARNING: Some mild adult content
8.5x11 inches

ISBN-13: 978-1479220885
$39.99 USD

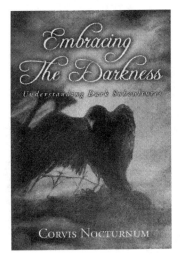

Embracing the Darkness: Understanding Dark Subcultures
Corvis Nocturnum

Author Corvis Nocturnum brings you an unprecedented collection of Satanists, vampires, modern primitives, dark pagans, and Gothic ic artists, all speaking to you in their own words. These are people who have taken something most others find frightening or destructive, and woven it into amazing acts of creativity and spiritual vision. Corvis himself is a dark artist and visionary, and so it is with the eye of a kindred spirit that he has sought these people out to share their stories with you.

ISBN-13: 978-0976698401
242 pages
$17.95 USD

Goth: The Guide For Babybats and Beyond
Ligeia, Adrienne Gomez

Dark Moon Press brings you an insight to life as a young member of the Gothic subculture, as told by Ligeia Resurrected. Her topics range from how to talk to your parents about being different, bullies and the public's negative reaction to Goths, relationships, makeup and fashion tips and much more.

ISBN-13: 978-1495251375
160 pages
$17.99 USD

Hail Thyself! Unlocking the secrets of control wealth and power
Reverend E.R. Vernor "Corvis Nocturnum"

Do you want to be Shirley Temple or Honey Boo Boo? Do you want to be the Barrymores or the Duck Dynasty? If you prefer the former to the latter, then, my friends, *Hail Thyself* has something for you.

This book contains lessons learned through life experiences, mentors of great fame and many expert authors quoted on money, sex and power. Learn all of this and more: The Inner You, Control - self control comes first. Building esteem and confidence. We DO judge a book by its cover, so learn to make yours shine, tips on appearance, the use of scent and color psychology to manipulate those around you. Fake it 'til You Make It (from Goodwill to Armani. The keys to getting others to do for you, reputation, seduction. Controlling the Masses. Etiquette, a Forgotten Relic.

220 Pages
$19.99 USD

Serial Killers Murders Next Door
Bud Weiser

The serial killer next door doesn't always get mass news coverage for decades like Jack the Ripper, Ted Bundy or Ed Gein. Often, killers who prey on massive amount of victims never even make much of a ripple in history.

ISBN-13: 978-1492988601
274 pages
$19.99 USD

Paranormal

Most Haunted: Scariest Places on Earth
Corvis Nocturnum

Join occult researcher and author Corvis Nocturnum, as he guides you through some of the most bizarre and creepy places on the face of the planet. Many have long been rumored to be haunted and all of them are chilling to see! Photographs and facts on places such as the Boney Church, Danvers State Mental Hospital which was the filming location and inspiration for the horror movie Session 9, Alcatraz, the skull lined catacombs under Paris and much more!
ISBN-13: 978-1470015480
148 pages
$16.95 USD

Paranormal Investigation Basics
Mark Davis

Mark Davis breaks through the mystiscm of paranormal investigation, simply and fully detailing the skills and equipment needed for anyone interested in exploring the spirit world. *Paranormal Investigations: The Basics* give a details history and terms of the field and offers a wealth of knowledge for this fascinating and popular field.

Mark Davis is the Co-host of *The Shadows Radio*

ISBN-13: 978-1475006087
200 pages
$19.95 USD

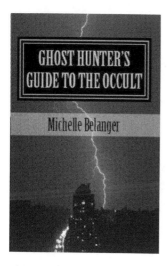

Ghost Hunter's Guide to the Occult
Michelle Belanger

How do you tell the difference between the symbol for the Order of the Eastern Star and a Pentagram? What does a Wiccan mean when she says she practices witchcraft? Paranormal State's Michelle Belanger explores the complex and sometimes confusing realm of the occult, outlining the history of the Western tradition, defining key terms, and exploring the meaning of a variety of icons and symbols. When paranormal investigation takes you into the realm of the unknown, this is the book to have at your side. With its quick-reference guide of terms and definitions, it will quickly become a must-have for all the members of your team.

ISBN-13: 978-1490567495
$19.99 USD
178 pages

Surviving Evidence: Memoir of an Extreme Haunting
Christopher Di Cesare

The legendary "C2D1 Haunting" – one of the most documented paranormal events in New York State history – comes to life in a newly-released memoir by Christopher Di Cesare, the college student who found himself at its horrifying epicenter. In *Surviving Evidence*, Di Cesare details the ghostly apparitions, disembodied voices, and damaging physical attacks that he and his college dorm mates had to endure in order to survive! Di Cesare's unique experience – which has been featured on the SyFy program *School Spirits*, and in the award winning independent film *Please, talk with me* – has quickly garnered national attention.

ISBN-13: 978-1496079169
$ 24.99 USD

Occult/New Age

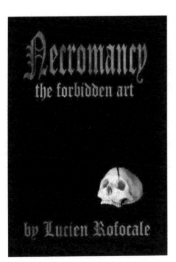

Necromancy the forbidden art
Lucien Rofocale

Discover the history of Demons and their magical sigils, how to work with them and those who have in the past.

ISBN-13: 978-1460972649
116 pages
$9.95 USD

232 pages
$19.95 USD

Promethean Flame
Corvis Nocturnum

Exploring the lineage of those who challenged dogmatic thinking, from the Renaissance and our modern day, Promethean Flame delves deep into religion, philosophy and the arts to explain the importance that the challengers of the past still have on our future. Covering the earliest secret societies such as the Templars and Chaos magicians to Rosicrucian Society, The Masonic Order, and key individuals such as Leonardo Da Vinci, The Hellfire Club all the way up to The Golden Dawn occultists. the Decadent Romantics such as Mary and Percy Shelly, Poe, and Lord Byron are examined.

ISBN-13: 978-0615242576

Collected Works of Eliphas Levi
Dark Moon Press

Collected is the written works of Eliphas Levi, containing in one volume *The Key of Mysteries and Dogma* and *Dogma et Ritual de la Haute Magie*, volumes one and two, all in one manual. Translations by Arthur E. Waite

600 pages
$29.99 USD

The Psychic Vampire s Guide to subtle Body Language &
Psionics
Lono F. Vespertillio

The powerful inter-connections of the body mundras as well as energy patterns we all have are easily explained and offer the reader basic and advanced techniques to alter our reality. Body language and how to work with others to manipulate situations from magic, to business to the bedroom.

ISBN-13: 978-1460970201
240 pages
$19.95 USD

The History of Witchcraft: From Salem to the Silver Screen
Corvis Nocturnum and Starr Morgayne

From old European Innqusition and midwives to modern herbalists and Neopaganism, witchcraft has a long history in the minds of people the world over. See the history of the ways of the wise ones evolve from days gone by to the popularity of this ancient path. Learn the difference between Wicca and Witchcraft, and see how Hollywood has used this iconic idea in everything from *Bewitched* and *Charmed* and beyond. Pages: TBA
Price: $19.99 USD
FALL 2014

Occult Philosophy
Henry Cornelius Agrippa

Heinrich Cornelius Agrippa von Nettesheim who lived from 486–1535. Dark Moon Press collects, examines and explains the works of the famed occultist and seeks to reveal the mysteries of the ancient wisdom he attempted to impart his thoughts on the world on magic. The acclaimed thinker provided the first definitive statement for occult philosophy in his masterwork, *De Occulta Philosophia Libri Tres,* published in 1533. The author felt occult philosophy was the synthetic side of philosophy, combined with skepticism, and believed that behind the natural world lay the celestial world of number the divine world of the angels, would reveal the truth of Christ's incarnation. In light of faith, through magical practice wedded with philosophical analysis, the magician and occult philosopher could achieve certain knowledge of the divine will.

Pages: TBA
Price: $29.99 USD
FALL 2014

Walking the Path of the Ancient Ways a collection of magic by various pagan authors
Corvis Nocturnum

Pagan authors from various backgrounds share their story on being pagan in the modern world. Insightful and thought provoking. With writings by Starr Morgayne, Corvis Nocturnum, Andrieh Vitimus and many more known and new voices.

ISBN-13: 978-1470034641
Pages: 200
$19.99 USD

Bewitching Beauty: Bringing out your inner Goddess, naturally
Starr Morgayne

Women of all ages are concerned about their skin, their bodies and growing older. In this book the author offers simple yet effective, personally tested recipes based on readily available ingredients, and her own unique perspective to help get you in touch with Mother Nature and yourself. Regardless of what stage of life you are in this book can be a positive addition to your journey.

ISBN-13: 978-1451585872
200 pages
$19.99 USD

How to make Infusions and Decoctions; Book One of the Herbal Preparations Series
Starr Morgayne

Starr Morgayne returns with her newest release as she instructs the reader on her secrets of making herbal infusions and other remedies from her kitchen to yours. In this book she describes how to make bath teas, steam facials, instructs you in how to make herbal syrups and much more. This certified herbalist has taken photos from her own herb garden to show the plants in bloom and clearly illustrate how she creates simple to make, yet effective, treatments such as clove toothache oil, mullein and garlic ear oil and a wide variety of teas.

ISBN-13: 978-1493503650
104 pages
$9.99 USD

How to make Salves; Book Two of the Herbal Preparations Series
Starr Morgayne

Starr Morgayne returns with her newest release as she instructs the reader on her secrets of making herbal infusions and other remedies from her kitchen to yours. In this book she describes how to make salves. This certified herbalist has taken photos from her own herb garden to show the plants in bloom and clearly illustrate how she creates simple to make, yet effective, for a wide variety of uses.

ISBN-13: 978-
102 pages
$9.99 USD

MAGICKAL MANNERS: A Guide to Magickal Etiquette
Puck Shadowdrake

"An extensive overview of the practices and etiquette of the entire Neo Pagan community. An excellent resource for chaplains as well as for students seeking a spiritual path." Kerr Cuhulain, author of *Pagan Religions: A Handbook for Diversity Training*

ISBN-13: 978-1481910958
Pages: 600
Price: $39.99 USD

JOURNEYS FROM THE MEADOW: *A Book of Guided Meditation*
Puck Shadowdrake

Puck Shadowdrake, the author of *MAGICKAL MANNERS: A Guide to Magickal Etiquette* brings you his collection of meditations to guide the modern witch through their various journeys through the path for relaxation, healing the body and contacting your deities, spirit guides and much more.
ISBN-13: 978-
Pages: TBA
Price: $19.99 USD

GUIDE TO SIGILS AND HOW TO MAKE THEM WORK FOR YOU
Vincent K Luce

Insightful and unique look at how and why sigils are important in workings. Detailed intricate illustrations show you how to develop them for your own use.

ISBN-13: 978-1492948797
Pages:152
Price: $19.99 USD

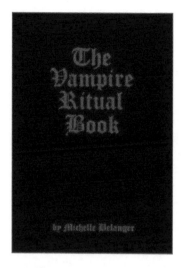

The Vampire Ritual Book
Michelle Belanger

The Vampire Ritual Book was originally commissioned for use within the *Sanguinarium*. Although many of the seasonal rites later appeared as calendar dates in the *Vampyre Almanac*, the rituals themselves were never widely distributed. In 2003, a limited-edition was prepared for print, but these rare books were circulated only to a very few. This book is a reprint of the 2003 limited edition.
ISBN-13: 978-1442118089
160 pages
$16.95 USD

Beneath the Sheltering Oak
Belfazaar Ashanitson

Beneath the Sheltering Oak is a guide of magic and vampirism by an Elder of the Real Vampire Community. Belfazaar Ashantison combines shielding techniques, simple wards and protection spells, from basic mantras to complex spells.

Well versed in archaic magic, Voodoo and Native American spirituality, Belfazaar is the founding member of the New Orleans Vampire Association (NOVA) and works at Voodoo Authentica in New Orleans when not helping the homeless.

ISBN-13: 978-1492782551
Pages: 208
Price: $16.99 USD

Voodoo through my eyes
Belfazaar Ashanitson

Beneath the Sheltering Oak author returns with his latest work, *Voodoo through My Eyes* is a Voodoo 101 from the New Orleans traditions. Within its pages you will find an introduction to the Orisha and Loa, descriptions of some of the "tools" used by many of the practitioners, workings for specific Spirits and recipes of my own creation.

ISBN-13: 978-
Pages: 208
Price: $16.99 USD

Rev. Zombies Common Sense Look At Divination
Tim Shaw & Marla Brooks

Radio host, Rev. Zombies Common Sense Look At Divination by Reverent Tim Shaw & Marla Brooks. A guide that will allow anyone to access the world of divination in a safe manner.

Pages: TBA

Price: $19.99 USD

FALL 2014

Spring 2014

Devil's Advocates
Corvis Nocturnum, Beelzebub

A collection of humorous and scathing thoughts from history's greatest writers, comedians and thinkers. From as far back as Niccoli Machiavelli, all the way up to Ayn Rand and Anton LaVey, this collection also has the sharp wit of Mark Twain, George Carlin and many others who have been the Devil's Advocates on Earth. Compiled by Corvis Nocturnum, and commentary by Ol' Scratch himself, you'll find reflections on his champions. It will make you both ponder and laugh at various aspects of the human condition.
180 pages
$17.99 USD

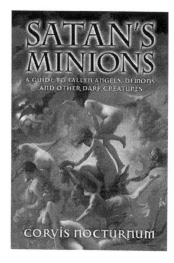

Satan's Minion's: A Guide to Fallen Angel's, Demons and other Dark Creatures
Corvis Nocturnum

Join occult researcher and author Corvis Nocturnum in the quest to uncover everything from the story and evolution of the mother of all dark creatures, Lilith to the Fallen Angels and many mythic creatures. Featuring artwork by the author, as well as fantasy artist, Joseph Vargo, and other classic artists.

ISBN-13: 978-1466484962
186 pages
$16.95 USD

Sumerian Exorcism: Mahick, Demons, and the Lost Art of Marduk
Michelle Belanger

Demonic possession, wicked spells, and ancient bindings all come together in this exploration of Sumerian magick and exorcism. Discover the roots of modern demonology and explore prayers and incantations from the very cradle of Western civilization. This book focuses on the original writings themselves, so you can read for yourself spells drawn from the Maklu Texts and other Sumerian magickal tablets. The translations present a fascinating view of Sumero-Babylonian religion, myth, and demonology. The gods Shamash, Marduk, and Ea play pivotal roles in the fight against the dark powers of Lilitum, Labartu, and the Utukku - a host of evil spirits dedicated to sowing destruction and disease amongst humanity.

ISBN-13: 978-1482521733
180 pages
$17.99 USD

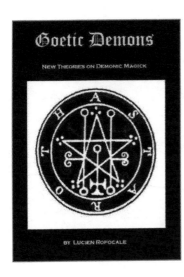

Goetic Demons: New theories on Demonic Magick
Lucien Rofocale

Get a glimpse into the ancient and forbidden art of necromancy and explore aspects of this Black Art history and practice of summoning spirits for spiritual protection to wisdom. Learn the tools and rituals needed in this fascinating work.

ISBN-13: 978-1466335295
100 pages
$9.95 USD

THESE AND 100 MORE TITLES ONLINE
www.darkmoonpress.com

Or use the handy order form on the next page to send in your order through the Postal Service. Please include your name and shipping address.

ORDER FORM

P.O. Box 11496
Fort Wayne, Indiana 46858-1496
www.DarkMoonPress.com

DarkMoon@DarkMoonPress.com

Qty	Title	Price	Total Price

	Shipping	
	Total	

Please make all checks/money orders payable to: Dark Moon Press. All checks/money orders returned for nonsufficient funds will be incur the cost of all fees by the bank plus $25.

*Shipping in the continental United States is $3.00 for the first book, and $2.00 per additional title. Please contact us for international postal rates, thank you!

Please allow for postal and federal holidays which will delay shipping. Wholesale accounts are available for special pricing, see vendor application.

Made in the USA
Middletown, DE
09 May 2016